Felix Emmanuel Schelling

A Book of Elizabethan Lyrics

Felix Emmanuel Schelling

A Book of Elizabethan Lyrics

ISBN/EAN: 9783744795296

Printed in Europe, USA, Canada, Australia, Japan

Cover: Foto ©Thomas Meinert / pixelio.de

More available books at **www.hansebooks.com**

Athenæum Press Series

A BOOK OF

ELIZABETHAN LYRICS

SELECTED AND EDITED

BY

FELIX E. SCHELLING

PROFESSOR OF ENGLISH LITERATURE IN THE UNIVERSITY OF PENNSYLVANIA

BOSTON, U.S.A.

GINN & COMPANY, PUBLISHERS

1895

PREFACE.

THE making of an anthology of any form of poetry is like the culling of a nosegay, a matter in which selection by color, form, and fragrance counts for much, and arrangement according to taste, prejudice, or caprice makes up the remainder. If this be not the method, it is likely to be that of the herbarium, in which appear both flowers and weeds with labelled completeness, in substance dull, in order categorical. It is too much to expect that the disadvantages attending these usual methods have been wholly avoided in the following pages. Every collection of poetry must be made on a plan primarily subjective, and some one will always be found to disapprove, to wonder at the omission of a favorite, or to criticise the editor's eccentricity of judgment. I accept with frankness all responsibility on this score, but hope that a diligent endeavor to become acquainted with the whole field of Elizabethan lyric verse, even in its humbler productions, together with the exercise of a conservative judgment in choice, may have accomplished somewhat in toning any too emphatic an accentuation of the personal note.

Employing the word Elizabethan in a broad sense and that usually accepted, this collection aims to cover the half century from the publication of *The Paradise of Dainty Devises*, 1576, to the death of John Fletcher, 1625. The selections have been drawn from the works of individual authors, from "novels," plays, and masques, and from the poetical miscellanies, song-books, and sonnet sequences of that age.   Each selection is given entire and by preference in the earliest form in which it received the supervision of the author.   Each poem, moreover, is referred to its earliest appearance in manuscript or print and to its probable date of writing; and these facts are noted in a heading above the title.   Later versions and variant readings are occasionally preferred, authority for both of which will be found in the notes.   An order approximately chronological is maintained, that the collection may be representative as far as consistent with a standard of high lyrical excellence.

Aside from numerous editions of Elizabethan poets and dramatists, many of the better collections and anthologies of English poetry have been consulted with reference to the notes and text, which latter has been collated with earlier editions where necessary.   The editings and collections of Dyce, Collier, Hazlitt, Grosart, Arber, and others, although of unequal merit, together with the publications of the several literary societies, have of course been found indispensable; and extended use has been made of Mr. Bullen's various books of Elizabethan songs and lyrics, collections that have rendered accessible much poetry till recently locked away in rare contemporary volumes or still rarer manuscripts.   It need scarcely be added that my many debts to previous editors will be found duly recorded in the Notes.

The introduction is concerned for the most part with two topics: (1) an account of the Elizabethan lyric of art in its nature, origin, and different modes, with comment on the authors and the literary tendencies involved; and (2) a consideration of the chief lyrical measures of the age from an organic as well as an historical point of view.   The foreign relations of Elizabethan poetry which, in the lyric, were exemplified largely in the pastoral mode and in the fashion for sonneting and writing lyrics to be set to music, are presented mainly in the discussion of Italian forms like the madrigal and the sonnet. A full consideration of these relations and of the origins of English metres in a broader sense, however interesting, is considered alien to the purpose of this book. It is hoped that the Notes may furnish such explanatory and biographical information as may not be readily accessible in the usual books of reference, and that the indices may guide the student, or the casual reader, in finding such assistance as he may reasonably demand. It was part of the original plan to furnish in an appendix a bibliography of the Elizabethan lyric; but the scope of this book was found unfitted to so extended an undertaking. I have endeavored, therefore, to supply this want by a Bibliographical Index to the Introduction and Notes, which contains a complete list of the sources and authorities on which this collection is based. No one recognizes more fully the utter futility of notes and glosses to supply taste or an appreciation of poetry, where taste or appreciation is wanting; and yet there seem to be times when the interpreter may well perform his services before the shrines of the oracles and translate — so far as translation is possible — the inspired language of "the literature of power," as De Quincey calls it, into the humbler terms of knowledge.

It is my pleasure to record here my indebtedness for the loan and use of books to the Harvard Library, the Library of Columbia College, and the Philadelphia Library. Private treasures of Marshall C. Lefferts, Esq., of New York, of Jacob Sulzberger, Esq., of Philadelphia, and of Dr. Horace Howard Furness too have been liberally at my disposal. Others to whom my acknowledgments are due are the Rev. Richard Hooper, of Didcot, England, Churton Collins, Esq., of London, Dr. S. Weir Mitchell of Philadelphia, Professor Gummere of Haverford College, and Professor Gayley of the University of California; among my colleagues, Professor

Lamberton and Dr. Gudeman. Lastly this book has been fortunate in the valuable and assiduous supervision of the general editors and in the cordial assistance in gathering and transcribing material which I have had at the hands of my more intimate colleagues of the University of Pennsylvania, Mr. Penniman, Mr. Homer Smith, and Mr. Quinn, Instructors in English.

UNIVERSITY OF PENNSYLVANIA,
November 19, 1894.

CONTENTS.

———❧———

INTRODUCTION.

I.

THE ELIZABETHAN LYRIC.

WHILE the prime conception of the term, lyric, is based upon the singing or song-like quality of this species of poetry as contrasted with the telling or epic quality of narrative verse, an accurate conception of the term contains another, perhaps even more important, consideration. The lyric is personal, concerned with the poet and with the interpretation of his thoughts, sentiments, and emotions. It is the inward world of passion and feeling that is here celebrated, as opposed to the outward world of sequence in time. It is the individual singer, dignified by the sincerity and potency of his art, that unfolds his own moods and emotions to our sympathy and understanding, not a mere voice, the instrument by which we are introduced to the protracted wanderings of Ulysses or the heroic deeds of Beowulf.

But it is not enough that the lyric deal with passion and emotion ; it must deal with both in their simplicity, and not call in, as does the drama, the strong aid of imitated action and heightened situation. Granting grasp and insight into the given mood, the success of a lyric poem will depend upon the poet's ability to exalt his mood to an independence of the ordinary considerations of time and place, and upon his fortunate treatment of the conditions of his theme in fitting and musical form. The elimination of most of those

elements which other forms of verse possess in common
with prose — elements, which can be justified in the lyric
only in the degree in which they make for intelligibility —
has led many to look upon the lyric as alone constituting
the true essence of poetry; the contention being that other
forms, as the epic and the drama, are poetry only in so far
as they contain the elements that add the soul of passion and
the wings of song. Be this as it may, the lyric element of
poetry is assuredly the most subtile and the most difficult
of approach; it is the last element mastered — if mastered
it ever is — by those whom we commonly describe as practical or unpoetical people; it is the element which resides
at the antipodes of what again we commonly describe as
hard matter of fact.[1]

As to form, the lyric, like other varieties of poetry, involves
the presentation of thought in metrical words, but partakes
more of the nature — if not of the limitations — of music in
reflecting a mood rather than in symbolizing an event or
presenting a picture. "Lyrical beauty," says Mr. Stedman,
"does not necessarily depend upon the obvious repetends
and singing-bars of a song or regular lyric. The purest
lyrics are not of course songs; the stanzaic effect, the use
of open vowel sounds, and other matters instinctive with
song-makers, need not characterize them. What they must
have is *quality*. That their rhythmic and verbal expression
appeals supremely to the finest sensibilities indicates, first,
that the music of speech is more advanced, because more
subtly varying, than that of song; or, secondly, that a more
advanced music, such as the German and French melodists

---

[1] We are concerned in this discussion wholly with the lyric of art,
the criterion of which is its personality. No one will deny the existence
in English, as in other tongues, of the impersonal *Volkslyrik*. See on
this subject in general Professor Gummere's *Introduction, Old English
Ballads, Athenæum Press Series*.

now wed to words, is required for the interpretation of the most poetic and qualitative lyric." [1]

Like good poetry of all classes, the lyric must combine universality of feeling with unity of form. In accord with the first, the poem must be neither narrative nor descriptive to a degree which will destroy the central idea. Less than any other form of literature conceivable should the lyric be didactic ; for by the intrusion of didacticism a particular instance, with its pendent maxim, is substituted for a general truth, and a product of fine art degraded into a mere utility. Again, the lyric must present the unity of a perfect art form, and "each poem," as Mr. Palgrave states it, must "turn on some single thought, feeling, or situation." [2] It is easy to see that by its very conditions the lyric must be short, as an emotion prolonged beyond a pleasurable length will defeat its own artistic aim. [3]

As to another canon of "the best poetry," much trumpeted of late, I feel less ready to give an unqualified assent. Doubtless it is no light thing to say of a poem that "no man's gravity hath been disturbed thereby," and the touchstone of "high seriousness" may perhaps be applied with much success to that group of classical productions which are far more admired than read. But there is a flash in the play of a familiar word about a remote idea, there is a joy that bursts into song and a mirth which rises into the bubble of nonsense, all of which are highly subversive of gravity, and yet very often much of the salt of that "consolation and stay" which literature affords us in the rough places of the world. Even cynicism of mood, though often dangerously intellectual, need not be destructive of lyric [4]

[1] *The Nature and Elements of Poetry*, p. 179.
[2] *Golden Treasury of English Lyrics.* Preface.
[3] Cf. E. A. Poe, *The Poetic Principle. Select Works*, ed. 1885, p. 641.
[4] Cf. Donne's *Song*, p. 97.

excellence. The following pages will be found far less grave than those of many such collections; and I have no apology to offer for the fact.

Inasmuch as the lyric demands a grasp of the subtler forms of human passion and emotion, combined with a consummate mastery of form and of the music of speech, it is but natural that all literatures should display the lyric amongst the latest of literary growths. Despite what must be admitted as to an impersonal lyrical quality inhering in much early popular poetry, an age in which the gift of lyric expression is widely diffused, must be alike removed from the simplicity and immaturity which is content to note in its literature the direct effects of the phenomena of the outside world and no more, and from that complexity of conditions and that tendency to intellectualize emotion which characterize a time like our own. In an age lyrically gifted, we may look for innumerable points of contact between the spirit of the time and its literature, for the most beautiful and fervent thoughts couched in the most beautiful and fervent language; in such an age we may expect the nicest adjustment and equilibrium of the real and the ideal, each performing its legitimate function and contributing in due proportion to the perfect realization of truth in its choicest form, beauty. Such an age was that of the Elizabethan Lyric, which bloomed with a flower-like diversity of form, color, and fragrance from the boyhood of Shakespeare to the accession of Charles I.

The Elizabethan lyric had its origin in culture, not among the people; and the culture of the England of the sixteenth century was the culture of Italy. No one who pretended to gentility could afford to be ignorant of the Italian language, and no one who claimed politeness could ignore her literature or her art. A familiar passage of Roger Ascham dilates upon "the enchantments of Circe, brought out of Italy, to mar men's manners in England, much by example of ill life, but more by precepts of fond books of late translated out of Italian into English, sold in every shop in London"; and laments that the young "have in more reverence the triumphs of Petrarch than the *Genesis* of Moses."[1] Indeed even the classical mania of the day came clothed in Italian garb, and the classics most imitated and admired in England were those most esteemed in Italy. But however widely diffused this superficial Italianism, literary culture was in the earlier decades of the century confined to the society surrounding princes, and Puttenham's term for the early English poets, "courtly makers," is thus peculiarly fitting.[2] We may thus disregard all earlier attempts and state that the history of the English lyric begins with the life of the first English court which felt the rays of the arisen sun of the Renaissance. That court was the court of Henry VIII, and *Tottel's Miscellany*, not printed until 1557, is the treasury into which was garnered the earliest lyrical harvest of England. The Earl of Surrey, Thomas Lord Vaux, Sir Thomas Wyatt, George Boleyn Lord Rochford, brother to the unfortunate Queen Anne, even Henry himself — who wrote, somewhat inconsistently, on constancy in love[3] — all were notable lyrical poets in their day ; and it is worthy of remembrance that few, if any, of the lyrists of *Tottel's Miscellany* were not courtiers themselves, or not under the immediate patronage of the court. As time went on, however, two other influences made

---

[1] *The Scholemaster*, ed. Arber, pp. 78, 92.

[2] "And in her Majesty's time that now is are sprong up another crew of courtly makers, noblemen and gentlemen of her Majesty's own servants, who have written excellently well," etc. Puttenham, *The Art of English Poetry*, ed. Arber, p. 75.

[3] See Flügel's *Liedersammlungen des XVI. Jahrhunderts, besonders aus der Zeit Heinrich's VIII, Anglia* XII, 225 f., and Chappell, *Old English Popular Music*, I, 42 f.

themselves felt in the lyric equally with other forms of literature. If culture was derived through the social life of the
court, the learning of the time, in which the courtiers shared
in no mean part, was based upon a study of the ancients. No
less were the scholars and courtiers Englishmen, and hence
before long we find the foreign lyrical graft, strengthened
by a real love and study of the classics, and rendered hardy
by the infusion of a genuine vernacular spirit. The combination of these elements, that of Italian, and, to a lesser
degree, French and Spanish culture, classic, especially
Roman learning, assimilated to English feeling and manner
of thought, give us the literary spirit of the age of Elizabeth.
In *Tottel's Miscellany* and *The Paradise of Dainty Devices*,
with the possible addition of Clement Robinson's *A Handful of Pleasant Delights*, will be found the bulk of the better
lyrics written before the accession of Queen Elizabeth.
These collections are representative because they are the
product of contemporary educated taste, selecting and
choosing from a considerable mass of material already
popular with a limited but cultivated audience of readers. A
wide diffusion of the gift of lyrical composition is always
accompanied by a far wider diffusion of appreciation for
lyric art. The work of these earlier miscellanies was prentice
work, much of it; but prentice work on good models and
not infrequently intrinsically of no mean standard. Many
of the older poets, such as Hunnis, Edwards, and the Earl
of Oxford, all contributors to *The Paradise*, and others, such
as Turberville, Googe, and Gascoigne, lived well into Elizabeth's reign, and did their part towards preparing the way
for the glorious outburst of song which followed the publication of *The Shepherds' Calendar* in 1579.

Few sovereigns have witnessed such social and literary
changes as Queen Elizabeth; indeed, the advance of half a
century in many other ages have scarcely equalled the strides

of a single decade in this singularly quickened time. This was more striking in literature than in almost any other field of activity. Elizabeth had gone to school to excellent Roger Ascham in childhood and laughed at the rude cleverness of Heywood the epigrammatist; she had sonneted in limping Poulter's measure in young womanhood; and lived to receive the literary homage of men like Sidney, Spenser, and Raleigh and to know the glories of the Shakespearean drama in the height of its splendor.

There is reason for placing the beginning of the Elizabethan outburst of lyrical poetry at 1575. In that year George Gascoigne, the most important literary figure between Surrey and Spenser, was still at the height of a popularity which seems to have been considerable, and which was based very largely upon a happy lyrical vein and a ready metrical facility. Gascoigne died two years later, and few of his poetical contemporaries long survived him, if we except Whetstone and Churchyard, who are both distinctly unlyrical, if not unpoetical. To this we may add the fact that, in 1576, *The Paradise of Dainty Devices* gathered up what was then regarded as the choicest lyrical poetry of the period just concluded. On the other hand, in 1575, Spenser, Greville, Lodge, Greene, and Harvey, the classical mentor of Spenser, were already at Cambridge, whilst Lyly, Peele, and Watson remained at Oxford, which Sidney had just quitted to be introduced at court and to proceed upon his foreign travels. The influences that made these men poets were thus at work while they were students at the Universities; for, setting aside the case of Spenser's contributions to *The Theatre of Voluptuous Worldlings*, in 1569, which not even Dr. Grosart's zeal has rendered wholly unapocryphal,[1] we know from the letters between the two that Harvey and Spenser were much

---

[1] See his ed. of Spenser, I, 15–23.

interested in poetry at Cambridge well before the eighties ;[1]
and it is likely that Lodge at least, if not Greene and Watson,
began to write before their departure for London. Within
the ten years that followed, each of the authors mentioned
had made a name for himself in literature.

The decade, 1580-1590, may be regarded as the period
of the supremacy of the pastoral. During this period *The
Shepherds' Calendar* and Sidney's *Arcadia* (although the latter
was not printed until 1590) were the most pervasive literary
influences. *Euphues* could alone question the supremacy of
these works, and *Euphues*, though not a pastoral, fell in with
the prevailing fashion in not a few particulars. At court,
too, Lyly and Peele were cultivating a species of the drama,
which, if largely classical in subject, was often pastoral in
form, in imagery, and the use of allegory. (*E.g.*, Peele's *The
Arraignment of Paris* or Lyly's *Gallathea*.) The *Arcadia*
is full of lyrical verse ; but Sidney is scarcely here at his
best, and there was in him a finer lyrical chord which
thrilled in the rich music of *Astrophel and Stella*. Though
surprisingly successful, especially in longer and statelier
pastoral lyrics (cf. the *Canzon Pastoral* in honor of Elizabeth, and the *Dirge* for the Shepherdess Dido, in *April*
and *November* respectively, of the *Shepherds' Calendar*),
Spenser too was so much more, that to him the pastoral
lyric became little beyond a passing mood. Notwithstanding then that to these two great poets the prevalence of
the mode is due, we must look to others for the more
limited and distinctive development of the pastoral lyric :
whether displayed in the dainty songs interspersed through
the dramas of Lyly and Peele, in the equally beautiful
amorous verse of the romances of Lodge and Greene, or
in the charming little idyls of Breton's poetical booklets.

---

[1] These letters were published by Harvey in 1580. See Dr. Grosart's
ed. of Harvey.

In the poetry of these men, and some few others, such as
Marlowe, Constable, Munday, and Barnfield in individual
poems, will be found the perfection of the English pastoral
lyric : its simplicity and *insouciance*, its music and metrical felicity, its sweet pathos and tenderness, its delicate
and artistic artificiality united with a genuine joy in the
beauties of nature. Of the forms of this class of lyrics
I shall have occasion to speak elsewhere ;[1] but I cannot
refrain from here urging all true lovers of poetry not to
neglect to read such exquisite lyrical artists as Greene,
Lodge, and Breton — the last two, even now only too little
known, and unobtainable in popular form.[2] The pastoral
mode continued in vogue to the end of Elizabeth's reign
and beyond, but in the following decades it ceased to be
the dominant lyrical strain.

But if this decade is superficially the period of the
pastoral, there is in its poetry a deeper undertone not
only in the artistic seriousness of Spenser, but in the
sincerity and passion of Sidney. In Sidney is struck,
for the first time unmistakably, that individual note, that
intense and passionate cry of the poet's very heart, that was
thenceforth to be the distinctive mark of the great literature
of Elizabeth. Lamb and Ruskin have united to lavish upon
the poetry of Sidney the most enthusiastic praise : and few
who know him well, will think this praise excessive. In the
lyric poetry too of Sidney's friend, Fulke Greville — the
period of the writing of which is doubtful, although probably
contemporaneous with Sidney — there is a new and independent spirit, a widening of the sphere of the lyric theme
to include non-erotic sentiment, and an all but complete

---

[1] See the second part of this Introduction.

[2] But see the scraps from the verse and prose of Greene and of
Breton, recently published by Dr. Grosart, *The Elizabethan Library*,
London, 1893 and 1894.

abandonment of the classic imagery and allusion which long continued elsewhere to be one of the chief excrescences of the ornate and elaborated style of the time. Far different in this respect is the poetry of Watson and Barnes, who continue the Italian impulse given to English poetry by Sidney, as Greville continued his strength, if not his fervor of thought. Both the former poets exhibit, with the more strictly pastoral lyrists just mentioned, that "passionate delight in beauty" which forms the "inspiring motive" of all the renaissance poets. In the words of Professor Dowden, who is writing, apropos of Barnes, of this class of poets in general:

" They do not need ideas, or abstractions, or memories of the past or hopes for the future ; it suffices them to be in presence of a bed of roses, or an arbor of eglantine, or the gold hair of a girl, or her clear eyes, bright lips, and little cloven chin, her fair shadowed throat, and budding breasts. She shall be a shepherdess, and the passionate shepherd will cull the treasures of earth, and of the heaven of the gods of Greece and Rome to lay them before her feet. . . . It is not only the Renaissance with its rehabilitation of the senses which we find in these poems ; there is in them also the Renaissance with its ingenuity, its fantasticality, its passion for conceits, and wit, and clever caprices and playing upon words. With this it is harder and perhaps not wholesome to attempt to enter into sympathy." [1]

The next decade, the last of the sixteenth century, is the time of the sonnet, long since introduced into English literature by Sir Thomas Wyatt and practiced in greater or less imitation of Italian models by his immediate successors, but not rendered a power until the masterly grasp of *Astrophel and Stella*, the earliest sonnet sequence in the language. Though written much earlier, this work

<hr/>

[1] *The Academy*, Sept. 2, 1876.

did not appear in print until Nashe's quasi-surreptitious edition of 1591. This included not only Sidney's sequence, but "sundry other rare sonnets of divers noblemen and gentlemen," notably twenty-seven sonnets of Samuel Daniel, who was then traveling abroad. Daniel resented this premature publication of his work, and in the following year put forth a true edition of his *Delia*, which included the sonnets published by Nashe, and others. Constable's *Diana* appeared in the same year and enjoyed a remarkable popularity. With this, sonneteering became the fashion, and sequence after sequence, in repeated editions, issued from the press. After Sidney, Daniel, and Constable, the last of whom subsequently wrote *Spiritual Sonnets to the Honor of God and His Saints*, and thus first turned the sonnet to "divine uses," came in 1593 Lodge's *Phyllis*, Watson's *Tears of Fancy*, Barnes' *Parthenophil and Parthenophe*, mixed with other lyric forms as were many of these collections, Drayton's *Idea* and Dr. Giles Fletcher's *Licia*. In 1594, appeared Percy's *Cælia* and the anonymous *Zepheria;* in 1595, Barnfield's *Cynthia*, Chapman's *A Coronet for his Mistress Philosophy*, and Barnes' *A Divine Century of Spiritual Sonnets;* in 1596, Griffin's *Fidessa*, Smith's *Chloris*, Lynche's *Diella*, and, most perfect of all, Spenser's *Amoretti*. Sonnets of Shakespeare were well known, as Meres tells us, before 1598; Breton's *The Soul's Harmony* appeared in 1600, Sir John Davies' *Sonnets to Philomel* in Davison's *Poetical Rhapsody*, in 1602; Donne's *Holy Sonnets* and Alexander's *Aurora* remain of uncertain date. Other works are frequently included in this list: as Watson's *Passionate Century of Love*, which was not written in quartorzains and falls too early to have been affected by the prevalent mode; J. C.'s *Alcilia* and Greville's *Cælica*, neither of which preserves the sonnet form although both are sequences; and Breton's *Arbor of Amorous Devices*, which, though containing some few sonnets, is not a sequence properly speaking. Willoughby's *Avisa* from its stanzaic structure, dialogue form, and satiric intent, not only belongs without the category of sonnets, but is not lyrical.

It will be noticed that these sonnet sequences fall naturally into certain well defined groups. The vast majority are devoted to the celebration of the passion of love: some, as Sidney's, Drayton's, Spenser's, and Shakespeare's, suggesting by means of successive lyrical moods a more or less connected love story, of greater or less probable basis in fact; another class dealing with the praises of a mistress or lamenting her hardness of heart as *Phyllis*, *Cynthia*, and *Diana* or Watson's *Tears of Fancy*. Yet another class are little more than loosely connected series of amatory verse, as Breton's *Arbor* or J. C.'s *Alcilia;* or even collections of poems amatory and other, as Greville's *Cælica*, having nothing in common with the sonnet except a certain unity of thought and brevity of form. On the much discussed question of the subjective significance of these sequences, I do not feel called upon to write here. Suffice it to say that in these cases it is as easy to interpret mere lyrical hyperbole into a *chronique scandaleuse* as it is tempting to etherialize real human passion into what Mr. Walter Bagehot called in a different connection "evanescent mists of lyrical energy."

The convenient length of the sonnet early suggested its use as occasional verse (cf. Raleigh's sonnet prefixed to *The Faery Queen*, or Barnfield's *In Praise of Music and Poetry*, p. 87), a use which continued throughout the period. Lastly, we find Constable, Barnes, Breton, and Donne turning the form to the expression of religious emotion in sequences of "Divine Sonnets." (For examples, see Barnes' *Talent*, and Donne's sonnet *To Death*, pp. 81 and 142.) Chapman's *A Coronet for his Mistress Philosophy* is probably the earliest attempt to write a sonnet sequence neither devotional nor amatory. Although the sonnet continued a popular form during the remainder of the reign of Elizabeth and that of her successor, excepting the work of William Drummond, a scholarly poet, who lived much in the past, and series like William Browne's *Cælia* and *Visions*, the writing of sonnet sequences went out of the literary fashion with the close of the former reign. The old sequences, however, continued in popularity, as the frequency of later editions attest, up to the time of Withers' *Phil'arete* and Habington's *Castara*, erotic sequences eschewing the sonnet form altogether.

Notwithstanding the surprising excellence of even the minor sonneteers of the time, the Elizabethan sonnet is a peculiarly restricted product, with its fixed form and a theme for the most part limited and conventionalized to a definite method of treating a single passion. Shakespeare recognized this, and, although himself not above practicing all these subtle arts and wiles, and outdoing the sugared similes and rapturous hyperboles of the sonnet tribe, did not hesitate to ridicule the school and its follies in the honest, direct sonnet, beginning :

> My mistress' eyes are nothing like the sun,
> Coral is far more red than her lips red ;

and ending

> And yet, by heaven, I think my love as rare
> As any she belied with false compare.[1]

Less known, though scarcely less excellent of its kind, is Chapman's rebuke, the first of his sonnets to " his Mistress Philosophy," which I quote here as representing the attitude of the more serious minds of the age towards the excessive ornament and eroticism of the time :

[1] See p. 87.

Muses that sing Love's sensual empery,
And lovers kindling your enragèd fires
At Cupid's bonfires burning in the eye,
Blown with the empty breath of vain desires,
You that prefer the painted cabinet
Before the wealthy jewels it doth store ye,
That all your joys in dying figures set,
And stain the living substance of your glory,
Abjure those joys, abhor their memory,
And let my love the honored subject be
Of love, and honor's complete history ;
Your eyes were never yet let in to see
The majesty and riches of the mind,
But dwell in darkness ; for your god is blind.[1]

This limitation of the sonnet in subject and treatment led
to no little repetition.   Indeed, many sonnets were written
in avowed competition, as the well-known series of tournament sonnets, as they are called, on Sleep,[2] on Death, the
Flight of Time, and others.   I believe that an examination
of the entire literature of the Elizabethan sonnet, with respect
to subject and sentiment, would result in the discovery of
an unusual number of such parallels, and exhibit, to an
extent scarcely yet recognized, that the versatility of much
of this species of poetry is a versatility of expression, not
a versatility of thought.

The cultivation of the sonnet had, on the other hand, a
beneficial effect on the English Lyric, as it demanded a greater
attention to the minutiæ of form, a greater regard for unity,
and, from the somewhat dignified tread of its decasyllables,
a greater care in the molding of the thought of the lyric in
distinction from the quality of mere song.   In the hands of
Sidney, Spenser, Daniel, and Shakespeare, the sonnet reached

---

[1] *Works of Chapman, Poems and Minor Translations,* ed. 1875, p. 38.
[2] See note on *Care-charmer Sleep,* p. 234.

an artistic height which was not surpassed until the conception of the scope of its subject was widened, and the beauty of the stricter Petrarchan form was reasserted by Milton, to be practiced by Wordsworth and Dante Gabriel Rossetti.

But, as in the case of the pastoral fashion, there were other currents of lyrical production, less directed by the conventionalities of the moment. Spenser aside, whose elaborated state does not lend itself readily to the shorter lyric, and whose singing robes are stiff with tissue of gold, wrought work, and gems inlaid, and Shakespeare, also, whose non-dramatic Muse is dedicated to thoughtful sonnet and mournful threnody, as well as to the sprightlier melodies of love, wine, and merriment, the most important poetical influence of this decade is that of that grave and marvelous man, Dr. John Donne. I would respectfully invite the attention of those who still persist with Dr. Johnson in regarding this great poet as the founder of a certain "Metaphysical School of Poetry,"[1] a man all but contemporary with Cowley, and a writer harsh, obscure, and incomprehensible in his diction, first to an examination of facts which are within the reach of all, and, secondly, to an honest study of his works. Ben Jonson told Drummond[2] that "Donne's best poems were written before he was twenty-five years old," *i.e.*, before 1598, and Francis Davison, apparently when collecting material for his *Poetical Rhapsody* in 1600, includes in a memorandum of "MSS. to get," certain poems of Donne.[3] The Carews, Crashaws, and Cowleys begin at least thirty years later, and, be their imitations of Donne's characteristics what they may, Donne himself is an Elizabethan in the strictest possible acceptation of that term, and far in fact as in time from the representative of a

---

[1] *Lives of the English Poets,* ed. Tauchnitz. I, 11.

[2] *Conversations, Sh. Soc. Pub.,* p. 8.

[3] *Poetical Rhapsody,* ed. Nicolas, p. xlv.

degenerate and false taste. It is somewhat disconcerting to find an author whom, like Savage Landor in our own century, the critic cannot glibly classify as the founder of a school or the product of a perfectly obvious series of literary influences. Donne is a man of this difficult type. For, just as Shakespeare touched life and man at all points, and, absorbing the light of his time, gave it forth a hundredfold, so Donne, withdrawn almost wholly from the influences affecting his contemporaries, shone and glowed with a strange light all his own.

Few lyrical poets have ever rivaled Donne in contemporary popularity. Mr. Edmund Gosse has recently given a reason for this, which seems worthy of attention, while by no means explaining everything. "Donne was, I would venture to suggest, by far the most modern and contemporaneous of the writers of his time. . . . He arrived at an excess of actuality of style, and it was because he struck them as so novel, and so completely in touch with his age, that his immediate coevals were so much fascinated with him."[1] A much bequoted passage of the *Conversations with Drummond* informs us that Ben Jonson "esteemeth Donne the first poet in the world in some things."[2] An analysis of these "some things," which space here forbids, will, I think, show them to depend, to a large degree, upon that deeper element of the modern lyric, poetic insight; the power which, proceeding by means of the clash of ideas familiar with ideas remote, flashes light and meaning into what has hitherto appeared mere commonplace. This, mainly, though with much else, is the positive originality of Donne. A quality no less remarkable is to be found in what may be called his negative originality, by which I mean that trait which caused Donne absolutely to give over

---

[1] *The Jacobean Poets,* p. 64.
[2] *Conversations,* as above, p. 8.

the current mannerisms of his time; to write neither in the usual Italian manner, nor in borrowed lyrical forms; indeed, to be at times wantonly careless of mere expression, and, above all, to throw away every trace of the conventional classic imagery and mannerisms which infected and conventional-ized the poetry of so many of his contemporaries. It seems to me that no one, excepting Shakespeare, with Sidney, Gre-ville, and Jonson in lesser measure, has done so much to develop intellectualized emotion in the Elizabethan lyric as John Donne. But Donne is the last poet to demand a proselyting zeal of his devotees, and all those who have learned to love his witching personality will agree to the charming sentiment of his faithful adorer, Izaak Walton, when he says: "Though I must omit to mention divers persons, . . . friends of Sir Henry Wotton; yet I must not omit to mention of a love that was there begun betwixt him and Dr. Donne, sometime Dean of Saint Paul's ; a man of whose abilities I shall forbear to say anything, because he who is of this nation, and pretends to learning or ingenuity, and is ignorant of Dr. Donne, deserves not to know him." [1]

But in the great age of Elizabeth, miracles were not the monopoly of the immortals. Strenuous Titans, such as those that wrought poetical cosmos out of the chaos of *Barons' Wars* or *Civil Wars*, out of disquisitions on state-craft and ponderous imitations of Senecan rhetoric, could also work dainty marvels in song. The lyrics of that most interesting and "difficult" of poets, Fulke Greville, have already been noticed, and are the more remarkable in their frequent grace of fancy, uncommon wit, originality, and real music of expression in that they are the sister products of the obscure and intricate musings and the often eccentric didac-ticism of *Mustapha* and *Alaham*. Of Daniel, a conscientious artist as he was a sensible theorist in verse, we might expect

---

[1] *Life of Wotton, Lives, etc.*, Amer. ed., 1846, p. 136.

the delicacy and elegance of the consummate lyrist ; but far
more extraordinary does it seem that the Drayton of later
years should have continued well skilled in the lighter lyrical
touch.   It would be difficult to find a more perfect union of
artistic feeling with fervent passion than is contained in
" I pray thee leave, love me no more," or in the finished
variation of the same theme in sonnet form : " Since
there's no help."[1]   In quite another sphere, Drayton has
achieved the best war-song of his age, if not of English literature, the familiar *Ode to the Cambro-Britans* on the Battle
of Agincourt.[2]

The real or affected reluctance of courtiers and gentlemen
to permit their poetical productions to appear in print, led
early to the practice of keeping poetical commonplace-books,
in which the lover of poetry was accustomed to copy out,
for his own pleasure and remembrance, such verses as met
his fancy.   These manuscript books are very numerous,
and often afford us not only variant readings of well-
known poems, but occasionally verses of great value not
elsewhere to be found.   As the number of those who read
poetry increased, two changes came about : the poetical
commonplace-book was printed, and became the anthology,
or miscellany, as they then called it ; and, secondly, as
necessity at times pressed upon the broken gentleman, the
literary hack was evolved, in such men as Churchyard and
Breton, possibly in Nicholas Grimald himself.   In character,
the Elizabethan poetical miscellanies differ widely ; from a
selection of verse, strictly lyrical, the work of various
authors, to work of very mixed character, and even to mere
collections of poetical quotations.   The miscellanies, more
strictly so-called, after *The Paradise of Dainty Devices*, are
A Gorgeous Gallery of Gallant Inventions, 1578 ; *Britton's
Bower of Delights*, a pirated work including amongst much

---

[1] See pp. 194, 196.   [2] See p. 136.

else poems of Nicholas Breton, 1591 ; *The Phoenix' Nest,*
an interesting collection, including much of Breton's and
Lodge's, and of unknown editorship, 1593 ; *The Passionate Pilgrim,* another pirated work, containing poetry by
Shakespeare, Barnfield, Griffin, Raleigh, Marlowe, and others,
1599 ; *England's Helicon,* possibly the richest and most
representative of all, projected by John Bodenham, who was
concerned in several other like ventures, 1600 ; and, lastly,
Francis Davison's admirable *Poetical Rhapsody.* Less strictly
anthologies are the appendix to Chester's *Love's Martyr,
The Turtle and Phoenix,* 1601, including poems by Shakespeare, Jonson, Marston, and Chapman ; and collections
of extracts like *Belvedere or the Garden of the Muses* and
England's Parnassus. Munday's *Banquet of Dainty Conceits,* an inferior production published in 1588,[1] and Breton's
Arbor of Amorous Devices, 1593–94, are the work of their
respective editors, who appear to have traded on titles
usually employed to convey the idea of an anthology by
various authors. After the death of the queen, few new
miscellanies appeared, although, as in the case of the
sonnet, the old miscellanies continued to be republished.
Such miscellanies as were printed in the reign of James are
mostly indiscriminate collections of ballads, lyrics, and
occasional verse. The lyrical anthology, in a word, had gone
out of the fashion, and other collections, especially those of
songs and madrigals, generally with the music attached, took
their place in the popular esteem.

As might be expected, the earlier miscellanies, which it
must be emphasized were the product of an educated literary
taste in selection, reflect the prevailing fashions in poetry of
these two decades. In *England's Helicon* (the poetry of
which though published in 1600 was written far earlier)
there is still not a little affectation of shepherds and shep-

---

[1] This I have not been able to procure.

herdesses, whilst *The Poetical Rhapsody*, which represents
poetry for the most part written a dozen years later, is full
of sonnets and madrigals. In *The Phoenix' Nest, England's
Helicon*, and Davison's *Rhapsody* will be found much of the
choicest lyrical poetry prior to the accession of James I ;
including, besides a considerable body of verse the authorship of which it is difficult or impossible to identify, work by
almost every important lyrical poet of the age. Except for
some minor names, the miscellanies published before 1600
exhibit only the work of tried and successful authors. It
was different with Davison's *Poetical Rhapsody*, which includes, besides work of this character, much that was new, as
Davison's own beautiful poetry, distinguishable by its erotic
fervor and directness, that of his two brothers, of Sir John
Davies, of Donne, Sylvester, Sir Henry Wotton, Campion,
and much anonymous verse. Altogether this collection
most fittingly opens a new period.

Taking Mr. Bullen's list of Elizabethan song books,[1]
appended to his admirable *Lyrics from Elizabethan Song
Books*,[1] I find that out of fifty-five song books of known date
of publication, falling between Byrd's *Psalms, Sonnets, and
Songs of Sadness and Piety*, 1588, and Pilkington's *Second
Set of Madrigals*, 1624, forty-one appeared between 1595
and 1615, and more than half of these in the central decade
1600–10. This seems to establish the fact that, upon the
waning of the fashion for sonnets, the attention of the minor
lyrists was directed chiefly to the writing of songs for music.

In a contemplation of the preëminence of the literature
under consideration, we are apt to forget that other arts too
came in to share in the vigorous life and aesthetic activity
that distinguished this most fortunate of ages. This is not
the place for more than a word as to the popular love of
music and the general culture of it as an art in the England

[1] Revised ed., p. 229.

of the sixteenth and seventeenth centuries. This popularity is witnessed by a long and honorable list of trained musicians and composers, and by the considerable number of their compositions which have been handed down to us. The estimation in which such men were held may be seen in Barnfield's sonnet *To Music and Poetry* (p. 86). That other nations have long since outstripped England in music, and that an entirely new school has gone on to achievements utterly undreamed of in this simple age of lutes and virginals, of madrigals and three-part catches, will not alter the historical fact that the English were a very musical people in the days of Henry VIII, of his children and their successor.[1] Our present interest in this popularity of a sister art is confined to the impetus which it seems to have given to the writing of lyrics to be set to music; for the Elizabethans were very particular as to the artistic quality of the words of their songs ; and did not consider, as we, that any nonsense is good enough to sing.

There is a large amount of this literature ; and, although much of it was either literally translated from Italian or at

---

[1] " During the long reign of Elizabeth, music seems to have been in universal cultivation, as well as universal esteem. Not only was it a necessary qualification for ladies and gentlemen, but even the city of London advertised the musical abilities of boys educated in Bridewell and Christ's Hospital, as a mode of recommending them as servants, apprentices, or husbandmen. . . . Tinkers sang catches ; milkmaids sang ballads ; carters whistled ; each trade, and even the beggars, had their special songs ; the base-viol hung in the drawing room for the amusement of waiting visitors; and the lute, cittern and virginals, for the amusement of waiting customers, were the necessary furniture of the barber's shop. They had music at dinner ; music at supper; music at weddings ; music at funerals ; music at dawn, music at night. . . . He who felt not, in some degree, its soothing influences, was viewed as a morose, unsocial being, whose converse ought to be shunned and regarded with suspicion and distrust." Chappell, *Old English Popular Music*, i. 59. See also Galliard's *Cantatas*, 1720, Preface.

least inspired by Italian models, the words as well as the music, there was yet some scope for originality. Considering all things, the literary worth of the Elizabethan song books is surprisingly great. It is the opinion of Mr. Bullen, who is certainly best entitled to speak on this subject, that "as a rule composers are responsible only for the music" of the song books published under their names. In consequence much of this beautiful verse remains unidentified as to authorship. Certain it is, however, that some of the composers were likewise poets. This is notably the case with Dr. Thomas Campion, a most accomplished and versatile man, at once a physician, a musician, a critic, and a lyrical poet of rare order in Latin and English verse. Mr. Bullen, to whose untiring zeal and industry we practically owe the rediscovery of Campion, ranks that poet with Shelley and Burns as a lyrist ; adding "for tenderness and depth of feeling, for happiness of phrase and for chaste, artistic perfection he is supreme. . . . As we read Campion's lyrics we feel that the poet could without effort beat out of our rough English speech whatever music he chose. . . . To every varying mood the lyre-strings are responsive. Never a false or jarring note ; no cheap tricks and mannerisms ; everywhere ease and simplicity."[1] Whether this seem the pardonable over-estimate of a discoverer or not, few poets have surpassed Campion in the highest quality of the songwriter : the writing of words that sing. Although not among the greater masters that have wrought most deeply in thought and emotion, Campion may take his place beside Herrick and Ben Jonson in lighter vein as one of the best Anacreontic lyrists in the language.

But the lyrics set to music were not confined to collections of airs, songs, or madrigals by musicians like Byrd, Dowland, Campion, and Jones ; they flourished in the drama and in

[1] Preface to *More Lyrics*, etc., p. vi.

the masque, which latter in the hands of Jonson and Daniel assumed a new dignity and beauty. The songs of the dramatists have long been recognized as amongst the best of English lyrics. Beginning with the rollicking old drinking song of *Gammer Gurton's Needle*, "Back and side go bare, go bare," which it is delightful to believe was the work of a prospective bishop, the practice of enlivening the drama with songs and other lyrics continued until developed into a consummate art in the hands of Lyly, Dekker, and Shakespeare. Indeed even with Shakespeare setting the standard, it is amazing what lyrics far lesser men could produce : Anthony Munday, an obscure and fertile literary hack, reeling out volume after volume of ordinary verse and yet more ordinary prose, yet reaching once or twice a rare level, which shall preserve his name from oblivion ; Thomas Heywood, facile and most productive of dramatists, visited at moments by the golden touch of lyric inspiration ; Thomas Nashe, the redoubtable " English Aretine," with the swagger of a bully in almost all his prose, yet leaving us but too few of the purest and saddest of lyrics ; Thomas Dekker, whose life was spent in alternation between the debtor's jail and the lower London theatres, in unremitting drudgery under the usurious, pawn-broking prince of the Elizabethan dramatic sweating system, Richard Henslowe, singing like a lark of " sweet content " and "golden numbers." Little wonder that such men should lament at times that "Virtue's branches wither, Virtue pines," or ask in heart-rending accents : "O sorrow, sorrow, say where dost thou dwell ? "

Owing to the wide popularity of the drama, these lyrics are far less the reflection of foreign models than the collections of the writers of madrigals ; but they reflected the immediate fashion in poetry even more faithfully. Thus the songs, interspersing the plays of Lyly and Peele, partook more or less of the pastoral and classical spirit preced-

ing 1590; whilst the earliest comedies of Shakespeare
exhibit the effects of the "humor" for sonnets.[1] The playwrights, however, almost at once perceived the need of a
wider scope of sentiment than was to be found in the
pastoral mode, and recognized the superior excellence of
shorter and sprightlier metrical forms over the slow-paced
sonnet. Hence we find the songs of the dramatists vying
in wealth of fancy and originality of form with the best
work of other lyrists. With the exception of Shakespeare,
whose lyrics, like all else that his hand touched, are beyond
comparison, no Elizabethan poet has produced so large a
number of exquisite songs as John Fletcher. His work
of this class displays the same facile grace and ease of
expression, the same mastery of effect combined with a
complete absence of effort that form the distinctive traits of
his dramatic works. Fletcher is not startling, nor very
original perhaps, but he has done what many have tried
and failed to do: he has united all but perfect beauty to all
but perfect naturalness. But Fletcher was not alone in this
or in the other graces that adorned the poetry of his age:
the gift of lyric song was general amongst the dramatists as
amongst other poets. From Chapman and Marston [2] alone

---

[1] "In *Love's Labour's Lost*," says Mr. Fleay, "he not only introduces
two sonnets proper which were published separately in *The Passionate
Pilgrim* as poems by him, but uses the sonnet form in the dialogue in
several instances." Cf. i, 1, 163–177, a passage which, however, is not
quite a sonnet; iv, 2, 109–122; 3, 60–73, etc. There are two sonnets
in *Romeo and Juliet*, one in *All's Well* and in *Henry V* (Fleay, *The
English Drama*, II, 224, and *Sh. Manual*, p. 135). Mr. T. Hall Caine
has discovered "the sextet of a Shakespearean sonnet" in *Rich. II*, ii,
1, 8–13. It will be noticed that all of these plays are early, *All's Well*
being the only one that falls after 1600. After this Shakespeare did not
use the sonnet in his plays.

[2] It is, perhaps, fair to state, as to Marston, that the songs which are
not infrequently indicated in his plays, have not come down to us.
Chapman, the great "Homeri Metaphrastes," needed the compass of

of them all is it difficult to get a lyric which is not at once good and representative. From all the rest comes music of varying melody and compass : the dainty lightness of Lyly, the sweet sincerity of Dekker, the delicate erotic sentiment of Beaumont and Fletcher, the weird and fanciful sorrow of Webster, the classical symmetry and nicety of Jonson, the rich variety and perfect mastery of Shakespeare : whether in the melodious lament for what is fair and fleeting, in the hearty bacchanal of good cheer and good fellowship, or in the love song with its flashing prismatic lights and deep, rich shadows, we have here the perfection of winged music, wedded to the perfection of lyrical emotion.

In the last years of the century an original and potent influence began to make itself felt. Ben Jonson is one of that interesting class of literary men that have a theory about literature; and Jonson's theory was a reasonable and consistent one. It was one view of the subject ; it was not the only view. While all art must ultimately resolve itself into an imitation of nature, in Aristotle's sense of that term, it is none the less true that few artists can afford to neglect the careful study of previous interpretations of nature. It was the amateurishness of contemporary art that Jonson criticised, which, when it copied at all, was apt to copy inferior models irresponsibly, and was continually running to excesses of all kinds, to over-ornament, bizarre treatment, carelessness as to construction, confusion of design, departures from simplicity and directness, of all of which his age furnished examples enough. Jonson contended, like Matthew Arnold in our own day, that only in a faithful,

---

"the vasty deep" in which to spread his "full and swelling sail"; he was stranded in the shallows of a calmly-flowing inland stream. It is notable that even his sonnet sequence *A Coronet in Praise of his Mistress Philosophy*, becomes little more than a continuous poem written in successive quatorzains.

though neither slavish nor affected, study of the ancients could English literature hope to acquire that professional touch, that sense of taste and proportion, of finish *ad unguem*, which industry, but no mere genius can supply. He was thus the first to feel theoretically the beginning of the reaction against the excesses of Romanticism run riot; and he was certainly as judicious in the application of his theories to his own poetry as he was injudicious in ventilating these theories at peculiarly inopportune moments. There has been in the history of literature, in consequence, a curious confusion of Jonson's theories, his practice and his manners. The last were often so bad as scarcely to be conceived worse; but there is much misapprehension still common about the other two. Now all this applies to Jonson's lyrics as well as to his other productions; for Jonson's lyrics are usually found by the critics to be wanting in something or other, if they are not called heavy, harsh, and stiff. The harshness, stiffness, and heaviness of the poetical diction of Ben Jonson is precisely as demonstrable as his undying enmity towards Shakespeare: both are the purest figments of the imagination. Not only shall I agree with Lowell when he tells us: "Yet Ben, with his principles off, could soar and sing with the best of them," but I shall not hesitate to affirm that Ben could soar and sing with his principles on, and possibly because of them. Many of the lyrics of Jonson are nearly perfect in their kind, and the reason for their perfection is, I think, to be found in the happy conjunction of a choice lyrical gift with the cultivated taste of genuine scholarship. To complete Lowell's words of Jonson: "There are strains in his lyrics which Herrick, the most Catullian of poets since Catullus, could imitate but never match."[1] I, at least, have no excuse to offer for having included a larger number of the lyrics of

[1] *Lessing,* Lowell's *Prose Works,* ed. 1890, II, 223.

Jonson in this collection than of any other poet except Shakespeare.

Jonson, Fletcher, and the later dramatists continued the lyric vein to the end of the reign of James and beyond ; and the lyrics written for music remained popular to the time of the later collections of Campion, Bateson, and Peerson ; whilst an occasional belated sequence of sonnets mixed with madrigals appeared, such as Drummond's. But the golden summer of the English lyric was now on the wane under stress of new and non-lyrical influences ; moreover a new and portentous growth had appeared, a species of applied literature, voluminous, nondescript verse devoted to things essentially unpoetical. For now came the days of the *Polyolbions* and *Purple Islands*, of verses topographical-mythological, and allegorical-anatomical : works that stand like huge Pelasgan walls, inexplicable from the hands of men as men now are. Naturally such works demanded a large attention, and this, with the growing interest in literary prose, took from the popular culture of the lyric, which languished somewhat in the hands of younger men, though still the native utterance of the surviving poets of an older generation.

It is a commonplace of the history of literature that the Jacobean poets wrote under three strong poetic influences, that of Spenser, that of Donne, and that of Jonson. Shakespeare less affected his immediate successors because he rose above mannerism and schools ; and yet it would hardly be unfair to say that the best lyrics of Beaumont, of Fletcher and Webster exhibit much of the Shakespearean manner. The lyrical tact and the classic certainty of Jonson's touch descended to several — not always the worthiest — of " the tribe of Ben," until the perfection of the hedonistic lyrical spirit in English poetry was reached in Campion, in Carew, and in Herrick. Donne, after no inconsiderable effect upon many of the minor poets and, indeed, upon Jonson himself, came in a new age to be regarded as more or less remotely the model whence were derived many of the blemishes, and not a few of the graces, of the poetry of Crashaw, Herbert, and others.

The Spenserians concern us less, as the Muse of Spenser is not so lyrical as imaginatively and elaborately idyllic. The shorter and more strictly lyrical poems, too, of William Browne and of Wither — who alone really succeeded in grafting a living shoot upon the pastoral stem of Spenser — are less derived from Spenser than from the more immediate models of Jonson or Campion.[1] Yet Browne had, notwithstanding, a true lyric quality of his own, which entitles him to a place of respect ; and, indeed, if we are to believe that he was actually the author of the famous *Epitaph on the Countess of Pembroke*, so long attributed to Jonson, Browne has certainly succeeded for once in rivaling his master at that master's best.[2] As to Wither whose verse, undistinguished from his poetry has long been painfully reprinting under the auspices of the Spenser Society (a task which indeed seems to have proved unhappily too much even for that long-lived association, and brought it of late to an untimely end), his heights and depths approach the heights and depths of Wordsworth ; whilst his fecundity is no less amazing than his metrical facility. Would that we had one more lyric like the immortal " Shall I wasting in despair " for many pages of eclogues and satires, excellent although many of them undoubtedly are.

Lastly we reach William Drummond of Hawthornden, whose sonnets are entirely after the earlier manner, Italian, sentimental, romantic, but touched with a delicate medita-

---

[1] Cf. Browne's *Song of the Siren*, p. 167 below, with Campion's *Hymn in praise of Neptune*, Bullen's *Campion*, p. 396.

[2] See the *Epitaph*, p. 201, and the note thereon.

tive imagination and a heightened sense of color that leads us to feel that in this poet we have the appropriate representative of the brilliant autumn of the Elizabethan year. Like Browne and Wither, Drummond was imitative in the best sense of that word, and displays with them a skillful and artistic employment of previous models to a larger degree than that spontaneous outburst of innate song which critics are wont to attribute to the earlier lyrists.[1] While recognizing this difference, I am sensible that it can easily be exaggerated and that "native wood-notes wild" are often in reality no more than that perfect art the crown of which is masterly concealment. A certain artificiality inheres in the artistic productions of all poets, and some there are, notably Herrick shortly after this, and Campion, Drummond, and Browne in this age, whose sense of artistic fitness has enabled them at times to surpass even the success of their masters.

The death of Fletcher may seem an arbitrary limit to put to a series of literary phenomena so unbroken as the lyrics of the sixteenth and seventeenth centuries. By the year 1625, however, almost every lyrist of importance who had written in the reign of Elizabeth, had either completed his best work or ceased altogether to write ; whilst of the Caroline poets that were to make the next reign musical, not one had yet begun to sing. Shakespeare and Beaumont were dead in 1616, Raleigh in 1618, Campion, Daniel, and Davison in the next year ; Donne, Drayton, and Jonson survived until the thirties, but their poetry, especially their lyrical poetry, was earlier ; and the most significant work of Browne, and even of Wither, and certainly of Drummond and the later song-writers, was concluded well before the accession of Charles.

---

[1] See the notes on Drummond's poems in this volume for several instances of his borrowings from Sidney and others below p. 296.

We have thus traversed in the merest sketch that period
of the history of English literature in which the lyric
flourished as it has never flourished before or since in
England. We found the Elizabethan lyric rising as one of
the products of the Renaissance, rapidly developing amidst
the culture of the court, thriving under the quickening
impulses of national and urban life, and proceeding through
a series of definite though superficial poetical fashions to
triumph after triumph in a thousand forms of new and
diverse beauty under the touch of men whose names must
remain immortal, whilst our language continues to be read.
Aside from the lofty and sustained excellence of this verse
as a whole, and its extraordinary variety of mood and treatment, its most striking peculiarity consists in the wide contemporary distribution of a matchless gift of song, which
like the rays of the sun shone impartially on all, from
lords and courtiers such as Oxford, Essex, or Raleigh to
the veriest literary hacks, Nashe, Munday, or Chettle ;
from the saintly Father Southwell to atheistical Marlowe ;
visiting busy dramatists, like Heywood, Dekker, or Field,
in the dull stretches of perfunctory toil ; adorning the
learning of Jonson and the scholarly leisure of Drummond ; courting the condemned traitor Tychborne in his
cell and the fallen statesman Bacon in his disgrace. Nor
was this general ability to write excellent lyrical verse
due to narrow interests or to the spirit of the *dilettante*,
which rejoices in artistic trifling. On the contrary, the
lyrical poetry of this incomparable age, with its sister-
blossoms, the pastoral, the romantic epic, the drama, and
its ample leafage of admirable prose, was the outcome of an
intense and potent national spirit, seeking an outlet for its
energies, not only in social, religious, and political channels,
but in intellectual and emotional activities as well. The
men that wrote these lyrics were often the men that bore

arms, or sat in the councils of their sovereign, men that scorned not the good opinion of their neighbors, nor the lands and beeves wherewith to support the shows of the world. It is an excellent thing to contemplate this great historical refutation of that inane theory which makes literature the pursuit of dreamers, or of abnormal departures from typical manhood, instead of a divine realization, by those who can see more deeply than the crowd, of the real image of man and of nature, towards which image the world is striving, but whereunto it reaches but seldom.

Not the least merit of Elizabethan literature, defining both words strictly, is its soundness and its health ; its very lapses from decorum are those of childhood, and its extravagances those of youth and heated blood, both as far as possible removed from the cold cynicism, the doubt of man and God, that crept into England in the train of King James, and came in time to chill and benumb the pulses of the nation. The best lyrics of this age are redolent with this soundness and health, and still joyous with the flush of youth and beauty. There is but one way in which to know them, and that is to read them and to re-read them ; to study them, not as the interesting products of an age to be patronized as unhappily not in the enjoyment of all the inestimable advantages of our own, but to recognize in them the living work of men, who were, save for their genius, much such men as we ; to learn to understand them and through understanding to love them as one of the most exquisite and priceless heritages handed down to posterity through the lapse of years.

II.

ELIZABETHAN LYRICAL MEASURES.

The metrical forms, in which the lyric of the age of Elizabeth sought utterance, have been little studied : beyond the sonnet, scarcely studied at all.   Even Dr. Schipper, whose excellent work on English Metres[1] is surprisingly full of matter of even minor detail, leaps from the lyrical forms of Sidney to those of Jonson, Donne, and Drummond, and offers us no word of the metres of anthologies later than *Tottel's Miscellany*, of the song-books, of lyrics of the dramatists, or of the lyrical achievements of such metrists as Greene, Lodge, Breton, Barnes, Campion, and Wither. This is not the place for an extended study of this interesting subject, more especially as the interest attaching to questions of organic literary form often runs quite distinct from aesthetic or historical considerations.

It is familiar to scholars that modern English verse is the resultant of three forces, all of them contemporaneous in their action, but not in their origin, and varying in relative intensity.   These forces or influences are represented (1) in the older national metre, the English representative of the original Teutonic metre ; (2) in the several foreign metrical systems, chiefly Italian and French, derived either directly or through Chaucer ; and (3) in the imitations of classical metres in English, for many years the experiment and diversion of the learned.   Although several of the lyrists of this age, as Watson and Campion, display a graceful command of the composition of Latin verses, which must materially have aided them in the acquisition of a like facility in the mother tongue, this last influence may be disregarded,

---

[1] *Englische Metrik*, 1889.

after emphasizing the great advantage that came from experiments of this kind, in disclosing the actual nature and limitations of the English language, and in improving the *technique* of verse. The older vernacular metres, too, exerted less influence on the lyric than might be supposed, although the earlier freedom as to number and distribution of syllables not infrequently asserts itself, or the mediæval fondness for the employment of alliteration for the sake of the jingle and not as a characteristic entering into the organism of the verse. It is to contemporary and earlier foreign models, then, that we must turn, if we are to find the chief motive, spirit, and much of the form of the Elizabethan lyric. Nor need this be understood to involve in question the genuine originality of the best of Elizabethan lyrists. The tree stood transplanting and flourished hardily until it became a new species in the colder air of England; but the tender scion long partook of the nature of the parent stem, and the lyric of England in the hands of mediocrity continued essentially an imitation of the lyric of Italy.

Reasons for this are not far to seek. The lyric must be neither learned nor provincial. Most of all forms of poetry must the lyric be the product of a refined and a cultivated taste. We have seen that the English lyric had its birth in cultivated courtly circles; for it was there that the artistic spirit was the purest, because it was there that it was closest to its source and inspiration, the Italy of the Renaissance, and least intermixed with extraneous elements. Indeed, after all, the English, no less than the Italians, were devotees of the new and passionate cult of beauty, delighting in glories of form and gorgeousness of color, whether displayed in glittering and jeweled robes of state, in splendid piles of fantastic and bizarre architecture, or in the flow and sweep of the sonorous and elaborated stanzas of *The Faery Queen*.

From an organic point of view the Elizabethan lyric

exhibits the greatest possible diversity. Although the
iambus[1] was regarded by the early critics of verse as the
only English foot,[2] and continues to-day overwhelmingly
the most usual, other movements are found very early.
Thus Puttenham gives a (possibly manufactured) instance
of trochaic measure in the verse :

> Craggy cliffs bring forth the fairest fountain.[3]

and Wyatt and Surrey exhibit an occasional verse of like
effect although no entire poem in that measure. With Greene
and Breton trochaics become not uncommon and—especially
in the popular heptasyllabic or truncated verse of four
accents — are familiar to the versification of Barnfield,
Shakespeare, the later song writers, Jonson, Fletcher, Browne,
and Wither.[4]

It seems reasonable to regard English trochaic measures,
not so much as attempts to follow a foreign metrical system,
as a continuance of the original freedom of English verse as
to the distribution of syllables. Most English trochaics
show a tendency to revert back to the more usual iambic
system by the addition of an initial unaccented syllable.
Thus in Greene's *Ode* on p. 54, of thirty-six verses, ten are

---

[1] I use these terms (*iambus, trochee,* etc.) in their usual acceptation
as to English verse, for the want of a better popular nomenclature.
Few metrists now deny that English metres are founded primarily on
accent ; although some still continue to question the important function
of quantity as a regulator of the time intervals in which the accented
and unaccented syllables are arranged. On this subject see Schipper,
Englische Metrik, I, 21 f., and Lanier's demonstration "that there can
be no rhythm in sounds, except through their relative time or duration,
quantity." *Science of English Verse,* p. 65.

[2] See Gascoigne's *Notes of Instruction,* ed. Arber, pp. 33, 34, and
King James' *Essays of a Prentice,* chap. iii.

[3] *Art of English Poetry,* ed. Arber, p. 144.

[4] Cf. pp. 36, 47, 54, 88, 120, 128, 133, 162, 168, 174, 178.

iambic, the rest trochaic. On the other hand, trochaic license may appear in iambic verse, as in Raleigh's *Pilgrimage*, p. 130:

> And when the grand twelve-million jury
> Of our sins with direful fury,
> 'Gainst our souls black verdicts give,
> Christ pleads his death, and then we live.

Here the norm is four iambic feet, making eight syllables ; but these lines number respectively nine, eight, seven, and eight, and only the last follows the norm. A later, familiar, example of this freedom is to be found in Milton's *L'Allegro*. It is scarcely necessary to remark that the prevailing foot will impart its character to the whole poem, despite occasional departure from the type.[1] An instance of admirably successful anapæsts will be found in *Pilgrim to Pilgrim*, p. 3, a poem the metrical parallel of which it would be difficult to find until far later. *E.g.:*

> His desire is a dureless content,
> And a trustless joy;
> He is won with a world of despair
> And is lost with a toy.

Jonson's anapæsts (see *The Triumph of Charis*, p. 183) are not very successful, though scarcely deserving of the scathing invective of Mr. Swinburne.[2] Dactyls too are rare, and seem to have been confined chiefly to experiments in the classical hexameter. The dactyl, however, was defended in argument for measures other than the hexameter by critics like Puttenham,[3] and used occasionally, like the anapæst in iambic measures, as a license in poems prevailingly trochaic. The employment of anapæstic and dactylic measures in this age for an entire poem is unusual;

---

[1] See Mayor, *Chapters on English Metre*, p. 91.
[2] *A Study of Ben Jonson*, p. 104, and see note, p. 287, below.
[3] *Art of English Poetry*, ed. Arber, p. 140.

but is, for a part of a stanza otherwise constructed, somewhat more frequent, especially in Shakespeare, who often
employs a change to a light tripping measure for his refrain,
as in the second and third examples which follow :

> I am slain by a fair cruel maid.

> Heigh-ho ! sing heigh-ho ! unto the green holly :
> Most friendship is feigning, most loving mere folly.

> Merrily, merrily shall I live now
> Under the blossom that swings on the bough.[1]

The measures of the Elizabethan lyric exhibit great
diversity, whether in verses of equal or unequal lengths.
The range extends from verses of two stresses : [2]

> Sing we and chant it
> While love doth grant it,[3]

to the long iambic fourteener or septenary, which, although
usually split into alternate verses of four and three accents
by a strong cæsura and so printed, occurs not infrequently
undivided. *E.g.*, from Robert Jones' *Ultimum Vale:*

> Wert thou the only world's admirèd thou canst love but one,
> And many have before been loved, thou art not loved alone ; [4]

or thus in trochaic measure :

> Thy well ordered locks ere long shall rudely hang neglected
> And thy lively pleasant cheer read grief on earth dejected.[5]

For an instance of the divided septenary see Southwell's
Burning Babe, p. 69, sometimes, as in the first edition, printed
undivided. The Alexandrine, another verse of early popularity consisting of six iambic feet, generally occurs, in

---

[1] Cf. pp. 122, 95, and 154.   [2] Cf. *M. N. D.* iii, 2, 448.
[3] *Bullen's Lyrics from Elizabethan Song Books*, p. 106.
[4] Bullen, *More Lyrics*, p. 28.   [5] Cf. p. 187.

lyrical poetry, divided into two verses of three stresses each. *E.g.*, these lines of Lodge :

> The gods that saw the good
> That mortals did approve,
> With kind and holy mood,
> Began to talk of Love.

Several examples of the undivided Alexandrine are to be found in trochaics as well as iambics, continuous or — more frequently — united with verses of other lengths : *e.g.*, from the first sonnet of *Astrophel and Stella*, which is entirely in Alexandrines :

> Thus, great with child to speak, and helpless in my throes,
> Biting my truant pen, beating myself for spite ;
> Fool, said my Muse to me, look in thy heart, and write ;

or thus in trochaics :

> When thy story, long time hence, shall be perusèd,
> Let the blemish of thy rule be thus excusèd,
> ' None ever lived more just, none more abusèd.' [1]

The final Alexandrine of the Spenserian stanza was not without its effect on lyric measures, and several lyric stanzas display this "sweet lengthening" of the concluding verse. (See Jonson, p. 113 ; and Jones, p. 121.) The combination of the septenary and the Alexandrine, the well-known poulter's measure, was becoming rare in serious poetry by the beginning of this period ; a specimen may be seen, however, in Oxford's poem, *Fancy and Desire*, p. 8 of this volume.

If the sonnet be included in the count with the many other stanzas in which decasyllabic measure occurs alone or in combination with other measures, the iambic verse of five stresses will be found the most common English lyrical measure, as it is the measure most frequently employed in

---

[1] Bullen's *Campion*, p. 49.

the drama and in epic poetry. But, the sonnet apart, verses of four stresses form the favorite lyrical measure of the age, whether in the usual iambic form, *e.g.* :

> At last he set her both his eyes,
> She won, and Cupid blind did rise,[1]

or in the limpid trochaics (usually truncated and hence consisting of but seven syllables) of Breton, Barnfield, or Shakespeare, *e.g.* :

> On a day, alack the day !
> Love, whose month is ever May,
> Spied a blossom passing fair,
> Playing in the wanton air.[2]

The lyrics of Shakespeare, Fletcher and the dramatists in general exhibit a great preponderance of octosyllabics and shorter measures ; decasyllables being reserved for their dramatic writings almost altogether. This is scarcely less true of the song-writers, who display the greatest freedom of choice and combination, but prefer the lighter and shorter measures. As already intimated above, variety of feet, except as an occasional license, rarely extends, in any of these measures, beyond the usual iambic and trochaic movement ; and the trochee is confined, for the most part, to heptasyllabics. Thus, whether slurred in pronunciation or not, a redundance results from the substitution of three syllables for two in the third foot of this line :

> Roses their sharp *spines being* gone ;

or take, as an extreme case, the line :

> Thus fain *woŭld Ĭ hăve hăd* a pretty thíng,

which is uttered in the same time interval as :

> O Lady, what a luck is this.[3]

---

[1] Cf. Lyly's *Apelles' Song*, p. 19 ; also Sidney's *Wooing Stuff*, p. 9.
[2] *LLL*, iv, 3, 101 ; see also pp. 47, 50, 54, 67, etc.   [3] P. 26.

On the other hand syllables are occasionally omitted, forming
what is technically known as the compensating pause,
although such departures from the norm are far rarer in
lyric than in contemporary dramatic verse. An illustration
of such a pause effecting emphasis is this, from Lyly :

> Thy bread be frowns ; thy drink be gall,
> (◡) *Such* as when you Phao call.[1]

See also Spenser's *Perigot and Willie's Roundelay*,[2] which is
written altogether upon a recognition of the principle that
the time intervals of successive or corresponding verses
being the same, any distribution of syllables (not destructive
of such time intervals), may be rhythmical, *e.g.* :

◡	—	◡	—	◡	—	◡	—
Hey		ho		hol - li		daye.
Hey		ho	the	high		hyll.
The while	the	shep-heards	selfe	did		spill.
The greene		is	for	may - dens		meet.

Here the normal scheme demands eight syllables, or four
iambuses ; but few verses of the answering refrain or burden
exhibit this quantum, a deft distribution of pauses keeping
the poem, however, perfectly rhythmical. An example of
the compensating pause regularly distributed with onomato-
poetic effect is found in Jonson's *Echo's Lament for Narcissus*,
p. 113 :

> O could I still
> Like melting snow upon some craggy hill
> *Drop, drop, drop, drop,*
> Since Nature's pride is now a withered daffodil.

Variety of feet entering into the organism of the stanza
— and not as a mere license for variety's sake — is less
frequent in Elizabethan lyrical stanzas than might be ex-

---

[1] P. 22.　　　　　[2] P. 5, below.

pected. Some of Shakespeare's songs are the best known instances, as *Silvia* (p. 56), where the verses seem alternately trochaic and iambic by reason of the distribution of the unaccented syllables, the tripping refrains of the two songs from *As You Like It* (p. 95), and, best of all, the change from the anapæsts of the first four verses of the Dirge from *Twelfth Night* (p. 122) to the regular iambics of the fifth and seventh verses. While other lyrists, too, display this quality of an organic variation of foot, Thomas Campion appears to me one of the most subtle masters of this as of many other metrical devices. Space permits but two examples. Notice the clever adaptation of the metre to the thought in both cases, especially in the metrical change between the third and fourth verses of the latter:

> What if a day, or a month, or a year
> Crown thy delights with a thousand sweet contentings?
> Cannot a chance of a night or an hour
> Cross thy desires with as many sad tormentings?
> Fortune, Honor, Beauty, Youth
> Are but blossoms dying;
> Wanton Pleasure, doting Love
> Are but shadows flying, etc.

> Break now, my heart, and die! O no, she may relent.
> Let my despair prevail! O stay, hope is not spent.
> Should she now fix one smile on thee, where were despair?
> The loss is but easy, which smiles can repair.
> A stranger would please thee, if she was as fair.[1]

Modes more usually employed to compass variety of cadence are found in the increasing freedom with which later Elizabethan lyrists used (1) the distribution of rime-correspondences with correspondences as to length of verse, and (2) their growing skill in phrasing and the employment

---

[1] Bullen's *Campion*, p. 95; and see p. 398.

of run-on lines. Take this early stanza from *A Handful of Pleasant Delights* (p. 25):

> It is not all the silk in Cheap,
>   Nor all the golden treasure,
> Nor twenty bushels on a heap,
>   Can do my lady pleasure.

Here the alternate lines correspond respectively in length, rime, and rhetorical pause (*i.e.*, 'sense pause'), and unite, with perfect regularity of stress and number of syllables, to carry out what may be termed the metrical scheme. In contrast, consider this stanza of Jonson :

> Mark, mark, but when his wing he takes   1
> How fair a flight he makes !
> How upward and direct !
> Whilst pleased Apollo
> Smiles in his sphere to see the rest affect
> In vain to follow.   5
> This swan is only his,
> And Phœbus' love cause of his blackness is.[1]

Here only two of the lines, which correspond in length, also correspond in rime ; whilst not only are the verses of several different lengths, but the *enjambement*, or 'overflow' of lines 1, 4, and 5 adds a still greater variety to the effect. These characteristics were so general and often so dependent upon a passing mood that they hardly call for individual specification. Greene and Lodge (but neither Breton nor Lyly) often show extreme diversity in the lengths of their verses.[2] Among later lyrists the same contrast is to be found in the verse of Davison and Drummond on the one hand and

---

[1] *Ode* ἀλληγορικὴ, *Jonson*, Riverside ed., p. 374.

[2] Cf. *Rosalind's Madrigal*, p. 29, *Menaphon's Song*, p. 35, or *Doron's Jig*, p. 38, with *Apelles' Song*, p. 19, *Olden Love-Making*, p. 27, or *Phyllida and Corydon*, p. 47.

Wither and Browne on the other.[1] Shakespeare in his very latest lyrics, Jonson and Fletcher at times, and Donne constantly, show much freedom and art in phrasing and in the employment of the overflow.[2]

The Elizabethan lyric, like all English verse, displays an overwhelming preference for single or masculine rimes as compared with double or feminine ones. This is demanded by the monosyllabic character of our tongue and that proclitic tendency which has come to make the iambus the usual foot in modern English.[3] Feminine rimes, however, are used not only to vary the effect by a redundant final syllable, as in :

> She, poor bird, as all forlorn,
> Leaned her breast up-till a thorn,
> And there sung the dolefullest *ditty*,
> That to hear it was great *pity ;* [4]

but also as entering into the organism of the stanza, as in this Madrigal from Bateson's collection :

[1] Cf. *Madrigal, to Cupid*, p. 72, Drummond's Madrigals, pp. 179, 206, with *Welcome, welcome*, p. 175, *A Round*, p. 176, or *Shall I Wasting in Despair*, p. 168.

[2] See Shakespeare's *Orpheus*, p. 164, Fletcher's *Bridal Song*, p. 160, or *Care-charming Sleep*, p. 173, Jonson's *Echo's Dirge*, p. 113, *Nymph's Passion*, p. 192, or *Dream*, p. 193, Donne's *Funeral*, p. 104, and the Sonnet on *Death*, p. 142. This subject seems to me worthy of greater attention than it has yet received except in the field of dramatic blank verse. Few points of metre offer so strong an index of poetic temperament and development if wisely investigated.

[3] As instances of this proclitic character, notice the obscure pronunciation of many common English words, *e.g.*, the mān, ǒf stēēl. Other reasons for our modern preference for the iambus are to be found in the fact that monosyllabic words compounded with a prefix usually retain the Teutonic root-accent : fŏrewārned, bĕcōme ; that in words of three or more syllables the secondary accent is likely to fall on alternate syllables: ĕxtĕnūāte ; and that many rules of collocation further make for this tendency.   [4] See p. 88 9-12.

> Sister awake, close not your eyes
> The day its light *discloses*
> And the bright morning doth arise
> Out of her bed of *roses;* [1]

Or this of John Fletcher:

> Away, delights ! go seek some other *dwelling,*
> For I must die.
> Farewell, false love ! thy tongue is ever *telling*
> Lie after lie.

Sidney, Breton, several of the madrigal writers, and others have written poems, the rimes of which are wholly feminine. *E.g.*, Breton's *A Farewell to Love:*

> Farewell, love and loving folly,
> All thy thoughts are too unholy :
> Beauty strikes thee full of blindness,
> And then kills thee with unkindness, etc.[2]

In a long poem, however, this at times becomes forced. The greatest possible variety as to the number and arrangement of rime correspondences is to be found in this literature; men like Lodge, Nashe, and Shakespeare did not hesitate to play upon a rime for emphasis, serious or sportive, to the extent of four, six, and even eight successive lines. Notice the effect produced by the following, which is further increased by the strong and regular terminal and internal caesura :

> Accurst be Love, and those that trust his trains !
> He tastes the fruit whilst others toil,
> He brings the lamp, we lend the oil,
> He sows distress, we yield him soil,
> He wageth war, we bide the foil.[3]

---

[1] P. 132.

[2] Bullen's *Lyrics from Elizabethan Romances*, p. 97.

[3] P. 60; see also pp. 29, 51, and *M. N. D.*, iii, 2, 102-109.

Internal rime is not very frequent, although it occurs occasionally as an organic characteristic, in Nashe's song *Spring*, p. 51, or Campion's lines :

Every *dame* affects good *fame*, whate'er her doings be,
But true *praise* is Virtue's *bays*, which none may wear but she ;[1]

or almost accidentally, as in Wither's *Sonnet* (p. 202):

My spirit *loathes*
Where gaudy *clothes*
And feignèd *oaths* may love obtain.

The refrain, too, was a frequent device, occurring in the final verse of the stanza (see pp. 113, 153, 162), internally, as in Sidney's two poems (pp. 11 and 15); and even initially, as in the poem, *Accurst be Love*, a stanza of which is quoted just above. Often the refrain takes the form of a recurring stanza of several lines, sometimes placed at the beginning of the poem as well as after each stanza. (*E.g.*, Dekker's *O Sweet Content*, p. 93, or Browne's *Song*, p. 175.) At the other extreme of these various devices of sound correspondence may be mentioned the rare instances of poems which preserve all the 'notes' of the lyric except rime. (See the unrimed quatorzain, *All in Naught*, p. 148, and Jonson's lines, p. 194.[2])

Lastly alliteration, one of the earliest inheritances of the English Muse, continued a familiar device of poetic style ; although few things better mark the growth of a chastened literary style than the contrast between the persistent and unnecessary " hunting of the letter " by Gascoigne, and even by Spenser in his earlier day, and the subtle and half-furtive use of these correspondences in sound by the later dramatic

---

[1] *Fourth Book of Airs*, Bullen's *Campion*, p. 115.

[2] See also the hendecasyllabic, unrimed verses subscribed ' A. W.' in *The Poetical Rhapsody* and there called " Phaleuciacks." (Ed. Bullen, pp. 38, 44, 76.)

lyrists and song writers. (Cf. on this point Gascoigne's *The Strange Passion of a Lover*, p. 1, with Webster's *Dirge*, p. 145, or Beaumont and Fletcher's *Aspatia's Song*, p. 148.)

We left the earlier Elizabethan lyrists experimenting and busily engaged in peopling the downs of Middlesex and Surrey with the supposed shepherds and shepherdesses of Piedmont and the Campagna ; not only transmuting their Madges and Maulkins into Lauras or at least Phyllidas, but likewise imitating the dainty poetic forms of Italy in sonnets, madrigals, terzines, canzons, and sestines. But a national literature can never be established upon the imitation of foreign models, however perfect ; and while several of these forms continued to be practiced with greater or less fidelity and success, it was only those which were molded into a distinctively English character in the hands of the greater masters of versification, that quickened with a later growth.

Historically as well as intrinsically, the three greatest metrists of the earlier part of this period are Sidney, Spenser, and Marlowe. Of these, Marlowe's achievements in dramatic blank verse do not concern us here. The stanza of *The Faery Queen* is only the most striking instance of the perfect taste and unerring metrical tact, which have enabled Spenser, more successfully than any other English poet, to choose or invent precisely that medium of poetic expression which was best fitted to the conveyance of his thought. Nothing could be finer than the liquid flow of the long stanzas of the *Prothalamion* (p. 76) or the diversified, musical phrasing of the *Dirge* for Dido in *November* of *The Shepherds' Calendar;* and we recognize at once that in form as well as in matter Spenser stands at the head of the pastoral lyrists. But, as remarked above, the Muse of Spenser is not so purely lyrical as imaginatively and elaborately idyllic, and hence we are not surprised to find him

rarely winging those short ecstatic flights which distinguish
so many of his minor contemporaries. The classical experiments of Spenser, Sidney, and their Areopagus Club,[1]
as already stated, little concerned the lyric; and yet the
metrical ingenuity of the young reformers was busied in
matters besides abortive sapphics and asclepiads; and the
Arcadia exhibits many imitations of contemporary Italian
metrical forms.   Sidney thus becomes for us the chief
representative of Italian metrical influence on the English
lyric.

The word pastoral is a generic term denoting a literary
mode, not a special literary form.   It is familiar that this
mode is common to verse and prose, the epic, dramatic, and
lyric form, and mingled with every other conceivable mode
which the teeming originality of an age which doted on
novelty could bring forth.   We have thus the pastoral
romance told in prose, *Rosalind* or *Pandosto;* exhibiting
simple bucolic life or mingled with deeds of valor and adventure as in the *Arcadia;* allegorized and told in verse as in
The Faery Queen. We have the pastoral drama mythologized
in *Midas* or *The Arraignment of Paris;* anglicized in *The Sad
Shepherd;* or maintaining the Italian flavor in *The Faithful
Shepherdess* or in *The Queen's Arcadia.*   Again, there are
narrative pastorals like *The Shepherds' Calendar;* the eclogues
of Drayton and Lodge with all the devices of dialogue and
musical contest, in the latter case diverted into a satirical
channel, at other times stretched into a rambling poem
describing much, narrating little, like *Britannia's Pastorals;*
forced into the mold of far-fetched allegory as *The Purple
Island;* or applied to "divine uses" as *Christ's Victory and*

---

[1] See Mr. Gosse's article on *Sidney, Contemporary Review,* I, 642,
Church's *Spenser,* pp. 18, 19, and the editor's *Poetic and Verse Criticism
of the Reign of Elizabeth, Publications of the University of Pennsylvania,
Series in Philology, Literature and Archaeology,* I, No. 1, pp. 27 f.

Triumph. Lastly we have the pastoral lyric in collections like Lodge's *Phyllis* and the poems of this species scattered through the anthologies and through longer works in verse and prose. These poems often exhibit very direct foreign influence in title and stanzaic form : the familiar *eclogue* and *idyl*, a term of infrequent occurrence among Elizabethan authors ; the *madrigal*, discussed below ; the *barginet*, more correctly the *bergeret*, a shepherd's song, in the specimen by Lodge in *England's Helicon*,[1] made up of a series of tercets. The only English metre which can be said to have become to any degree identified with the pastoral mode, is the octo-syllabic iambic measure riming either in couplets or alternately with its derivative, the heptasyllabic trochaics, extremely common in the works of Breton. These metres, however, are almost as frequently employed in other lyrical modes.[2]

On the other hand, *England's Helicon*, which may be regarded as typical of the pastoral mode, lavishes the greatest variety of titles indiscriminately upon poems little distinguished as to form. Thus *sonnet* is applied to anything, whether a quatorzain or of other length, whilst long stanzaic poems equally with short ones are called *madrigals, ditties, idyllia, songs*, or simply *pastorals*. The last word too is affixed to any term : as *pastoral ode, pastoral song, pastoral sonnet*, or *canzon pastoral*. Many titles of pastoral songs and their corresponding words are derived from popular terms for dances : as the *jig*, a merry, irregular song in short measure, more or less comic, and often sung and danced by the clown to an accompaniment of pipe and tabor ; the *branle*, Eng-lished *brawl* and confused with a very different significance of the same word ; the *roundelay*, a light poem, originally a shepherd's dance, in which an idea or phrase is repeated,

---

[1] Ed. Bullen, p. 46.
[2] Cf. pp. 114, 119, 120, 162, 168, 172.

often as a verse, or stanzaic refrain.[1] Lastly several titles
are distinctly English, or at least translations of foreign
titles into English equivalents : as *passion*, used especially
by Watson, *contention*, *complaint*, and *lament*, all in their meanings sufficiently obvious. It is useless to attempt the pres-
ervation of distinctions wholly artificial. Similar conditions
produce similar results ; and we do not need the Provençal
tenzone to account for the English *brawl* nor the *alba*
and *serena* to explain morning songs and serenades. A few
metrical forms yet remain, which, however far some of
them ultimately departed from their originals, are none the
less Italian in source and interesting in themselves. These
are the *madrigal*, the *terzine*, the *sestine*, the *canzon*, and the
sonnet.

The Italian *madrigal* is described by Körting [2] as an epigrammatic lyric preserving no absolute rule as to form.
From Dr. Schipper,[3] however, we learn that the madrigal
originally consisted of a combination of two or three tercets
variously arranged as to rime, followed by one or by two
couplets, or occasionally even by a quatrain, the measure
being usually hendecasyllabic. Schipper gives eight varieties
of the madrigal based upon these principles and the most
common in the fifteenth century. From these examples it
appears that the number of verses was not less than eight
nor more than eleven, and that the favorite arrangement of
the tercets was that in which the second and third verses
rimed, the first corresponding with the fourth or not, as the
case might be. (*E.g.*, *a b b, a c c,* or *a b b, c d d;* plus a couplet,
e e, or couplets, *e e, f f.*) An examination of the short poems
contained in Oliphant's *Musa Madrigalesca*, Mr. Bullen's
two volumes of *Lyrics from Elizabethan Song Books*, Davi-

---

[1] For the jig see p. 38 ; for the roundelay, pp. 5, 20, 21, etc.
[2] *Encyklopädie und Methodologie der romanischen Philologie*, III, 672.
[3] *Englische Metrik*, II, 887.   •

son's *Poetical Rhapsody*, and the poems, entitled madrigals, by Sidney, Barnes, Alexander, Drummond, and some others, exhibits some eighty or more examples approximating the madrigal forms given by Dr. Schipper, scarcely a score representing the actual Italian arrangement of rimes, and but one, and that not one of this number, preserving the hendecasyllabics of the original metre throughout.[1] As results, we find (1) the range of the madrigal extended from six verses to fifteen, and even sixteen, whilst Barnes, who wrote twenty-six poems in this form, has madrigals of nineteen, twenty-seven, and even one of forty-two lines, although his average range is from ten to sixteen ; (2) the metre is constantly varied, for the most part independently of the rimes, with verses of differing lengths, preferably lines of five accents and of three ; (3) considerable freedom is displayed in the arrangement of the rimes of the tercets ; and (4) there is an endeavor, especially among writers of madrigals to be set to music, to preserve the effect of Italian iambics by means of a preference for feminine rimes.

The majority of these madrigals on Italian models occur in the earlier collections of Byrd, Morley, and Dowland, and in the *Musica Transalpina*, which purports to be a mere translation. In these collections, and far more frequently in later ones, are found a large number of short poems otherwise constructed as to rime, and yet exhibiting the characteristics of the madrigal, and often so entitled. Some of these display other Italian verse forms, *e.g.*, a quatrain followed by one or by two couplets, a single or double quatrain, or a short succession of couplets, all of these varieties of the *Rispetto* and other Italian folk-verse. To what extent these simple forms are merely due to prevailing English metrical influences, it is, of course, impossible to say. In several

---

[1] Cf. *Musa Madrigalesca*, p. 88, which exhibits *abb*, *cdd*, a truncated form omitting the concluding couplet.

instances of metrical variation from Dr. Schipper's Italian madrigal forms, Oliphant gives the original, and the English shows a close metrical reproduction. This proves, what we know from other sources, that the English writers were only following in the madrigal, as in other forms, the greater freedom which Italian verse had assumed among their contemporaries of the latter half of the sixteenth century.

I quote the following madrigal from *Canzonets, or little short Songs to three voices, newly published,* by Thomas Morley, 1593. It preserves a usual Italian form, except for the variation of metre:

> Say, gentle nymphs, that tread these mountains,
> Whilst sweetly you sit playing,
> Saw you my Daphne straying
>
> Along your crystal fountains?
> If that you chance to meet her,
> Kiss her and kindly greet her;
>
> Then these sweet garlands take her,
> And say from me, I never will forsake her.[1]

Here is another illustrating a form consisting only of tercets. It appears prefixed to Morley's *Ballets to Five Voices,* and is signed M. M. D., which has been thought to stand for Master Michael Drayton:

> Such was old Orpheus' cunning,
> That senseless things drew near him
> And herds of beasts to hear him.
>
> The stock, the stone, the ox, the ass, came running.
> Morley! but this enchanting
> To thee, to be the music god, is wanting;

---

[1] *Musa Madrigalesca,* p. 79.

And yet thou needst not fear him;
Draw thou the shepherds still, and bonny lasses,
And envy him not stocks, stones, oxen, asses.[1]

Eventually the freer forms superseded those more closely imitating the Italian, until verses termed madrigals became indistinguishable from other short poems. Drummond, following the earlier work of his friend, Sir William Alexander, attempted a revival of the madrigal as of the sonnet. The madrigals of Drummond range from five to fifteen verses, and are composed, for the most part, on the general system of tercets, followed by a concluding couplet; they are very irregular in rime arrangement, and confined almost entirely to a free alternation of verses of five accents and of three, and to masculine rimes.[2] It is hardly necessary to state that the madrigal was commonly set to music.[3]

The *terzine* is a continuous measure of five accents riming *a b a*, *b c b*, *c d c*, etc., introduced into English by Wyatt and Surrey. It is a narrative rather than a lyric measure, and is rare in Elizabethan poetry, although used by Sidney, Daniel, Jonson, and Drummond, for eclogues, occasional verse, and once in a somewhat lyrical song by the first.[4] Sidney, followed by Spenser, Barnes, Alexander, Drummond,

---

[1] *Percy Society Publications*, XIII, 21; the same volume contains three madrigals of Watson's, one of them in *ottava rima*, another in couplets. Watson appears to have left other poems in this form; these I have been unable to see. For further illustrations of the madrigal in its various English forms see pp. 83, 90, 112, 127, 132, 133, 155, 161, 179-81, and 193. The epigrammatic nature of the form is nicely preserved in Jonson's *Hour Glass*, p. 193, and in the madrigal from Greaves' *Songs*, p. 132.

[2] Cf. pp. 179-81, 206.

[3] An excellent work on the bibliography of English Song Books is the *Bibliotheca Madrigaliana*, by E. F. Rimbault, 1847. See, also, Oliphant's *A Short Account of Madrigals*, London, 1836, and an article in the *British and Foreign Review* for 1845.

[4] Grosart's *Sidney*, III, 50.

and others, also employs the highly artificial *sestine* in its
various modifications, for an explanation of the structure of
which I must refer the reader to Dr. Schipper.[1]

The *canzon*,[2] which in the hands of Petrarch had consisted
of a highly organized lyrical form extending from five to ten
stanzas of from nine to twenty verses, each with an added
commiato or *envoy*, was rarely practiced by the English poets
of this age. Barnabe Barnes affords the best specimens,
notably in his *Canzon III*, the rimes of which exactly repro-
duce the arrangement of those of the second *Canzone* of
Petrarch : *O aspettata in ciel, beata e bella ;* although Barnes
uses only decasyllabic or hendecasyllabic verses, whilst
Petrarch employs here, as customarily, a metre occasionally
varied with shorter verses. Barnes' canzon is made up of
seven stanzas of fifteen verses, the rimes of which are
arranged upon this system : *a b c b a c, c d e e d e f d f;* the
two parts forming what is technically known as the *fronte*
and the *sirima*, followed by a *commiato* or conclusion, which
reproduces the rime arrangement of the *sirima*. The other
canzons of Barnes, and those of Sir William Alexander,[3]
are freer in construction ; and other similar long stanzaic
structures shade off into irregular odes, epithalamia or
other stanzas, losing entirely any sense of an original,
Italian, classical, or English. The term thus came to be
loosely employed, as may be seen by reference to Bolton's
two stanzas on p. 109, or Greene's canzone in common
metre.[4] As to the diminutive *canzonet*, the term is of

---

[1] *Engl. Metr.*, II, 902 *seq.* ; for examples see Barnes' *Parthenophil
and Parthenope*, Arber's *English Garner*, V, 406–479 *passim ;* also Sidney's *Arcadia*, Grosart's *Poems of Sidney*, III, 48, and II, 197 and 202,
where still greater metrical refinements are practiced in the double
sestine and "a Crown of Dizaines and Pendent."

[2] Italian *canzone*, originally a song unaccompanied.

[3] *Aurora*, 1604, ed. 1870, pp. 1, 28.

[4] *Poems of Greene*, ed. Bell, p. 61.

infrequent use in English poetry, and seems to have been employed much, as in Provençal and Italian, to denote any short lyric, generally not exceeding a single stanza. Drayton uses the term for a poem of three stanzas of double quatrains,[1] and elsewhere for a quatorzain.[2]

So much has been written, wisely and unwisely, on the *sonnet*, that some excuse must be offered for here repeating the particulars of an often repeated tale. For minuter matters I must refer the reader to Leigh Hunt's charming essay, prefixed to his *Book of the Sonnet*, to Schipper, as above, and to the many excellent discussions of this fertile theme elsewhere ;[3] some repetition cannot be avoided. Mr. Waddington very properly objects to the customary terms " Italian sonnet," or " Petrarchan sonnet," applied to a certain type, as other types were nearly as popular and quite as Italian, whilst the type in question " was written by Guittone many years before Petrarch adopted it as his model."[4] Even more objectionable than these mere inaccuracies are the opprobrious epithets frequently applied to those English quatorzains which depart from the various Italian types, the more especially that even among those English sonnets which most minutely observe the number and arrangement of the Petrarchan rimes, there are few which do not violate other rules of the Italian sonnet as strict, if not so obvious.

The term, sonnet, is very elastic as employed by Elizabethan writers ; and it was commonly used, as originally in Italy, to signify a short lyric of almost any form, or as a sort of generic term including the canzon, madrigal, ode,

---

[1] See p. 196 below.

[2] *Idea, Son.* lxi, ed. 1605.

[3] See also L. Biadene, *Morfologia del Sonetto nei secoli XIII e XIV*, in Monaci's *Studj di Filologia Romanza*, IV, 1–234.

[4] *English Sonnets by Living Writers*, p. 201.

and what not.[1] By the more careful, however, the term
came more and more to be restricted to signify a quartor-
zain or integral form of fourteen verses[2] devoted to the
expression of a single thought or passion, ordinarily that
of love. The classical Italian sonnet, which is always
hendecasyllabic except for comic effect, was composed of
two metrical systems, — the octave, consisting of two quatrains or *basi*, and the sestet, consisting of two tercets or
volte. Each system has its own rimes; the quatrains, two,
either 'enclosed' (*a b b a*), or alternate (*a b a b*), generally
both alike, though occasionally otherwise arranged (as
a b a b, b a b a); the tercets, two or three, commonly alternate (*c d c, d c d* or *c d c, c d c*), though several other arrangements were allowable, even a concluding couplet in one
form. It may be added that the earliest Italian form was
composed upon four rimes, alternate throughout the two
systems.

With such a freedom in bondage for a model, with a
monosyllabic tongue like English, in which rimes are far
less frequent than in Italian, and in which metrical tra-
ditions such as the quatrain and the riming couplet already
existed, certain results might be expected in the attempt to
transplant the sonnet. (1) The metre would adjust itself
to the language, and exhibit a preponderance of masculine
rimes, thus becoming decasyllabic. (2) The alternate rime
would be preferred to the enclosed rime throughout, (3) with
a change of rime rather than a frequent repetition of the
same rime. (4) Lastly, the Italian restraint, that sought
the avoidance of a closing couplet that the unity of the
entire poem might not be destroyed by an undue prom-
inence of any part, would be sacrificed to the more

---

[1] Cf. the forms called sonnets by Greene, Watson, Greville, or
Breton.

[2] Cf. the title, Drayton's *Idea's Mirror: Amours in Quatorzains.*

apparent effect of climax and epigrammatic vigor. The result is before us: a series of three quatrains, riming independently, followed and closed by a couplet (*a b a b, c d c d, e f e f, g g*), the form of the sonnet of Shakespeare and of the majority of contemporary sonneteers.

But it is not to be supposed that all this was accomplished without experiment. The forms of the Elizabethan quatorzain, to say nothing of derivative stanzas of other lengths, are almost endless. Thus Wyatt practiced many sonnet forms, for the most part preserving the Italian structure of the octave, though falling in the sestet into the final couplet; whilst Surrey soon hit upon the form afterwards adopted by Shakespeare, and practiced it almost to the exclusion of all others. Again Sidney, who was intimate with Italian literature, good and indifferent, experimented with the sonnet, and has probably produced it in a greater diversity of form than any other Elizabethan. While prevailingly strict as to the number and arrangement of his rimes, Sidney too falls into the usual preference for the concluding couplet. On the other hand, Spenser characteristically invented the only original English quatorzain, a link sonnet running *a b a b, b c b c, c d c d, e c*, undoubtedly suggested by his exercise of the stanza of his *Faery Queen*, and practiced it practically to the exclusion of all other forms.[1] Among later sonneteers, the form which Surrey had introduced became overwhelmingly the most popular, affecting even such Italianate poets as Barnes; while Daniel, Drayton, Shakespeare, and the host of minor and occasional writers of sonnets are given wholly over to this form. Constable, who

---

[1] Of Spenser's linked form of sonnet Leigh Hunt writes: "It is surely not so happy as that of the Italian sonnet. The rime seems at once less responsive and always interfering; and the music has no longer its major and minor divisions." (*Book of the Sonnet*, I, 74.) It may be doubted if every one will agree with this verdict.

lived much abroad and whose sonnets were greatly admired
in his day, was almost alone in insisting upon the Italian
types ; and even he was not proof against Surrey's arrangement of rimes or against the seductive closing couplet.[1]

Without entering into the details of the diversities of the
Elizabethan quatorzain, the following data may be sufficient
to indicate their extent. Quatorzains in blank verse were
written by Spenser in his earlier translations of the *Visions
of Bellay;*[2] on one and on two rimes — occasionally on the
same word or words — by Sidney, Surrey, and Wyatt;[3] on
three rimes by Sidney.[4] Four and five rimes constitute the
normal Italian number, while Spenser's linked sonnet and
some others exhibit five, and Daniel the exceptional number, six.[5] Seven is the ordinary number of rimes in the
sonnet of Surrey and Shakespeare. Again, besides (1) the
three quatrains and a couplet of this common form, and
(2) the two quatrains and sestet variations of the Italian
types, the rime arrangement of the Elizabethan quatorzain
exhibits occasionally (3) a series of seven couplets : *a a, b b,
c c, d d, e e, f f, g g;*[6] (4) a series of four triplets followed by
a couplet : *a a a, b b b, c c c, d d d, e e;*[7] (5) two sestets followed by a couplet — if, indeed, it be not better described
as an alternation of couplets and quatrains — a very unusual
structure of Gascoigne's : *a a, b c b c, d d, e f e f, g g.*[8] Lastly,

---

[1] For specimens of the Italian type see his *Diana,* Nos. 11, 13, 21,
23, 25, etc.   [2] Ed. Grosart, III, Appendix, p. 231.

[3] See a highly successful example on two rimes in this vol., p. 11 ; on
two words *Astrophel and Stella,* Son. lxxxix.

[4] Ed. Grosart, III, 1.   [5] *Delia,* Son. li.

[6] Cf. Drummond's *Urania,* Son. ix, *Works,* ed. 1856, p. 86; and
Donne, *To Mr. I. L.,* Riverside ed., p. 40.

[7] Cf. Donne, *To Mr. T. W.* and *Incerto, ibid.,* pp. 34, 35.

[8] Cf. Hazlitt's Gascoigne, I, 426, and the present editor's monograph
on that poet, *Publications of the University of Pennsylvania, Series in
Philology, Literature and Archaeology,* II, No. 4, pp. 34, 35.

(6) Greene and Drayton have in diverse ways achieved the feat of dividing a quatorzain into two equal parts; Greene by a simple combination of two stanzas of the rime royal: *a b a b b c c, d e d e e ff,* Drayton by a more complex succession of couplets and triplets: *a a b b c c c, d d e e f f f.*[1] As to rime, as already stated, modern English demands that the majority of rimes be masculine, and most English sonnets are constructed on such rimes alone; a mixture of feminine rimes, however, is not infrequent; whilst Shakespeare and others have written quatorzains wholly in hendecasyllabics.[2] Sir Thomas Wyatt wrote a quatorzain with a sonnet-like arrangement of rimes in octosyllabics, and was followed by Shakespeare.[3] A more frequent departure is the quatorzain in Alexandrines practiced several times by Sidney with the rime arrangement of the sonnet, and with remarkable success.[4] Raleigh's *Vision upon the Faery Queen* in a quatorzain of seven poulter's measures with the verses of twelve, fifteen, and more lines written upon the general analogy of the sonnet, certainly takes us beyond the most indulgent range that could be granted this topic.

The Italian division of the sonnet into two systems by a pause in the sense at the conclusion of the octave, and the Italian avoidance of *enjambement* or overflow between the quatrains and the tercets were never closely observed in the Elizabethan sonnet, which from the very first asserted its freedom in these particulars, and its right to be consid-

----

[1] Cf. Greene's *Poems,* ed. Bell, p. 110, and Drayton's *Idea,* Son. lxii, ed. 1603. See also the verses from Wilbye's *Second Set of Madrigals,* p. 148 of this volume, in which a quatorzain, also divided into stanzas, exhibits the following mixture of rimed and unrimed verses: *a b c d e ff, g h i j k l l.*

[2] Cf. Shakespeare's Son. xx, and Greville's quatorzain, p. 17 of this volume.   [3] Wyatt, Aldine ed., p. 20, and Shakespeare, Son. cxlv.

[4] *Astrophel and Stella,* Son. i, lxxvi, lxxvii, and cii.

ered indigenous. It is curious that Spenser's unrimed sonnets are stricter in these matters than his later *Amoretti*.
It was but natural that the practice of three quatrains
of independent rimes should obliterate the distinction
between the two systems, and that the closing couplet
should have a tendency to draw the whole poem to a final
climax. As Mr. T. Hall Caine has well pointed out,
"the metrical structure is plainly determined by the intellectual modeling. . . . Apart from all regard for structural
divergence, we have merely to set side by side the intellectual plotting of a sonnet by Petrarch and that of a
sonnet by Spenser, to see clearly that this form of verse in
England is a distinct growth. In the one, we perceive a
conscious centralization of some idea systematically sub-
divided, with each of its parts allotted a distinctive place, so
that to dislodge anything would be to destroy the whole.
In the other, we recognize a facet of an idea or sentiment,
so presented as to work up from concrete figure to abstract
application. The one constitutes a rounded unity, the other
is a development; the one is thrown off at the point at which
it has become quintessential and a thing in itself, the other
is still in process of evolution." [1]

I quote the following sonnet of Constable as a fair
specimen of the stricter Italian method of maintaining the
stanzaic structure of the two systems. No really great sonnet ever preserved the syllogistic requirements of Quadrio,
by which the first quatrain stated the proposition, the second
proved it, the tercets successively confirming the proposition
and drawing the conclusion :

> Dear, though from me your gracious looks depart,
>   And of that comfort do myself bereave,
>   Which both I did deserve and did receive;
> Triumph not over much in this my smart.

---

[1] *Sonnets of Three Centuries*, Preface, pp. xi and xii.

Nay rather, they which now enjoy thy heart
For fear just cause of mourning should conceive,
Lest thou inconstant shouldst their trust deceive,
Which like unto the weather changing art.

For in foul weather birds sing often will
In hope of fair, and in fair time will cease,
For fear fair time will not continue still :

So they may mourn which have thy heart possessed,
For fear of change, and hope of change may ease
Their hearts whom grief of change doth now molest.[1]

For a contrast to the phrasing of this sonnet, and for the independence, spirit, and beauty of many an Elizabethan quatorzain which has cast the restrictions of Italy to the winds, I may confidently refer the student to even the small number of sonnets from the Elizabethan masters contained in this volume.

The acceptance of the Italian madrigal and sonnet as models, their adaptation to the demands of the English language and habit of thought, and their value in training English poets to an utterance more truly their own, may be taken as typical of the literary trend of the singularly versatile age which could evolve a great national drama out of the frigidities of Senecan tragedy and the trivialities of contemporary Italian comedy. We may regard the influence of Italy, as far as the lyric is concerned, as completely assimilated by even the weaker poets towards the close of Elizabeth's reign. There was now a demand for something more than imitation, and the greater men rose to the occasion, although seeking different means for the accomplishment of the same end. Thus Shakespeare, though now passing out of his distinctively lyrical period, found his way in an increasing and masterly freedom ; Jonson, in a scarcely

[1] *Sonnets from Todd's MS.*, ed. Pickering, p. 29.

less masterly restraint; whilst Donne displayed the daring
of an individualism that enabled him, while his poems
were yet in manuscript, to exercise upon his contemporaries
the effect of an accepted classic.

The story of Shakespeare's gradual enfranchisement from
the trammels of imitation and the adherence to ephemeral
rules of art has been often told, and is as true of his work,
considered metrically, as from any other point of view. With
increasing grasp of mind came increasing power and aban-
don in style and versification; and this applies to the
incidental lyrics of his plays (as far as the data enables us
to judge), as it applies to the sweep and cadence of his
blank verse.[1]

On the other hand, Jonson, despite his unusual versatility in the invention and practice of new and successful
lyrical forms, displays the conservative temper throughout,
in avoiding mixed meters, stanzas of irregular structure or
of differing lengths, and in such small matters as his careful
indication of elision where the syllable exceeds the strict
number demanded by the verse-scheme.   Many of Jonson's
utterances, too, attest his detestation of license (*e.g.*, "that
Donne, for not keeping of accent, deserved hanging"); his
esteem of the formal element in literature (*e.g.*, "that Shakespeare wanted art"); or his dislike to innovation.[2]   Towards
the close of his life, Jonson grew increasingly fond of the
decasyllabic rimed couplet, the meter which was to become
the maid of all work in the next generation.   This meter
it was that he defended in theory against the heresies
of Campion and Daniel,[3] and it was in this meter that he

---

[1] There is a wide step in versification between *Silvia* or the *Song*
from the *Merchant of Venice* (pp. 56 and 82), and the free cadenced
songs of the *Tempest* (p. 154).

[2] See *Jonson's Conversations*, Sh. Soc. Publ., p. 3.

[3] See, especially, the opening passage of the *Conversations* concerning his Epic, "all in couplets, for he detesteth all other rimes. Said he

wrote, at times with a regularity of accent and antithetical form that reminds us of the great hand of Dryden in the next age.[1] Jonson's tightening of the reins of regularity in the couplet and in lyric forms — in which latter, despite his inspiration, Herrick followed his master with loving observance of the law — is greatly in contrast with the course of dramatic blank verse, which, beginning in the legitimate freedom of Shakespeare, descended, through the looseness of Fletcher and Massinger, to the license of Davenant and Crowne.

By far the most independent lyrical metrist of this age was John Donne, who has been, it seems to me, quite as much misunderstood on this side as on the side of his eccentricities of thought and expression. In a recent chapter on Donne, in several other respects far from satisfactory, Mr. Edmund Gosse has treated this particular topic very justly. Speaking of Donne's "system of prosody," he says : "The terms 'irregular,' 'unintelligible' and 'viciously rugged,' are commonly used in describing it, and it seems even to be supposed by some critics that Donne did not know how to scan. This last supposition may be rejected at once; what there was to know about poetry was known to Donne. But it seems certain that he intentionally introduced a revolution into English versification. It was doubtless a rebellion against the smooth and somewhat nerveless iambic flow of Spenser and the earliest contemporaries of Shakespeare, that Donne invented his violent mode of breaking up the line into quick and slow beats." Mr. Gosse

had written a Discourse of Poesie, both against Campion and Daniel, . . . where he proves couplets to be the bravest sort of verse, especially when they are broken like hexameters," *i.e.*, exhibit a strong medial cæsura.

[1] See, especially, the later epistles and occasional verses, such as the *Epigrams* to the Lord Treasurer of England, *To my Muse*, etc.

finds this innovation the result of a desire for "new and more varied effects," adding : "The iambic rimed line of Donne has audacities such as are permitted to his blank verse by Milton, and although the felicities are rare in the older poet instead of being almost incessant, as in the later, Donne at his best is not less melodious than Milton."[1]   We need not be detained by the query, whether it was not the strange personality of the poet rather than any unusual desire for "new and more varied effects" which produced a result so unusual.   It is certain, that for inventive variety, fitness, and success, the lyrical stanzas of Donne are surpassed by scarcely any Elizabethan poet.   In short, Donne seems to have applied to the lyric the freedom of the best dramatic verse of his age, and stood as the exponent of novelty and individualism in form precisely as Jonson stood for classic conservatism.

We have thus seen how in form as well as in thought the governing influence upon the English Elizabethan lyric was the influence of Italy, the Italy of the Renaissance ; how, organically considered, there was a steady advance towards greater variety of measure and inventiveness in stanzaic form, and a general growth of taste in such matters as alliteration, the distribution of pauses, and the management of rime.   As might be expected, the analogies of certain forms of verse to certain forms of thought were far less rigidly preserved in the English literature of this day than in that of Italy ; and there is scarcely a form of English verse, of which it can be said that it was restricted to a given species of poetry.   Spenser less completely than Sidney is the exponent of the Italianate school of poetry in England ; for in Sidney is to be found not only its pastoral presentation, but the sonnet sequence and the madrigal, both long to remain the favorite utterance of contemporary lyrists.   But

[1] *The Jacobean Poets*, p. 61 f.

even if Sidney was the representative of the Italianate school, the lyric took almost at once in his hands, and in those of Spenser and Shakespeare, the characteristics of a genuine vernacular utterance which it afterwards maintained, adapting itself in the minutiæ of style and versification as in the character of thought and theme. The Italian influence, although completely assimilated especially among dramatists like Dekker, Fletcher, and Beaumont, and in Browne and the later poetry of Drayton, still continued dominant in poets such as Davison, Drummond, and the writers of madrigals; but failed, as the classic influence too failed, to reach Donne. It was here that the new classic influence arose with Ben Jonson, an assimilated classicism—as far as possible removed from the imitative classicism of Harvey and Spenser in the days of the Areopagus; and it was this spirit that came finally to prevail—not that of Donne which substituted one kind of radicalism for another;—it was this spirit of conservative nicety of style and regularity of versification that led on through Herrick and Sandys to the classicism of Dryden and Pope.

ELIZABETHAN LYRICS.

GEORGE GASCOIGNE, *The Adventures of Master Ferdinando Ieronimi, Posies,* 1575.

SONNET.

THE stately dames of Rome their pearls did wear
About their necks to beautify their name :
But she whom I do serve, her pearls doth bear
Close in her mouth, and, smiling, shew the same.
No wonder, then, though every word she speaks   5
A jewel seem in judgment of the wise,
Since that her sugared tongue the passage breaks
Between two rocks, bedecked with pearls of price.
Her hair of gold, her front of ivory —
A bloody heart within so white a breast —   10
Her teeth of pearl, lips ruby, crystal eye,
Needs must I honor her above the rest,
Since she is formèd of none other mould
But ruby, crystal, ivory, pearl and gold.

GEORGE GASCOIGNE, *Posies, Flowers,* 1575.

THE STRANGE PASSION OF A LOVER.

AMID my bale I bathe in bliss,
I swim in heaven, I sink in hell ;
I find amends for every miss
And yet my moan no tongue can tell.

I live and love, what would you more?   5
As never lover lived before.

I laugh sometimes with little lust,
    So jest I oft and feel no joy;
Mine ease is builded all on trust,
    And yet mistrust breeds mine annoy.   10
I live and lack, I lack and have,
I have and miss the thing I crave.

These things seem strange, yet are they true;
    Believe me, sweet, my state is such,
One pleasure which I would eschew   15
    Both slakes my grief and breeds my grutch.
So doth one pain which I would shun
Renew my joys, where grief begun.

Then like the lark that passed the night
    In heavy sleep, with cares oppressed,   20
Yet when she spies the pleasant light
    She sends sweet notes from out her breast:
So sing I now because I think
How joys approach when sorrows shrink.

And as fair Philomene, again,   25
    Can watch and sing when others sleep,
And taketh pleasure in her pain
    To wray the woe that makes her weep:
So sing I now for to bewray
The loathsome life I lead alway.   30

The which to thee, dear wench, I write,
    That know'st my mirth, but not my moan.
I pray God grant thee deep delight,
    To live in joys when I am gone.
I cannot live, it will not be,   35
I die to think to part from thee.

SIR WALTER RALEIGH (?) in
M.S. Rawl. 85, fol. 124, date
uncertain.

PILGRIM TO PILGRIM.

As you came from the holy land
   Of Walsinghame,
Met you not with my true love
   By the way as you came?

How shall I know your true love,   5
   That have met many one.
As I went to the holy land,
   That have come, that have gone?

She is neither white nor brown,
   But as the heavens fair ;   10
There is none hath a form so divine
   In the earth or the air.

Such a one did I meet, good sir,
   Such an angel-like face,
Who like a queen, like a nymph, did appear,   15
   By her gait, by her grace.

She hath left me here all alone,
   All alone, as unknown,
Who sometimes did me lead with herself,
   And me loved as her own.   20

What's the cause that she leaves you alone,
   And a new way doth take,
Who loved you once as her own,
   And her joy did you make?

I have loved her all my youth,   25
   But now old, as you see,
Love likes not the falling fruit
   From the withered tree.

Know that Love is a careless child,
   And forgets promise past ;   30
He is blind, he is deaf when he list,
   And in faith never fast.

His desire is a dureless content,
   And a trustless joy ;
He is won with a world of despair   35
   And is lost with a toy.

Of womankind such indeed is the love,
   Or the word love abusèd,
Under which many childish desires
   And conceits are excusèd.   40

But true love is a durable fire,
   In the mind ever burning,
Never sick, never old, never dead,
   From itself never turning.

———•◦•———

        THOMAS LODGE, *Scilla's Meta-*
        morphosis, etc., 1589 ; written
        about 1577.

LAMENT.

THE earth, late choked with showers,
   Is now arrayed in green,
Her bosom springs with flowers,
   The air dissolves her teen ;
     The heavens laugh at her glory,   5
     Yet bide I sad and sorry.

The woods are decked with leaves,
  And trees are clothèd gay,
And Flora, crowned with sheaves,
  With oaken boughs doth play;   10
    Where I am clad in black,
    The token of my wrack.

The birds upon the trees
  Do sing with pleasant voices,
And chant in their degrees   15
  Their loves and lucky choices;
    When I, whilst they are singing,
    With sighs mine arms am wringing.

The thrushes seek the shade,
  And I my fatal grave;   20
Their flight to heaven is made,
  My walk on earth I have;
    They free, I thrall; they jolly,
    I sad and pensive wholly.

———◦◦◦———

EDMUND SPENSER, *The Shep-
heardes Calender, August,* 1579.

PERIGOT AND WILLIE'S ROUNDELAY.

IT fell upon a holly eve,
  Hey ho hollidaye,
When holly fathers wont to shrieve:
  Now gynneth this roundelay.
Sitting upon a hill so hye,   5
  Hey ho the high hyll,
The while my flocke did feede thereby,
  The while the shepheard selfe did spill:

I saw the bouncing Bellibone,
　　Hey ho Bonibell,　　　　　　　　　10
Tripping over the dale alone,
　　She can trippe it very well :
Well decked in a frocke of gray,
　　Hey ho gray is greete,
And in a kirtle of greene saye,　　　　15
　　The greene is for maydens meete :
A chapelet on her head she wore,
　　Hey ho chapelet,
Of sweete violets therein was store,
　　She sweeter then the violet.　　　　20
My sheepe did leave theyr wonted foode,
　　Hey ho seely sheepe,
And gazd on her, as they were wood,
　　Woode as he, that did them keepe.
As the bonilasse passed bye,　　　　　25
　　Hey ho bonilasse,
She rovde at me with glauncing eye,
　　As cleare as the christall glasse :
All as the sunnye beame so bright,
　　Hey ho the sunne beame,　　　　　30
Glaunceth from Phœbus face forthright,
　　So love into my hart did streame :
Or as the thonder cleaves the cloudes,
　　Hey ho the thonder,
Wherein the lightsome levin shroudes,　35
　　So cleaves thy soule asonder :
Or as Dame Cynthias silver raye
　　Hey ho the moonelight,
Upon the glyttering wave doth playe :
　　Such play is a pitteous plight.　　　40
The glaunce into my heart did glide,
　　Hey ho the glyder,

Therewith my soule was sharply gryde,
   Such woundes soone wexen wider.
Hasting to raunch the arrow out,   45
   Hey ho Perigot,
I left the head in my hart roote :
   It was a desperate shot.
There it ranckleth ay more and more,
   Hey ho the arrowe,   50
Ne can I find salve for my sore :
   Love is a carelesse sorrowe.
And though my bale with death I bought,
   Hey ho heavie cheere,
Yet should thilk lasse not from my thought :   55
   So you may buye gold to deare.
But whether in paynefull love I pyne,
   Hey ho pinching payne,
Or thrive in welth, she shalbe mine.
   But if thou can her obteine.   60
And if for gracelesse greefe I dye,
   Hey ho gracelesse griefe,
Witnesse, shee slewe me with her eye :
   Let thy follye be the priefe.
And you, that sawe it, simple shepe,   65
   Hey ho the fayre flocke,
For priefe thereof, my death shall weepe,
   And mone with many a mocke.
So learnd I love on a hollye eve,
   Hey ho holidaye,   70
That ever since my hart did greve.
   Now endeth our roundelay.

EDWARD VERE, Earl of Oxford,
in Breton's *Bower of Delights*,
ed. before 1592; written before 1580.

FANCY AND DESIRE.

COME hither, shepherd's swain ;
  Sir, what do you require ?
I pray thee shew to me thy name.
  My name is Fond Desire.

When wert thou born, Desire?   5
  In pride and pomp of May.
By whom, sweet boy, wert thou begot?
  By Self-Conceit, men say.

Tell me, who was thy nurse?
  Fresh Youth in sugared joy.   10
What was thy meat and daily food?
  Sad sighs and great annoy.

What hadst thou then to drink?
  Unfeignèd lovers' tears.
What cradle wert thou rockèd in?   15
  In hope devoid of fears.

What lulled thee to thy sleep?
  Sweet thoughts which liked one best.
And where is now thy dwelling place?
  In gentle hearts I rest.   20

Doth company displease?
  It doth in many one.
Where would Desire then choose to be?
  He loves to muse alone.

What feedeth most thy sight?   25
    To gaze on beauty still.
Whom findest thou [the] most thy foe?
    Disdain of my good will.

Will ever age or death
    Bring thee unto decay?   30
No, no, Desire both lives and dies
    A thousand times a day.

Then, Fond Desire, farewell,
    Thou art no make for me,
I should be loath, methinks, to dwell   35
    With such a one as thee.

SIR PHILIP SIDNEY, from *MS.*
Cottoni Posthuma, date uncertain.

WOOING STUFF.

FAINT Amorist, what! dost thou think
To taste love's honey, and not drink
One dram of gall? or to devour
A world of sweet and taste no sour?
Dost thou ever think to enter   5
The Elysian fields, that dar'st not venture
In Charon's barge? a lover's mind
Must use to sail with every wind.
He that loves, and fears to try,
Learns his mistress to deny.   10
Doth she chide thee? 'tis to shew it
That thy coldness makes her do it.
Is she silent? is she mute?

Silence fully grants thy suit.
Doth she pout, and leave the room?   15
Then she goes to bid thee come.
Is she sick? Why then be sure
She invites thee to the cure.
Doth she cross thy suit with No?
Tush, she loves to hear thee woo.   20
Doth she call the faith of man
In question? Nay, she loves thee than ;
And if ere she makes a blot,
She's lost if that thou hit'st her not.
He that after ten denials   25
Dares attempt no further trials,
Hath no warrant to acquire
The dainties of his chaste desire.

———•◦•———

Sir Philip Sidney, quoted in
Puttenham's *The Art of English Poesy,* 1589; written about
1580.

DITTY: HEART EXCHANGE.

My true-love hath my heart, and I have his,
By just exchange one for the other given :
I hold his dear, and mine he cannot miss,
There never was a bargain better driven.
     My true-love hath my heart, and I have his.   5

His heart in me keeps him and me in one,
My heart in him his thoughts and senses guides.
He loves my heart, for once it was his own,
I cherish his because in me it bides.
     My true-love hath my heart, and I have his.   10

Sir Philip Sidney, *The Countess of Pembroke's Arcadia,* ed. 1598; written about 1580.

SONNET: TO SLEEP.

Lock up, fair lids, the treasure of my heart,
Preserve those beams, this age's only light ;
To her sweet sense, sweet Sleep, some ease impart —
Her sense too weak to bear her spirit's might.
And while, O Sleep, thou closest up her sight !   5
Her sight, where Love did forge his fairest dart, —
O harbor all her parts in easeful plight ;
Let no strange dream make her fair body start
But yet, O dream, if thou wilt not depart
In this rare subject from thy common right,   10
But wilt thyself in such a seat delight :
Then take my shape and play a lover's part,
Kiss her from me, and say unto her sprite,
Till her eyes shine I live in darkest night.

Sir Philip Sidney, *Astrophel and Stella,* 1591 ; written before 1582.

FIRST SONG.

Doubt you to whom my Muse these notes intendeth,
Which now my breast surcharged to music lendeth !
  To you, to you, all song of praise is due,
Only in you my song begins and endeth.

Who hath the eyes which marry state with pleasure !   5
Who keeps the key of Nature's chiefest treasure !
  To you, to you, all song of praise is due,
Only for you the heaven forgat all measure.

Who hath the lips where wit in fairness reigneth !
Who womankind at once both decks and staineth ! 10
   To you, to you, all song of praise is due,
Only by you Cupid his crown maintaineth.

Who hath the feet, whose step all sweetness planteth !
Who else, for whom Fame worthy trumpets wanteth !
   To you, to you, all song of praise is due, 15
Only to you her sceptre Venus granteth.

Who hath the breast, whose milk doth patience nourish ! '
Whose grace is such, that when it chides doth cherish !
   To you, to you, all song of praise is due,
Only through you the tree of life doth flourish. 20

Who hath the hand, which without stroke subdueth !
Who long-dead beauty with increase reneweth !
   To you, to you, all song of praise is due,
Only at you all envy hopeless rueth.

Who hath the hair, which loosest fastest tieth ! 25
Who makes a man live then glad when he dieth !
   To you, to you, all song of praise is due,
Only of you the flatterer never lieth.

Who hath the voice, which soul from senses sunders !
Whose force but yours the bolts of beauty thunders ! 30
   To you, to you, all song of praise is due,
Only with you not miracles are wonders.

Doubt you to whom my Muse these notes intendeth,
Which now my breast o'ercharged to music lendeth !
   To you, to you, all song of praise is due, 35
Only in you my song begins and endeth.

SONNETS.

XXXI.

WITH how sad steps, O moon, thou climb'st the skies !
How silently, and with how wan a face !
What, may it be that even in heavenly place
That busy archer his sharp arrows tries !
Sure, if that long-with-love-acquainted eyes   5
Can judge of love, thou feel'st a lover's case,
I read it in thy looks; thy languished grace,
To me, that feel the like, thy state descries.
Then ev'n of fellowship, O moon, tell me,
Is constant love deemed there but want of wit ?   10
Are beauties there as proud as here they be '
Do they above love to be loved, and yet
Those lovers scorn whom that love doth possess ?
Do they call virtue there ungratefulness ?

XXXIX.

COME, Sleep ! O Sleep, the certain knot of peace,
The baiting-place of wit, the balm of woe,
The poor man's wealth, the prisoner's release,
The indifferent judge between the high and low ;
With shield of proof shield me from out the prease   5
Of these fierce darts Despair at me doth throw :
O make in me those civil wars to cease ;
I will good tribute pay, if thou do so.
Take thou of me smooth pillows, sweetest bed,
A chamber deaf of noise and blind of light,   10
A rosy garland and a weary head :
And if these things, as being thine in right,
Move not thy heavy grace, thou shalt in me,
Livelier than elsewhere, Stella's image see.

LXXXIV.

HIGH way, since you my chief Parnassus be,
And that my Muse, to some ears not unsweet,
Tempers her words to trampling horses' feet
More oft than to a chamber-melody ;
Now blessèd you bear onward blessèd me   5
To her, where I my heart, safe-left, shall meet ;
My Muse and I must you of duty greet
With thanks and wishes, wishing thankfully.
Be you still fair, honored by public heed,
By no encroachment wronged, nor time forgot,   10
Nor blamed for blood, nor shamed for sinful deed ;
And that you know I envy you no lot
Of highest wish, I wish you so much bliss, —
Hundreds of years you Stella's feet may kiss.

XC.

STELLA, think not that I by verse seek fame,
Who seek, who hope, who love, who live but thee ;
Thine eyes my pride, thy lips mine history :
If thou praise not, all other praise is shame.
Nor so ambitious am I as to frame   5
A nest for my young praise in laurel tree :
In truth, I swear, I wish not there should be
Graved in my epitaph a poet's name.
Ne, if I would, could I just title make,
That any laud thereof to me should grow,   10
Without my plumes from others' wings I take :
For nothing from my wit or will doth flow,
Since all my words thy beauty doth endite,
And Love doth hold my hand and makes me write.

Sir Philip Sidney, *Certain Sonnets, The Arcadia,* ed. 1598.

A DIRGE: LOVE IS DEAD.

RING out your bells, let mourning shews be spread;
   For Love is dead:
All Love is dead, infected
With plague of deep disdain:
   Worth, as nought worth, rejected,   5
And Faith fair scorn doth gain.
   From so ungrateful fancy,
   From such a female franzy,
   From them that use men thus,
   Good Lord, deliver us!   10

Weep, neighbors, weep; do you not hear it said
   That Love is dead?
His death-bed, peacock's folly,
His winding-sheet is shame,
   His will, false-seeming holy,   15
His sole exec'tor, blame.
   From so ungrateful fancy,
   From such a female franzy,
   From them that use men thus,
   Good Lord, deliver us!   20

Let dirge be sung, and trentals rightly read,
   For Love is dead;
   Sir Wrong his tomb ordaineth
My mistress' marble heart,
   Which epitaph containeth,   25
'Her eyes were once his dart.'
   From so ungrateful fancy,
   From such a female franzy,
   From them that use men thus,
   Good Lord, deliver us!   30

Alas, I lie: rage hath this error bred ;
  Love is not dead ;
Love is not dead, but sleepeth
In her unmatchèd mind,
  Where she his counsel keepeth,   35
Till due deserts she find.
Therefore from so vile fancy,
To call such wit a franzy,
  Who Love can temper thus,
Good Lord, deliver us !   40

————◦◦◦————

FULKE GREVILLE, LORD BROOKE,
Cælica, in *Certain Learned and*
Elegant Works, 1633; written 15?

SONNETS.

XVII.

TO CYNTHIA.

CYNTHIA, whose glories are at full forever,
  Whose beauties draw forth tears, and kindle fires,
Fires, which kindled once are quenchèd never :
  So beyond hope your worth bears up desires.
Why cast you clouds on your sweet-looking eyes?   5
  Are you afraid, they show me too much pleasure?
Strong Nature decks the grave wherein it lies,
  Excellence can never be expressed in measure.
Are you afraid because my heart adores you,
  The world will think I hold Endymion's place?   10
Hippolytus, sweet Cynthia, kneeled before you ;
  Yet did you not come down to kiss his face.
Angels enjoy the Heaven's inward choirs :
Star-gazers only multiply desires.

XXII.

MYRA.

I, WITH whose colors Myra dressed her head,
  I, that ware posies of her own hand-making,
I, that mine own name in the chimneys read
  By Myra finely wrought ere I was waking:
Must I look on, in hope time coming may   5
With change bring back my turn again to play?

I, that on Sunday at the church-stile found
  A garland sweet with true-love knots in flowers,
Which I to wear about mine arms was bound,
  That each of us might know that all was ours: 10
Must I lead now an idle life in wishes,
And follow Cupid for his loaves and fishes?

I, that did wear the ring her mother left,
  I, for whose love she gloried to be blamed,
I, with whose eyes her eyes committed theft, 15
  I, who did make her blush when I was named:
Must I lose ring, flowers, blush, theft, and go naked,
Watching with sighs till dead love be awakèd?

I, that when drowsy Argus fell asleep,
  Like Jealousy o'erwatchèd with Desire, 20
Was ever warnèd modesty to keep
  While her breath speaking kindled Nature's fire:
Must I look on a-cold while others warm them?
Do Vulcan's brothers in such fine nets arm them?

Was it for this that I might Myra see 25
  Washing the water with her beauties white?
Yet would she never write her love to me:
  Thinks wit of change when thoughts are in delight?
Mad girls may safely love, as they may leave:
No man can print a kiss; lines may deceive. 30

LV.

TO CYNTHIA.

CYNTHIA, because your horns look divers ways,
  Now darkened to the east, now to the west,
Then at full glory once in thirty days,
  Sense doth believe that change is nature's rest.
Poor earth, that dare presume to judge the sky :   5
  Cynthia is ever round, and never varies ;
Shadows and distance do abuse the eye,
  And in abusèd sense truth oft miscarries :
Yet who this language to the people speaks,
Opinion's empire sense's idol breaks.   10

LXXXVII.

FORSAKE THYSELF, TO HEAVEN TURN THEE.

THE earth, with thunder torn, with fire blasted,
  With waters drowned, with windy palsy shaken,
Cannot for this with heaven be distasted,
  Since thunder, rain, and winds from earth are taken.
Man, torn with love, with inward furies blasted,   5
  Drowned with despair, with fleshly lustings shaken,
Cannot for this with heaven be distasted :
  Love, fury, lustings out of man are taken.
Then man, endure thyself, those clouds will vanish.
  Life is a top which whipping Sorrow driveth,   10
Wisdom must bear what our flesh cannot banish,
  The humble lead, the stubborn bootless striveth :
Or, man, forsake thyself, to heaven turn thee,
Her flames enlighten nature, never burn thee.

LXXXVIII.

A CONTRAST.

WHENAS man's life, the light of human lust,
  In socket of his earthly lanthorn burns,
That all his glory unto ashes must,
  And generations to corruption turns,
Then fond desires that only fear their end,   5
Do vainly wish for life, but to amend.
But when this life is from the body fled,
  To see itself in that eternal glass,
Where time doth end, and thoughts accuse the dead,
  Where all to come is one with all that was ;   10
Then living men ask how he left his breath,
That while he livèd never thought of death.

———◆◆◆———

JOHN LYLY, *Alexander and Cam-*
paspe, 1584; acted 1581.

APELLES' SONG.

CUPID and my Campaspe played
At cards for kisses, — Cupid paid ;
He stakes his quiver, bow and arrows,
His mother's doves, and team of sparrows :
Loses them too ; then down he throws   5
The coral of his lip, the rose
Growing on's cheek (but none knows how) ;
With these the crystal of his brow,
And then the dimple of his chin :
All these did my Campaspe win.   10
At last he set her both his eyes ;
She won, and Cupid blind did rise.
O Love, has she done this to thee?
What shall, alas ! become of me?

GEORGE PEELE, *The Arraignment of Paris,* 1584 ; acted
before 1582.

CUPID'S CURSE.

Œnone.   FAIR and fair, and twice so fair,
As fair as any may be ;
The fairest shepherd on our green,
A love for any lady.

Paris.   Fair and fair, and twice so fair,   5
As fair as any may be ;
. Thy love is fair for thee alone
And for no other lady.

Œn.   My love is fair, my love is gay,
As fresh as bene the flowers in May,   10
And of my love my roundelay,
My merry, merry roundelay,
Concludes with Cupid's curse, —
They that do change old love for new
Pray gods they change for worse !   15

Ambo simul. They that do change old love for new
Pray gods they change for worse !

Œn.   Fair and fair, and twice so fair,
As fair as any may be ;
The fairest shepherd on the green,   20
A love for any lady.

Par.   Fair and fair, and twice so fair,
As fair as any may be ;
Thy love is fair for thee alone
And for no other lady.   25

Œn.   My love can pipe, my love can sing,
My love can many a pretty thing,
And of his lovely praises ring
My merry, merry roundelays.

Amen to Cupid's curse, — 30
They that do change old love for new
Pray gods they change for worse !
Ambo simul. They that do change old love for new
Pray gods they change for worse !

COLIN'S PASSION OF LOVE.

O GENTLE Love, ungentle for thy deed,
Thou mak'st my heart
A bloody mark
With piercing shot to bleed.

Shoot soft, sweet Love, for fear thou shoot amiss, 5
For fear too keen
Thy arrows bene,
And hit the heart where my belovèd is.

Too fair that fortune were, nor never I
Shall be so blest, 10
Among the rest,
That love shall seize on her by sympathy.

Then since with Love my prayers bear no boot,
This doth remain
To ease my pain, 15
I take the wound and die at Venus' foot.

JOHN LYLY, *Sappho and Phao,*
1584 ; acted 1582.

SAPPHO'S SONG.

O CRUEL Love, on thee I lay
My curse, which shall strike blind the day ;
Never may sleep with velvet hand
Charm thine eyes with sacred wand ;

Thy jailors shall be hopes and fears ;   5
Thy prison-mates groans, sighs, and tears ;
Thy play to wear out weary times,
Fantastic passions, vows, and rimes ;
Thy bread be frowns ; thy drink be gall,
Such as when you Phao call ;   10
The bed thou liest on be despair,
Thy sleep fond dreams, thy dreams long care ;
Hope, like thy fool, at thy bed's head,
Mock thee, till madness strike thee dead,
As, Phao, thou dost me with thy proud eyes ;   15
In thee poor Sappho lives, for thee she dies.

VULCAN'S SONG:

IN MAKING OF THE ARROWS.

My shag-hair Cyclops, come, let's ply
Our Lemnian hammers lustily.
        By my wife's sparrows,
        I swear these arrows
        Shall singing fly   5
Through many a wanton's eye.

These headed are with golden blisses,
These silver ones feathered with kisses,
        But this of lead
        Strikes a clown dead,   10
        When in a dance
        He falls in a trance,
To see his black-brow lass not buss him,
And then whines out for death t'untruss him.
So, so : our work being done, let's play :   15
Holiday ! boys, cry holiday !

THOMAS WATSON, *The* 'Εκατομ-παθία, *or Passionate Century of Love,* 1582.

PASSIONS.

XXXVII.

IF Jove himself be subject unto Love
And range the woods to find a mortal prey;
If Neptune from the seas himself remove,
    And seek on sands with earthly wights to play:
        Then may I love my peerless choice by right,   5
        Who far excells each other mortal wight.

If Pluto could by love be drawn from hell,
    To yield himself a silly virgin's thrall ;
If Phœbus could vouchsafe on earth to dwell,
    To win a rustic maid unto his call :   10
        Then how much more should I adore the sight
        Of her, in whom the heavens themselves delight?

If country Pan might follow nymphs in chase,
    And yet through love remain devoid of blame ;
If Satyrs were excused for seeking grace   15
    To joy the fruits of any mortal dame :
        Then, why should I once doubt to love her still
        On whom ne Gods nor men can gaze their fill?

C.

RESOLVED to dust entombed here lieth Love,
    Through fault of her, who here herself should lie ;
He struck her breast, but all in vain did prove
    To fire the ice : and doubting by and by
        His brand had lost his force, he gan to try   5
        Upon himself ; which trial made him die.

In sooth no force ; let those lament who lust,
  I'll sing a carol song for obsequy ;
For, towards me his dealings were unjust,
  And cause of all my passèd misery: 10
    The Fates, I think, seeing what I had passed
    In my behalf wrought this revenge at last.

But somewhat more to pacify my mind,
  By illing him, through whom I lived a slave,
I'll cast his ashes to the open wind,   15
  Or write this epitaph upon his grave :
    Here lieth Love, of Mars the bastard son,
    Whose foolish fault to death himself hath done.

From CLEMENT ROBINSON'S *A
Handful of Pleasant Delights*,
1584.

A PROPER SONG.

*FAIN would I have a pretty thing
  To give unto my Lady :
I name no thing, nor I mean no thing,
  But as pretty a thing as may be.*

Twenty journeys would I make,   5
  And twenty ways would hie me,
To make adventure for her sake,
  To set some matter by me :
    But I would fain have a pretty thing, etc.

Some do long for pretty knacks,   10
  And some for strange devices :
God send me that my lady lacks,
  I care not what the price is.
    Thus fain, etc.

Some go here, and some go there,   15
    Where gazes be not geason ;
And I go gaping everywhere,
    But still come out of season.
        Yet fain, etc.

I walk the town and thread the street,   20
    In every corner seeking :
The pretty thing I cannot meet,
    That's for my lady's liking.
        Fain would, etc.

The mercers pull me, going by,   25
    The silk-wives say, "What lack ye?"
"The thing you have not," then say I,
    " Ye foolish fools, go pack ye ! "
        But fain, etc.

It is not all the silk in Cheap,   30
    Nor all the golden treasure,
Nor twenty bushels on a heap
    Can do my lady pleasure.
        But fain, etc.

The gravers of the golden shows   35
    With jewels do beset me ;
The sempsters in the shops that sews,
    They do no thing but let me.
        But fain, etc.

But were it in the wit of man   40
    By any means to make it,
I could for money buy it than,
    And say " Fair Lady, take it."
        Thus fain, etc.

O Lady what a luck is this,   45
  That my good willing misseth
To find what pretty thing it is
  That my good lady wisheth.
Thus fain would I have had this pretty thing
  To give unto my lady :   50
I said no harm, nor I meant no harm,
  But as pretty a thing as may be.

———◦◦◦———

ROBERT GREENE, *Arbasto, the*
Anatomy of Fortune, 1584.

DORALICIA'S DITTY.

IN time we see that silver drops
  The craggy stones make soft ;
The slowest snail in time we see
  Doth creep and climb aloft.

With feeble puffs the tallest pine   5
  In tract of time doth fall ;
The hardest heart in time doth yield
  To Venus' luring call.

Where chilling frost alate did nip,
  There flasheth now a fire ;   1c
Where deep disdain bred noisome hate,
  There kindleth now desire.

Time causeth hope to have his hap ;
  What care in time not eased?
In time I loathed that now I love,   15
  In both content and pleased.

CHIDICK TYCHBORNE, in *Verses
of Praise and Joy . . . written
upon her Majesty's Preserva-
tion,* 1586.

LAMENT.

My prime of youth is but a frost of cares,
  My feast of joy is but a dish of pain,
My crop of corn is but a field of tares,
  And all my good is but vain hope of gain :
My life is fled and yet I saw no sun,   5
And now I live, and now my life is done.

The spring is past and yet it hath not sprung,
  The fruit is dead, and yet the leaves be green,
My youth is gone and yet I am but young,
  I saw the world and yet I was not seen :   10
My thread is cut and yet it is not spun,
And now I live, and now my life is done.

I sought my death, and found it in my womb,
  I looked for life, and saw it was a shade,
I trod the earth and knew it was my tomb,   15
  And now I die, and now I am but made :
The glass is full and now my glass is run,
And now I live, and now my life is done.

———◦◦◦———

NICHOLAS BRETON, from *Cosens'
MS.,* after 1586.

OLDEN LOVE-MAKING.

IN time of yore when shepherds dwelt
  Upon the mountain rocks,
And simple people never felt
  The pain of lover's mocks ;

But little birds would carry tales   5
    'Twixt Susan and her sweeting.
And all the dainty nightingales
    Did sing at lovers' meeting:
Then might you see what looks did pass
    Where shepherds did assemble,   10
And where the life of true love was
    When hearts could not dissemble.

Then *yea* and *nay* was thought an oath
    That was not to be doubted,
And when it came to *faith* and *troth*   15
    We were not to be flouted.
Then did they talk of curds and cream,
    Of butter, cheese and milk,
There was no speech of sunny beam
    Nor of the golden silk.   20
Then for a gift a row of pins,
    A purse, a pair of knives,
Was all the way that love begins;
    And so the shepherd wives.

But now we have so much ado,   25
    And are so sore aggrievèd,
That when we go about to woo
    We cannot be believèd;
Such choice of jewels, rings and chains,
    That may but favor move,   30
And such intolerable pains
    Ere one can hit on love ;
That if I still shall bide this life
    'Twixt love and deadly hate,
I will go learn the country life   35
    Or leave the lover's state.

THOMAS LODGE, *Rosalind, Euphues' Golden Legacy*, 1590; written 1587.

ROSALIND'S MADRIGAL.

LOVE in my bosom like a bee,
  Doth suck his sweet,
Now with his wings he plays with me,
  Now with his feet.
  Within mine eyes he makes his nest,   5
  His bed amidst my tender breast,
  My kisses are his daily feast ;
  And yet he robs me of my rest :
   Ah wanton, will ye?

And if I sleep, then percheth he   10
  With pretty flight,
And makes his pillow of my knee
  The livelong night.
  Strike I my lute, he tunes the string,
  He music plays if so I sing,   15
  He lends me every lovely thing ;
  Yet cruel he my heart doth sting :
   Whist, wanton, still ye !

Else I with roses every day
  Will whip you hence,   20
And bind you, when you long to play,
  For your offence ;
  I'll shut mine eyes to keep you in,
  I'll make you fast it for your sin,
  I'll count your power not worth a pin :   25
  Alas, what hereby shall I win,
   If he gainsay me?

What if I beat the wanton boy
    With many a rod ?
He will repay me with annoy,   30
    Because a god.
Then sit thou safely on my knee,
And let thy bower my bosom be,
Lurk in mine eyes, I like of thee ;
O Cupid, so thou pity me,   35
    Spare not, but play thee.

ROSALIND'S DESCRIPTION.

LIKE to the clear in highest sphere
    Where all imperial glory shines,
Of selfsame color is her hair
    Whether unfolded or in twines :
        Heigh ho, fair Rosaline !   5
Her eyes are sapphires set in snow,
    Refining heaven by every wink ;
The gods do fear whenas they glow,
    And I do tremble when I think.
        Heigh ho, would she were mine !   10

Her cheeks are like the blushing cloud
    That beautifies Aurora's face,
Or like the silver crimson shroud
    That Phœbus' smiling looks doth grace ;
        Heigh ho, fair Rosaline !   15
Her lips are like two budded roses
    Whom ranks of lilies neighbor nigh,
Within which bounds she balm incloses
    Apt to entice a deity :
        Heigh ho, would she were mine !   20

Her neck is like a stately tower
  Where love himself imprisoned lies,
To watch for glances every hour
  From her divine and sacred eyes:
    Heigh ho, fair Rosaline!   25
Her paps are centres of delight,
  Her breasts are orbs of heavenly frame,
Where Nature moulds the dew of light
  To feed perfection with the same:
    Heigh ho, would she were mine!   30

With orient pearl, with ruby red,
  With marble white, with sapphire blue
Her body every way is fed,
  Yet soft in touch and sweet in view:
    Heigh ho, fair Rosaline!   35
Nature herself her shape admires;
  The gods are wounded in her sight;
And Love forsakes his heavenly fires
  And at her eyes his brand doth light:
    Heigh ho, would she were mine!   40

Then muse not, Nymphs, though I bemoan
  The absence of fair Rosaline,
Since for her fair there is fairer none,
  Nor for her virtues so divine:
    Heigh ho, fair Rosaline;   45
Heigh ho, my heart! would God that she were mine!

PHŒBE'S SONNET.

'*Down a down!*'
  Thus Phyllis sung
    By fancy once distressèd:

'Whoso by foolish love are stung,
Are worthily oppressèd.   5
And so sing I, with a down, a down a.'

When Love was first begot
   And by the mover's will
Did fall to human lot
   His solace to fulfil,   10
Devoid of all deceit,
   A chaste and holy fire
Did quicken man's conceit,
   And woman's breast inspire.
The gods that saw the good   15
   That mortals did approve,
With kind and holy mood,
   Began to talk of Love.

'Down a down!'
   Thus Phyllis sung,   20
      By fancy once distressèd:
'Whoso by foolish love are stung,
   Are worthily oppressèd.
And so sing I, with a down, a down a.'

But during this accord,   25
   A wonder strange to hear;
Whilst Love in deed and word .
   Most faithful did appear,
False Semblance came in place,
   By Jealousy attended,   30
And with a double face
   Both Love and Fancy blended.
Which makes the gods forsake,
   And men from fancy fly,
And maidens scorn a make,   35
   Forsooth and so will I.

'Down a down!'
  Thus Phyllis sung
    By fancy once distressèd:
'Whoso by foolish love are stung,   40
    Are worthily oppressèd.
And so sing I, with down, a down, a down a.'

——•◦•——

EDWARD VERE, EARL OF OX-
FORD, in William Byrd's
*Psalms, Sonnets, and Songs
of Sadness and Piety.* 1588.

IF WOMEN COULD BE FAIR AND YET NOT FOND.

IF women could be fair and yet not fond,
  Or that their love were firm, not fickle still,
I would not marvel that they make men bond
  By service long to purchase their good will;
But when I see how frail those creatures are,   5
I laugh that men forget themselves so far.

To mark the choice they make, and how they change,
  How oft from Phœbus they do flee to Pan;
Unsettled still, like haggards wild they range,
  These gentle birds that fly from man to man;   10
Who would not scorn and shake them from the fist,
And let them fly, fair fools, which way they list?

Yet for our sport we fawn and flatter both,
  To pass the time when nothing else can please,
And train them to our lure with subtle oath,   15
  Till, weary of their wiles, ourselves we ease;
And then we say when we their fancy try,
To play with fools, O what a fool was I!

ROBERT GREENE, *Perimedes the
Blacksmith.* 1588.

FAIR IS MY LOVE FOR APRIL IN HER FACE.

FAIR is my love for April in her face,
   Her lovely breasts September claims his part,
And lordly July in her eyes takes place,
   But cold December dwelleth in her heart ;
Blest be the months that set my thoughts on fire,   5
Accurst that month that hindereth my desire.

Like Phœbus' fire, so sparkle both her eyes,
   As air perfumed with amber is her breath,
Like swelling waves, her lovely [breasts] do rise,
   As earth her heart, cold, dateth me to death :   10
Aye me, poor man, that on the earth do live,
When unkind earth death and despair doth give.

In pomp sits mercy seated in her face,
   Love 'twixt her breasts his trophies doth imprint,
Her eyes shine favor, courtesy and grace,   15
   But touch her heart, ah that is framed of flint !
Therefore my harvest in the grass bears grain ;
The rock will wear, washed with a winter's rain.

——◆——

ROBERT GREENE, *Pandosto, the
Triumph of Time,* before 1588 (?).

AH, WERE SHE PITIFUL AS SHE IS FAIR.

AH, were she pitiful as she is fair,
   Or but as mild as she is seeming so,
Then were my hopes greater than my despair,
   Then all the world were heaven, nothing woe.

Ah, were her heart relenting as her hand,   5
  That seems to melt even with the mildest touch,
Then knew I where to seat me in a land,
  Under wide heavens, but yet [there is] not such.
So as she shows, she seems the budding rose,
  Yet sweeter far than is an earthly flower,   10
Sovereign of beauty, like the spray she grows,
  Compassed she is with thorns and cankered bower,
Yet were she willing to be plucked and worn,
She would be gathered, though she grew on thorn.

Ah, when she sings, all music else be still,   15
  For none must be comparèd to her note ;
Ne'er breathed such glee from Philomela's bill,
  Nor from the morning-singer's swelling throat.
Ah, when she riseth from her blissful bed,
  She comforts all the world, as doth the sun,   20
And at her sight the night's foul vapor's fled ;   .
  When she is set, the gladsome day is done.
O glorious sun, imagine me the west,
Shine in my arms, and set thou in my breast !

—◦◦—

ROBERT GREENE, *Menaphon,* 1589.

MENAPHON'S SONG.

SOME say Love,
Foolish Love,
  Doth rule and govern all the gods :
I say Love,
Inconstant Love,   5
  Sets men's senses far at odds.
Some swear Love,
Smooth-faced Love,

Is sweetest sweet that men can have :
I say Love,   10
Sower Love,
    Makes virtue yield as beauty's slave.
A bitter sweet, a folly worst of all,
That forceth wisdom to be folly's thrall.

Love is sweet.   15
Wherein sweet?
    In fading pleasures that do pain.
Beauty sweet :
Is that sweet
    That yieldeth sorrow for a gain?   20
If Love's sweet,
Herein sweet,
    That minute's joys are monthly woes :
'Tis not sweet,
That is sweet   25
    Nowhere but where repentance grows.
Then love who list, if beauty be so sower ;
Labor for me, Love rest in prince's bower.

SEPHESTIA'S SONG TO HER CHILD.

WEEP not, my wanton, smile upon my knee,
When thou art old there's grief enough for thee.
    Mother's wag, pretty boy,
    Father's sorrow, father's joy ;
    When thy father first did see   5
    Such a boy by him and me,
    He was glad, I was woe,
    Fortune changèd made him so,
    When he left his pretty boy,
    Last his sorrow, first his joy.   10

Weep not, my wanton, smile upon my knee,
When thou art old there's grief enough for thee.
 Streaming tears that never stint,
 Like pearl drops from a flint,
 Fell by course from his eyes,   15
 That one another's place supplies ;
 Thus he grieved in every part,
 Tears of blood fell from his heart,
 When he left his pretty boy,
 Father's sorrow, father's joy.   20

Weep not, my wanton, smile upon my knee,
When thou art old there's grief enough for thee.
 The wanton smiled, father wept,
 Mother cried, baby leapt ;
 More he crowed, more we cried,   25
 Nature could not sorrow hide :
 He must go, he must kiss
 Child and mother, baby bliss,
 For he left his pretty boy,
 Father's sorrow, father's joy.   30
Weep not my wanton, smile upon my knee,
When thou art old there's grief enough for thee.

DORON'S DESCRIPTION OF SAMELA.

LIKE to Diana in her summer weed,
 Girt with a crimson robe of brightest dye,
  Goes fair Samela ;
Whiter than be the flocks that straggling feed,
 When washed by Arethusa Fount they lie,   5
  Is fair Samela ;

As fair Aurora in her morning-grey,
  Decked with the ruddy glister of her love,
      Is fair Samela ;
Like lovely Thetis on a calmèd day,   10
· Whenas her brightness Neptune's fancy move,
      Shines fair Samela ;

Her tresses gold, her eyes like glassy streams,
  Her teeth are pearl, the breasts are ivory
      Of fair Samela ;   15
Her cheeks like rose and lily yield forth gleams,
  Her brow's bright arches framed of ebony ;
      Thus fair Samela

Passeth fair Venus in her bravest hue,
  And Juno in the show of majesty,   20
      For she is Samela ;
Pallas in wit, all three, if you will view,
  For beauty, wit, and matchless dignity
      Yield to Samela.

DORON'S JIG.

THROUGH the shrubs as I can crack
  For my lambs, little ones,
  'Mongst many pretty ones, —
Nymphs I mean, whose hair was black
    As the crow: 5
    Like the snow
Her face and browès shined I ween ! —
  I saw a little one,
  A bonny pretty one,
As bright, buxom, and as sheen   10
    As was she
    On her knee

That lulled the god, whose arrow warms
  Such merry little ones,
  Such fair-faced pretty ones   15
As dally in love's chiefest harms:
      Such was mine,
      Whose grey eyne
Made me love. I gan to woo
  This sweet little one,   20
  This bonny pretty one.
I wooed hard a day or two,
      Till she bade
      'Be not sad,
Woo no more, I am thine own,   25
  Thy dearest little one,
  Thy truest pretty one.'
Thus was faith and firm love shown,
      As behoves
      Shepherds' loves.   30

From WILLIAM BYRD'S *Songs
of Sundry Natures,* 1589, author unknown.

PHILON, THE SHEPHERD, HIS SONG.

WHILE that the sun with his beams hot
  Scorchèd the fruits in vale and mountain,
Philon, the shepherd, late forgot,
  Sitting beside a crystal fountain
In shadow of a green oak tree,   5
Upon his pipe this song played he :
  Adieu Love, adieu Love, untrue Love,
  Untrue Love, untrue Love, adieu Love ;
  Your mind is light, soon lost for new love.

So long as I was in your sight,   10
  I was your heart, your soul, your treasure;
And evermore you sobbed and sighed,
  Burning in flames beyond all measure :
Three days endured your love for me,
And it was lost in other three.   15
    Adieu Love, adieu Love, untrue Love, .
    Untrue Love, untrue Love, adieu Love ;
    Your mind is light, soon lost for new love.

Another shepherd you did see,
  To whom your heart was soon enchainèd ;   20
Full soon your love was leapt from me,
  Full soon my place he had obtainèd :
Soon came a third, your love to win ;
And we were out and he was in.
    Adieu Love, adieu Love, untrue Love,   25
    Untrue Love, untrue Love, adieu Love ;
    Your mind is light, soon lost for new love.

Sure you have made me passing glad
  That you your mind so soon removèd,
Before that I the leisure had   30
  To choose you for my best belovèd :
For all your love was past and done
Two days before it was begun.
    Adieu Love, adieu Love, untrue Love,
    Untrue Love, untrue Love, adieu Love ;   35
    Your mind is light, soon lost for new love.

JOHN LYLY. *Midas,* 1592 ; acted
1590.

A SONG OF DAPHNE TO THE LUTE.

My Daphne's hair is twisted gold,
Bright stars a-piece her eyes do hold,
My Daphne's brow enthrones the graces,
My Daphne's beauty stains all faces ;
On Daphne's cheeks grow rose and cherry,   5
On Daphne's lip a sweeter berry,
Daphne's snowy hand but touched does melt,
And then no heavenlier warmth is felt ;
My Daphne's voice tunes all the spheres,
My Daphne's music charms all ears.   10
Fond am I thus to sing her praise,
These glories now are turned to bays.

HYMN TO APOLLO.

Sing to Apollo, god of day,
Whose golden beams with morning play,
And make her eyes as brightly shine,
Aurora's face is called divine ;
Sing to Phœbus and that throne   5
Of diamonds which he sits upon.
   Io pæans let us sing
   To physic's and to poesy's king !

Crown all his altars with bright fire,
Laurels bind about his lyre,   10
A Daphnean coronet for his head,
The Muses dance about his bed ;
When on his ravishing lute he plays,
Strew his temple round with bays.
   Io pæans let us sing   15
   To the glittering Delian king !

JOHN LYLY, *Mother Bombie*,
1594 ; acted about 1590.

HYMN TO CUPID.

O CUPID ! monarch over kings,
Wherefore hast thou feet and wings ?
It is to shew how swift thou art,
When thou wound'st a tender heart ;
Thy wings being clipped and feet held still,   5
Thy bow so many could not kill.

It is all one in Venus' wanton school,
Who highest sits, the wise man or the fool :
    Fools in love's college
    Have far more knowledge   10
    To read a woman over,
    Than a neat prating lover :
      Nay, 'tis confessed,
      That fools please women best.

GEORGE PEELE, *Polyhymnia*,
1590.

FAREWELL TO ARMS.

HIS golden locks time hath to silver turned ;
    O time too swift, O swiftness never ceasing !
His youth 'gainst time and age hath ever spurned,
    But spurned in vain ; youth waneth by increasing :
Beauty, strength, youth, are flowers but fading seen,   5
Duty, faith, love, are roots, and ever green.

His helmet now shall make a hive for bees,
    And, lovers' sonnets turned to holy psalms,
A man-at-arms must now serve on his knees,
    And feed on prayers, which are age his alms :   10
But though from court to cottage he depart,
His saint is sure of his unspotted heart.

And when he saddest sits in homely cell,
    He'll teach his swains this carol for a song —
' Bless'd be the hearts that wish my sovereign well,   15
    Cursed be the souls that think her any wrong.'
Goddess, allow this aged man his right,
To be your beadsman now that was your knight.

----•◦•----

WILLIAM SHAKESPEARE, *Love's Labour's Lost*, acted 1590.

WINTER.

WHEN icicles hang by the wall
    And Dick the shepherd blows his nail,
And Tom bears logs into the hall,
    And milk comes frozen home in pail ;
When blood is nipt, and ways be foul,   5
Then nightly sings the staring owl,
        Tuwhit, tuwhoo,
        A merry note,
While greasy Joan doth keel the pot.

When all around the wind doth blow,   10
    And coughing drowns the parson's saw,
And birds sit brooding in the snow,
    And Marian's nose looks red and raw ;

When roasted crabs hiss in the bowl,
Then nightly sings the staring owl,   15
     Tuwhit, tuwhoo,
     A merry note,
While greasy Joan doth keel the pot.

———•◦•———

THOMAS DEKKER, *The Pleasant
Comedy of Old Fortunatus,*
acted 1590 (?).

HYMN TO FORTUNE.

FORTUNE smiles, cry holiday!
     Dimples on her cheeks do dwell.
Fortune frowns, cry well-a-day!
     Her love is heaven, her hate is hell.
Since heaven and hell obey her power,   5
Tremble when her eyes do lower:
     Since heaven and hell her power obey,
     When she smiles cry holiday!
         Holiday with joy we cry,
         And bend, and bend, and merrily   10
         Sing hymns to Fortune's deity,
         Sing hymns to Fortune's deity.

Let us sing merrily, merrily, merrily!
     With our song let heaven resound,
     Fortune's hands our heads have crowned: 15
Let us sing merrily, merrily, merrily!

SONG.

VIRTUE'S branches wither, Virtue pines,
     O pity, pity, and alack the time;
Vice doth flourish, Vice in glory shines,
     Her gilded boughs above the cedar climb.

Vice hath golden cheeks, O pity, pity,   5
   She in every land doth monarchize ;
Virtue is exiled from every city,
   Virtue is a fool, Vice only wise.

O pity, pity, Virtue weeping dies,
   Vice laughs to see her faint, alack the time.   10
This sinks, with painted wings the other flies :
   Alack that best should fall, and bad should climb.

O pity, pity, pity, mourn, not sing,
   Vice doth flourish, Vice in glory shines,
Vice is a saint, Virtue an underling ;   15
   Virtue's branches wither, Virtue pines.

—◦◦◦—

ROBERT GREENE, *The Mourn-*
ing Garment, 1590.

THE SHEPHERD'S WIFE'S SONG.

Ah, what is love?   It is a pretty thing,
As sweet unto a shepherd as a king ;
     And sweeter too :
For kings have cares that wait upon a crown,
And cares can make the sweetest love to frown.   5
     Ah then, ah then,
If country loves such sweet desires do gain,
What lady would not love a shepherd swain ?

His flocks are folded, he comes home at night,
As merry as a king in his delight,   10
     ˙ And merrier too :
For kings bethink them what the state require,
Where shepherds careless carol by the fire.
     Ah then, ah then,
If country loves such sweet desires do gain,   15
What lady would not love a shepherd swain ?

He kisseth first, then sits as blithe to eat
His cream and curds as doth the king his meat;
   And blither too:
For kings have often fears when they do sup,   20
Where shepherds dread no poison in their cup.
   Ah then, ah then,
If country loves such sweet desires do gain,
What lady would not love a shepherd swain?

To bed he goes, as wanton then, I ween,   25
As is a king in dalliance with a queen;
   More wanton too:
For kings have many griefs affects to move,
Where shepherds have no greater grief than love.
   Ah then, ah then,   30
If country loves such sweet desires do gain,
What lady would not love a shepherd swain?

Upon his couch of straw he sleeps as sound,
As doth the king upon his beds of down;
   More sounder too: 35
For cares cause kings full oft their sleep to spill,
Where weary shepherds lie and snort their fill.
   Ah then, ah then,
If country loves such sweet desires do gain,
What lady would not love a shepherd swain?   40

Thus with his wife he spends the year, as blithe
As doth the king at every tide or sithe;
   And blither too:
For kings have wars and broils to take in hand,
When shepherds laugh and love upon the land.   45
   Ah then, ah then,
If country loves such sweet desires do gain,
What lady would not love a shepherd swain?

ROBERT GREENE, *Farewell to Folly*, 1591.

CONTENT.

SWEET are the thoughts that savor of content,
  The quiet mind is richer than a crown,
Sweet are the nights in careless slumber spent,
  The poor estate scorns fortune's angry frown :
Such sweet content, such minds, such sleep, such bliss, 5
Beggars enjoy, when princes oft do miss.

The homely house that harbors quiet rest,
  The cottage that affords no pride nor care,
The mean that grees with country music best,
  The sweet consort of mirth and modest fare,   10
Obscurèd life sets down a type of bliss :
A mind content both crown and kingdom is.

NICHOLAS BRETON, in *The Honorable Entertainment given to the Queen's Majesty*, 1591.

PHYLLIDA AND CORYDON.

IN the merry month of May,
In a morn by break of day,
With a troop of damsels playing
Forth the wood, forsooth a Maying :
When anon by the wood side   5
There I spièd all alone,
Phyllida and Corydon.
Much ado there was, God wot !
He would love and she would not.

She said, never man was true;   10
He said, none was false to you.
He said, he had loved her long;
She said, Love should have no wrong.
Corydon would kiss her then;
She said, maids must kiss no men,   15
Till they did for good and all;
Then she made the shepherd call
All the heavens to witness truth
Never loved a truer youth.
Thus with many a pretty oath,   20
Yea and nay, and faith and troth,
Such as silly shepherds use
When they will not love abuse,
Love, which had been long deluded,
Was with kisses sweet concluded;   25
And Phyllida, with garlands gay,
Was made the lady of the May.

———◆◆———

SAMUEL DANIEL, *Sonnets after
Astrophel*, 1591.

SONNET XI.

RESTORE thy tresses to the golden ore,
Yield Cytherea's son those arcs of love,
Bequeath the heavens the stars that I adore,
And to the orient do thy pearls remove,
Yield thy hands' pride unto the ivory white,   5
To Arabian odors give thy breathing sweet,
Restore thy blush unto Aurora bright,
To Thetis give the honor of thy feet;
Let Venus have thy graces her resigned,
And thy sweet voice give back unto the spheres; 10

But yet restore thy fierce and cruel mind
To Hyrcan tigers and to ruthless bears ;
Yield to the marble thy hard heart again :
So shalt thou cease to plague, and I to pain.

———•◊•———

Samuel Daniel, *Delia, Containing Certain Sonnets,* 1592.

SONNETS.

XXXI.

Look, Delia, how we esteem the half-blown rose,
The image of thy blush and summer's honor,
Whilst in her tender green she doth inclose
That pure, sweet beauty Time bestows upon her.
No sooner spreads her glory to the air,   5
But straight her full-blown pride is in declining ;
She then is scorned that late adorned the fair :
So clouds thy beauty, after fairest shining.
No April can revive thy withered flowers,
Whose blooming grace adorns thy glory now ;   10
Swift, speedy Time, feathered with flying hours,
Dissolves the beauty of the fairest brow.
O let not then such riches waste in vain,
But love, whilst that thou may'st be loved again.

XLII.

Beauty, sweet love, is like the morning dew,
Whose short refresh upon the tender green
Cheers for a time, but till the sun doth shew,
And straight 'tis gone as it had never been.
Soon doth it fade that makes the fairest flourish,   5
Short is the glory of the blushing rose,

The hue which thou so carefully dost nourish,
Yet which at length thou must be forced to lose.
When thou surcharged with burthen of thy years,
Shalt bend thy wrinkles homeward to the earth,   10
And that in beauty's lease expired appears
The date of age, the Kalends of our death.
But ah ! no more, this must not be foretold,
For women grieve to think they must be old.

XLV.

CARE-CHARMER Sleep, son of the sable Night,
Brother to Death, in silent darkness born :
Relieve my languish and restore the light ;
With dark forgetting of my care, return,
And let the day be time enough to mourn   5
The shipwrack of my ill-adventred youth :
Let waking eyes suffice to wail their scorn
Without the torment of the night's untruth.
Cease dreams, the images of day desires,
To model forth the passions of the morrow ;   10
Never let rising sun approve you liars,
To add more grief to aggravate my sorrow.
Still let me sleep, embracing clouds in vain,
And never wake to feel the day's disdain.

From the same.

AN ODE.

Now each creature joys the other,
    Passing happy days and hours,
One bird reports unto another
    In the fall of silver showers,
Whilst the earth, our common mother,   5
    Hath her bosom decked with flowers.

Whilst the greatest torch of heaven
  With bright rays warms Flora's lap,
Making nights and days both even,
  Cheering plants with fresher sap: 10
My field of flowers quite bereaven,
  Wants refresh of better hap.

Echo, daughter of the air,
  Babbling guest of rocks and hills,
Knows the name of my fierce fair,   15
  And sounds the accents of my ills.
Each thing pities my despair,
  Whilst that she her lover kills.

Whilst that she, O cruel maid,
  Doth me and my true love despise ;   20
My life's flourish is decayed,
  That depended on her eyes:
But her will must be obeyed,
  And well he ends for love who dies.

———•◦•———

THOMAS NASHE, *Summer's Last
Will and Testament,* 1600 ;
acted 1592.

FADING SUMMER.

FAIR summer droops, droop men and beasts therefore,
So fair a summer look for nevermore :
  All good things vanish less than in a day,
  Peace, plenty, pleasure, suddenly decay.
    Go not yet away, bright soul of the sad year,   5
    The earth is hell when thou leav'st to appear.

What, shall those flowers that decked thy garland erst,
Upon thy grave be wastefully dispersed?
  O trees, consume your sap in sorrow's source,
  Streams, turn to tears your tributary course.   10
    Go not yet hence, bright soul of the sad year,
    The earth is hell when thou leav'st to appear.

SPRING.

SPRING, the sweet Spring, is the year's pleasant king;
Then blooms each thing, then maids dance in a ring,
Cold doth not sting, the pretty birds do sing,
  Cuckoo, jug, jug, pu-we, to-witta-woo!

The palm and May make country houses gay,   5
Lambs frisk and play, the shepherds pipe all day,
And we hear aye birds tune this merry lay,
  Cuckoo, jug, jug, pu-we, to-witta-woo!

The fields breathe sweet, the daisies kiss our feet,
Young lovers meet, old wives a sunning sit   10
In every street, these tunes our ears do greet,
  Cuckoo, jug, jug, pu-we, to-witta-woo!
    Spring, the sweet spring!

DEATH'S SUMMONS.

Adieu, farewell earth's bliss,
This world uncertain is:
Fond are life's lustful joys,
Death proves them all but toys.
None from his darts can fly: 5
I am sick, I must die.
    Lord have mercy on us!

Rich men, trust not in wealth,
Gold cannot buy you health;

Physic himself must fade,   10
All things to end are made ;
The plague full swift goes by :
I am sick, I must die.
　　Lord have mercy on us !

Beauty is but a flower,   15
Which wrinkles will devour ;
Brightness falls from the air,
Queens have died young and fair,
Dust hath closèd Helen's eye :
I am sick, I must die.   20
　　Lord have mercy on us !

Strength stoops unto the grave,
Worms feed on Hector brave,
Swords may not fight with fate,
Earth still holds ope her gate.   25
Come, come, the bells do cry,
I am sick, I must die.
　　Lord have mercy on us !

Wit with his wantonness,
Tasteth death's bitterness ;   30
Hell's executioner
Hath no ears for to hear
What vain art can reply.
I am sick, I must die.
　　Lord have mercy on us !   35

Haste therefore each degree
To welcome destiny ;
Heaven is our heritage
Earth but a player's stage,
Mount we unto the sky :   40
I am sick, I must die.
　　Lord have mercy on us !

ROBERT GREENE, *Philomela,*
The Lady Fitzwater's Night-
ingale, 1592.

PHILOMELA'S ODE THAT SHE SUNG

IN HER ARBOR.

SITTING by a river side,
Where a silent stream did glide,
Muse I did of many things,
That the mind in quiet brings.
I gan think how some men deem   5
Gold their god ; and some esteem
Honor is the chief content
That to man in life is lent.
And some others do contend,
Quiet none like to a friend.   10
Others hold there is no wealth
Compared to a perfit health.
Some man's mind in quiet stands,
When he is lord of many lands ;
But I did sigh, and said all this   15
Was but a shade of perfit bliss ;
And in my thoughts I did approve
Naught so sweet as is true love.
Love 'twixt lovers passeth these,
When mouth kisseth and heart grees,   20
With folded arms and lips meeting,
Each soul another sweetly greeting ;
For by the breath the soul fleeteth,
And soul with soul in kissing meeteth.
If love be so sweet a thing,   25
That such happy bliss doth bring,

Happy is love's sugared thrall;
But unhappy maidens all,
Who esteem your virgins' blisses
Sweeter than a wife's sweet kisses.   30
No such quiet to the mind,
As true love with kisses kind.
But if a kiss prove unchaste,
Then is true love quite disgraced.
Though love be sweet, learn this of me :   35
No sweet love but honesty.

———•◦•———

THOMAS LODGE, *A Margarite
of America,* 1596; written
1592.

THE SOLITARY SHEPHERD'S SONG.

O SHADY vales, O fair enrichèd meads,
O sacred woods, sweet fields, and rising mountains ;
O painted flowers, green herbs, where Flora treads,
Refreshed by wanton winds and wat'ry fountains.
O all you wingèd choiristers of wood,   5
That perched aloft your former pains report,
And straight again recount with pleasant mood
Your present joys in sweet and seemly sort.
O all you creatures, whosoever thrive
On mother earth, in seas, by air, or fire,   10
More blest are you than I here under sun :
Love dies in me, whenas he doth revive
In you ; I perish under beauty's ire,
Where after storms, winds, frosts, your life is won.

WILLIAM SHAKESPEARE, *The
Two Gentlemen of Verona,*
1598 ; acted about 1592–93.

SILVIA.

WHO is Silvia? what is she,
   That all our swains commend her?
Holy, fair and wise is she ;
   The heaven such grace did lend her,
That she might admirèd be.   5

Is she kind as she is fair,
   For beauty lives with kindness?
Love doth to her eyes repair,
   To help him of his blindness,
And being helped inhabits there.   10

Then to Silvia let us sing,
   That Silvia is excelling ;
She excels each mortal thing
   Upon the dull earth dwelling :
To her let us garlands bring.   15

—◦◦—

BARNABE BARNES, *Parthenophil
and Parthenope,* 1593.

SONNET LXVI.

AH, sweet Content, where is thy mild abode?
Is it with shepherds and light-hearted swains,
Which sing upon the downs and pipe abroad,
Tending their flocks and cattle on the plains?

Ah, sweet Content, where dost thou safely rest ?   5
In heaven with angels which the praises sing
Of him that made and rules at his behest
The minds and hearts of every living thing?
Ah, sweet Content, where doth thine harbor hold?
Is it in churches with religious men   10
Which please the gods with prayers manifold,
And in their studies meditate it then ? ·
Whether thou dost in heaven, or earth appear,
Be where thou wilt, thou wilt not harbor here !

———◆◆◆———

CHRISTOPHER MARLOWE, in
The Passionate Pilgrim, 1599;
written before 1593.

THE PASSIONATE SHEPHERD TO HIS LOVE.

COME live with me, and be my love,
And we will all the pleasures prove,
That valleys, groves, hills and fields,
Woods or steepy mountains yields.

And we will sit upon the rocks,   5
Seeing the shepherds feed their flocks
By shallow rivers, to whose falls
Melodious birds sing madrigals.

And I will make thee beds of roses,
And a thousand fragrant posies,   10
A cap of flowers and a kirtle
Embroidered all with leaves of myrtle :

A gown made of the finest wool
Which from our pretty lambs we pull ;

Fair-linèd slippers for the cold,   15
With buckles of the purest gold ;

A belt of straw and ivy-buds,
With coral clasps and amber studs :
An if these pictures may thee move,
Come live with me and be my love.   20

The shepherd swains shall dance and sing
For thy delight each May morning :
If these delights thy mind may move,
Then live with me and be my love.

————◆◇◆————

THOMAS LODGE, *Phyllis honored*
with Pastoral Sonnets, 1593.

SONNETS.

XIII.

LOVE'S WANTONNESS.

LOVE gilds the roses of thy lips
    And flies about them like a bee ;
If I approach he forward skips,
    And if I kiss he stingeth me.

Love in thine eyes doth build his bower,   5
    And sleeps within their pretty shine ;
And if I look the boy will lower,
    And from their orbs shoot shafts divine.

Love works thy heart within his fire,
    And in my tears doth firm the same ;   10
And if I tempt it will retire,
    And of my plaints doth make a game.

Love, let me cull her choicest flowers,
    And pity me, and calm her eye,
Make soft her heart, dissolve her lowers,   15
    Then will I praise thy deity.

But if thou do not, Love, I'll truly serve her
In spite of thee, and by firm faith deserve her.

XV.

TO PHYLLIS, THE FAIR SHEPHERDESS.

My Phyllis hath the morning sun,
    At first to look upon her ;
And Phyllis hath morn-waking birds
    Her risings for to honor.
My Phyllis hath prime-feathered flowers   5
    That smile when she treads on them ;
And Phyllis hath a gallant flock
    That leaps since she doth own them.
But Phyllis hath so hard a heart,
    Alas that she should have it,   10
As yields no mercy to desart,
    Nor grace to those that crave it.
Sweet sun, when thou look'st on,
    Pray her regard my moan ;
Sweet birds, when you sing to her,   15
    To yield some pity, woo her ;
Sweet flowers whenas she treads on,
    Tell her, her beauty deads one,
And if in life her love she nill agree me,
Pray her before I die she will come see me.   20

THOMAS LODGE, in *The Phœnix' Nest,* 1593.

ACCURST BE LOVE.

ACCURST be Love, and those that trust his trains !
He tastes the fruit whilst others toil,
He brings the lamp, we lend the oil,
He sows distress, we yield him soil,
He wageth war, we bide the foil.   5

Accurst be Love, and those that trust his trains !
He lays the trap, we seek the snare,
He threat'neth death, we speak him fair,
He coins deceits, we foster care,
He favoreth pride, we count it rare.   10

Accurst be Love, and those that trust his trains !
He seemeth blind, yet wounds with art,
He sows content, he pays with smart,
He swears relief, yet kills the heart,
He calls for truth, yet scorns desart.   15
Accurst be Love, and those that trust his trains !
Whose heaven is hell, whose perfect joys are pains.

FOR PITY, PRETTY EYES, SURCEASE.

FOR pity, pretty eyes, surcease
To give me war, and grant me peace.
Triumphant eyes, why bear you arms
Against a heart that thinks no harms?
A heart already quite appalled,   5
A heart that yields and is enthralled?

Kill rebels, proudly that resist ;
Not those that in true faith persist,
And conquered serve your deity.
Will you, alas ! command me die ?   10
Then die I yours, and death my cross ;
But unto you pertains the loss.

————◦◦————

SIR WALTER RALEIGH (?) in
the same.

NOW WHAT IS LOVE.

Now what is love, I pray thee, tell ?
　It is that fountain and that well
Where pleasure and repentance dwell ;
　It is perhaps the sauncing bell
　That tolls all into heaven or hell :   5
And this is love, as I hear tell.

Yet what is love, I prithee, say ?
　It is a work on holiday,
　It is December matched with May,
When lusty bloods in fresh array   10
　Hear ten months after of the play :
And this is love, as I hear say.

Yet what is love, good shepherd sain?
　It is a sunshine mixed with rain,
　It is a toothache or like pain,   15
　It is a game where none hath gain ;
　The lass saith no, yet would full fain :
And this is love, as I hear sain.

Yet, shepherd, what is love, I pray?
  It is a yes, it is a nay,   20
  A pretty kind of sporting fray,
  It is a thing will soon away.
  Then, nymphs, take vantage while ye may :
  And this is love, as I hear say.

Yet what is love, good shepherd, show?   25
  A thing that creeps, it cannot go,
  A prize that passeth to and fro,
  A thing for one, a thing for moe,
  And he that proves shall find it so :
  And, shepherd, this is love, I trow.   30

———•◦•———

EDMUND SPENSER, *Amoretti*,
1595; written 1592–94.

SONNETS.

XXXVII.

WHAT guile is this, that those her golden tresses
She doth attire under a net of gold ;
And with sly skill so cunningly them dresses,
That which is gold or hair may scarce be told?
Is it that men's frail eyes, which gaze too bold,   5
She may entangle in that golden snare ;
And, being caught, may craftily enfold
Their weaker hearts, which are not well aware?
Take heed, therefore, mine eyes, how ye do stare
Henceforth too rashly on that guileful net,   10
In which, if ever ye entrappèd are,
Out of her bands ye by no means shall get.
Fondness it were for any, being free,
To covet fetters, though they golden be.

LV.

So oft as I her beauty do behold,
And therewith do her cruelty compare,
I marvel of what substance was the mould,
The which her made at once so cruel fair.
Not earth, for her high thoughts more heavenly are ;   5
Not water, for her love doth burn like fire ;
Not air, for she is not so light or rare ;
Not fire, for she doth freeze with faint desire.
Then needs another element inquire
Whereof she mote be made — that is, the sky ;   10
For to the heaven her haughty looks aspire,
And eke her mind is pure immortal high.
Then, sith to heaven ye likened are the best,
Be like in mercy as in all the rest.

LXV.

The doubt which ye misdeem, fair love, is vain,
That fondly fear to lose your liberty ;
When, losing one, two liberties ye gain,
And make him bond that bondage erst did fly.
Sweet be the bands, the which true love doth tie,   5
Without constraint, or dread of any ill :
The gentle bird feels no captivity
Within her cage, but sings, and feeds her fill.
There pride dare not approach, nor discord spill
The league 'twixt them that loyal love hath bound,   10
But simple truth, and mutual good will,
Seeks with sweet peace to salve each other's wound:
There Faith doth fearless dwell in brazen tower,
And spotless Pleasure builds her sacred bower.

LXXXI.

FAIR is my love, when her fair golden hairs
With the loose wind ye waving chance to mark ;
Fair, when the rose in her red cheeks appears ;
Or in her eyes the fire of love does spark.
Fair, when her breast, like a rich-laden bark,   5
With precious merchandise she forth doth lay ;
Fair, when that cloud of pride, which oft doth dark
Her goodly light, with smiles she drives away.
But fairest she, when so she doth display
The gate with pearls and rubies richly dight ;   10
Through which her words so wise do make their way
To bear the message of her gentle sprite.
The rest be works of nature's wonderment :
But this the work of heart's astonishment.

————•◦•————

NICHOLAS BRETON, *The Arbor
of Amorous Devises*, 1593-94.

A SWEET LULLABY.

COME, little babe, come, silly soul,
    Thy father's shame, thy mother's grief,
Born as I doubt to all our dole,
    And to thyself unhappy chief :
        Sing lullaby and lap it warm,   5
        Poor soul that thinks no creature harm.

Thou little think'st and less dost know
    The cause of this thy mother's moan ;
Thou want'st the wit to wail her woe,
    And I myself am all alone :   10
        Why dost thou weep? why dost thou wail,
        And know'st not yet what thou dost ail?

Come, little wretch, ah silly heart,
  Mine only joy, what can I more?
If there be any wrong thy smart, 15
  That may the destinies implore :
    'Twas I, I say, against my will;
    I wail the time, but be thou still.

And dost thou smile? O, thy sweet face,
  Would God himself he might thee see! 20
No doubt thou soon wouldst purchase grace,
  I know right well, for thee and me :
    But come to mother, babe, and play,
    For father false is fled away.

Sweet boy, if it by fortune chance 25
  Thy father home again to send,
If death do strike me with his lance,
  Yet mayst thou me to him commend :
    If any ask thy mother's name,
    Tell how by love she purchased blame. 30

Then will his gentle heart soon yield,
  I know him of a noble mind ;
Although a lion in the field,
  A lamb in town thou shalt him find :
    Ask blessing, babe, be not afraid, 35
    His sugared words hath me betrayed.

Then mayst thou joy and be right glad,
  Although in woe I seem to moan ;
Thy father is no rascal lad,
  A noble youth of blood and bone ; 40
    His glancing looks, if he once smile,
    Right honest women may beguile.

Come, little boy, and rock a-sleep,
  Sing lullaby and be thou still ;
I that can do naught else but weep,   45
  Will sit by thee and wail my fill :
    God bless my babe, and lullaby,
    From this thy father's quality.

A SONNET.

THOSE eyes that hold the hand of every heart,
  That hand that holds the heart of every eye,
That wit that goes beyond all nature's art,
  The sense too deep for wisdom to descry :
That eye, that hand, that wit, that heavenly sense   5
Doth shew my only mistress' excellence.

O eyes that pierce into the purest heart !
  O hands that hold the highest thoughts in thrall !
O wit that weighs the depth of all desart !
  O sense that shew the secret sweet of all !   10
The heaven of heavens with heavenly power preserve thee,
Love but thyself, and give me leave to serve thee.

To serve, to live to look upon those eyes,
  To look, to live to kiss that heavenly hand,
To sound that wit that doth amaze the mind,   15
  To know that sense, no sense can understand,
To understand that all the world may know,
Such wit, such sense, eyes, hands, there are no moe.

A PASTORAL OF PHYLLIS AND CORYDON.

On a hill there grows a flower,
   Fair befall the dainty sweet !
By that flower there is a bower,
   Where the heavenly Muses meet.

In that bower there is a chair,   5
   Fringèd all about with gold ;
Where doth sit the fairest fair,
   That did ever eye behold.

It is Phyllis fair and bright,
   She that is the shepherds' joy ;   10
She that Venus did despite,
   And did blind her little boy.

This is she, the wise, the rich,
   And the world desires to see ;
This is *ipsa quae* the which   15
   There is none but only she.

Who would not this face admire ?
   Who would not this saint adore ?
Who would not this sight desire,
   Though he thought to see no more ?   20

O, fair eyes ! yet let me see,
   One good look, and I am gone ;
Look on me, for I am he,
   Thy poor silly Corydon.

Thou that art the shepherd's queen,   25
   Look upon thy silly swain ;
By thy comfort have been seen
   Dead men brought to life again.

SCORN NOT THE LEAST.

Where wards are weak and foes encount'ring strong,
  Where mightier do assault than do defend,
The feebler part puts up enforcèd wrong,
  And silent sees that speech could not amend.
Yet higher powers must think, though they repine,   5
When sun is set, the little stars will shine.

While pike doth range the seely tench doth fly,
  And crouch in privy creeks with smaller fish ;
Yet pikes are caught when little fish go by,
  These fleet afloat while those do fill the dish.   10
There is a time even for the worm to creep,
And suck the dew while all her foes do sleep.

The merlin cannot ever soar on high,
  Nor greedy greyhound still pursue the chase ;
The tender lark will find a time to fly,   15
  And fearful hare to run a quiet race :
He that high growth on cedars did bestow,
Gave also lowly mushrumps leave to grow.

In Aman's pomp poor Mardocheus wept,
  Yet God did turn his fate upon his foe ;   20
The lazar pined while Dives' feast was kept,
  Yet he to heaven, to hell did Dives go.
We trample grass, and prize the flowers of May,
Yet grass is green when flowers do fade away.

THE BURNING BABE.

As I in hoary winter's night
  Stood shivering in the snow,
Surprised I was with sudden heat,
  Which made my heart to glow;
And lifting up a fearful eye   5
  To view what fire was near,
A pretty babe, all burning bright,
  Did in the air appear,
Who, scorchèd with excessive heat,
  Such floods of tears did shed,   10
As though his floods should quench his flames
  Which with his tears were fed.
'Alas,' quoth he, 'but newly born,
  In fiery heats I fry;
Yet none approach to warm their hearts   15
  Or feel my fire but I.
My faultless breast the furnace is,
  The fuel, wounding thorns,
Love is the fire, and sighs the smoke,
  The ashes, shame and scorns.   20
The fuel Justice layeth on,
  And Mercy blows the coals,
The metal in this furnace wrought
  Are men's defilèd souls,
For which, as now on fire I am   25
  To work them to their good,
So will I melt into a bath
  To wash them in my blood.'
With this he vanished out of sight
  And swiftly shrunk away;   30
And straight I callèd unto mind
  That it was Christmas-day.

ROBERT SOUTHWELL, *Mœoniæ*,
1595.

MAN'S CIVIL WAR.

My hovering thoughts would fly to heaven
    And quiet nestle in the sky,
Fain would my ship in Virtue's shore
    Without remove at anchor lie.

But mounting thoughts are halèd down   5
    With heavy poise of mortal load,
And blustring storms deny my ship
    In Virtue's haven secure abode.

When inward eye to heavenly sights
    Doth draw my longing heart's desire,   10
The world with jesses of delights
    Would to her perch my thoughts retire,

Fond Fancy trains to Pleasure's lure,
    Though Reason stiffly do repine ;
Though Wisdom woo me to the saint,   15
    Yet Sense would win me to the shrine.

Where Reason loathes, there Fancy loves,
    And overrules the captive will ;
Foes senses are to Virtue's lore,
    They draw the wit their wish to fill.   20

Need craves consent of soul to sense,
    Yet divers bents breed civil fray ;
Hard hap where halves must disagree,
    Or truce of halves the whole betray !

O cruel fight ! where fighting friend   25
  With love doth kill a favoring foe,
Where peace with sense is war with God,
  And self-delight the seed of woe !

Dame Pleasure's drugs are steeped in sin,
  Their sugared taste doth breed annoy ;   30
O fickle sense ! beware her gin,
  Sell not thy soul to brittle joy !

———◦◦◦———

HENRY CHETTLE, *Piers Plain-
ness Seven Years' Prenticeship,*
1595.

WILY CUPID.

TRUST not his wanton tears,
  Lest they beguile ye ;
Trust not his childish sigh,
  He breatheth slily.
Trust not his touch,   5
  His feeling may defile ye ;
Trust nothing that he doth,
  The wag is wily.
If you suffer him to prate,
You will rue it over-late.   10
  Beware of him, for he is witty ;
Quickly strive the boy to bind,
Fear him not, for he is blind :
  If he get loose, he shows no pity.

FRANCIS DAVISON, *The Poetical Rhapsody*, 1602; written, 1595–96.

MADRIGAL.

TO CUPID.

LOVE, if a god thou art,
  Then evermore thou must
  Be merciful and just.
If thou be just, O wherefore doth thy dart
Wound mine alone, and not my Lady's heart?   5

If merciful, then why
  Am I to pain reserved,
  Who have thee truly served ;
While she, that by thy power sets not a fly,
Laughs thee to scorn and lives in liberty?   10

Then, if a god thou wouldst accounted be,
Heal me like her, or else wound her like me.

THREE EPITAPHS UPON THE DEATH OF A RARE CHILD OF SIX YEARS OLD.

I.

WIT's perfection, Beauty's wonder,
Nature's pride, the Graces' treasure,
Virtue's hope, his friends' sole pleasure,
  This small marble stone lies under ;
    Which is often moist with tears   5
    For such loss in such young years.

II.

Lovely boy ! thou art not dead,
But from earth to heaven fled ;
For base earth was far unfit
For thy beauty, grace, and wit.　　　　10

III.

Thou alive on earth, sweet boy,
Hadst an angel's wit and face ;
And now dead, thou dost enjoy,
In high Heaven, an angel's place.

ODE X.

DISPRAISE OF LOVE AND LOVER'S FOLLIES.

If love be life, I long to die,
　Live they that list for me ;
And he that gains the most thereby,
　A fool at least shall be.
But he that feels the sorest fits,　　　　5
'Scapes with no less than loss of wits :
　　An happy life they gain,
　　Which love do entertain.

In day by feignèd looks they live,
　By lying dreams in night,　　　　10
Each frown a deadly wound doth give,
　Each smile a false delight.
If 't hap their lady pleasant seem,
It is for others' love they deem ;
　　If void she seem of joy,　　　　15
　　Disdain doth make her coy.

Such is the peace that lovers find,
Such is the life they lead,
Blown here and there with every wind,
Like flowers in the mead ;   20
Now war, now peace, now war again,
Desire, despair, delight, disdain :
Though dead, in midst of life,
In peace, and yet at strife.

ODE.

My only star,·
Why. why are your dear eyes,
Where all my life's peace lies,
With me at war?
Why to my ruin tending,   5
Do they still lighten woe
On him that loves you so,
That all his thoughts in you have birth and ending ?

Hope of my heart,
O wherefore do the words,   10
Which your sweet tongue affords,
No hope impart?
But cruel without measure,
To my eternal pain,
Still thunder forth disdain   15
On him whose life depends upon your pleasure.

Sunshine of joy,
Why do your gestures, which
All eyes and hearts bewitch,
My bliss destroy?   20
And pity's sky o'erclouding,
Of hate an endless shower
On that poor heart still pour,
Which in your bosom seeks his only shrouding?

Balm of my wound,   25
Why are your lines, whose sight
Should cure me with delight,
    My poison found?
Which, through my veins dispersing,
Doth make my heart and mind   30
And all my senses, find
A living death in torments past rehearsing.

Alas! my fate
Hath of your eyes deprived me,
Which both killed and revived me   35
    And sweetened hate ;
Your sweet voice and sweet graces,
Which clothed in lovely weeds
Your cruel words and deeds,
Are intercepted by far distant places.   40

But, O the anguish
Which presence still presented,
Absence hath not absented,
    Nor made to languish ;
No, no, to increase my paining,   45
The cause being, ah! removed
For which the effect I loved,
The effect is still in greatest force remaining.

O cruel tiger !
If to your hard heart's center   50
Tears, vows, and prayers may enter,
    Desist your rigor ;
And let kind lines assure me,
Since to my deadly wound
No salve else can be found,   55
That you that kill me, yet at length will cure me.

EDMUND SPENSER, *Prothalamion, or A Spousal Verse*, 1596.

PROTHALAMION.

CALM. was the day, and through the trembling air
Sweet-breathing Zephyrus did softly play
A gentle spirit, that lightly did delay
Hot Titan's beams, which then did glister fair ;
When I (whom sullen care,   5
Through discontent of my long fruitless stay
In princes' court, and expectation vain
Of idle hopes, which still do fly away
Like empty shadows, did afflict my brain)
Walked forth to ease my pain   10
Along the shore of silver-streaming Thames ;
Whose rutty bank, the which his river hems,
Was painted all with variable flowers,
And all the meads adorned with dainty gems,
Fit to deck maidens' bowers,   15
And crown their paramours
Against the bridal day, which is not long:
   Sweet Thames, run softly, till I end my song.

There, in a meadow, by the river's side,
A flock of nymphs I chancèd to espy,   20
All lovely daughters of the flood thereby,
With goodly greenish locks, all loose untied
As each had been a bride ;
And each one had a little wicker basket
Made of fine twigs, entrailèd curiously,   25
In which they gathered flowers to fill their flasket,
And with fine fingers cropped full feateously
The tender stalks on high.

Of every sort which in that meadow grew
They gathered some; the violet, pallid blue,   30
The little daisy, that at evening closes,
The virgin lily, and the primrose true,
With store of vermeil roses,
To deck their bridegrooms' posies
Against the bridal day, which was not long: 35
    Sweet Thames, run softly, till I end my song.

With that I saw two swans of goodly hue
Come softly swimming down along the Lee;
Two fairer birds I yet did never see;
The snow which doth the top of Pindus strew   40
Did never whiter shew,
Nor Jove himself, when he a swan would be
For love of Leda, whiter did appear;
Yet Leda was, they say, as white as he,
Yet not so white as these, nor nothing near;   45
So purely white they were,
That e'en the gentle stream the which them bare
Seemed foul to them, and bade his billows spare
To wet their silken feathers, lest they might
Soil their fair plumes with water not so fair,   50
And mar their beauties bright,
That shone as heaven's light,
Against their bridal day, which was not long:
    Sweet Thames, run softly, till I end my song.

Eftsoons the nymphs, which now had flowers their fill, 55
Ran all in haste to see that silver brood,
As they came floating on the crystal flood;
Whom when they saw, they stood amazèd still,
Their wondring eyes to fill;
Them seemed they never saw a sight so fair,   60
Of fowls so lovely that they sure did deem
Them heavenly born, or to be that same pair

Which through the sky draw Venus' silver team
For sure they did not seem
To be begot of any earthly seed,   65
But rather angels, or of angels' breed ;
Yet were they bred of summer's heat, they say,
In sweetest season, when each flower and weed
The earth did fresh array ;
So fresh they seemed as day,   70
Even as their bridal day, which was not long :
    Sweet Thames, run softly, till I end my song.

Then forth they all out of their baskets drew
Great store of flowers, the honor of the field,
That to the sense did fragrant odors yield,   75
All which upon those goodly birds they threw
And all the waves did strew,
That like old Peneus' waters they did seem,
When down along by pleasant Tempe's shore,
Scattred with flowers, through Thessaly they stream,   80
That they appear, through lilies' plenteous store,
Like a bride's chamber-floor.
Two of those nymphs meanwhile two garlands bound
Of freshest flowers which in that mead they found,
The which presenting all in trim array,   85
Their snowy foreheads therewithal they crowned ;
Whilst one did sing this lay
Prepared against that day,
Against their bridal day, which was not long :
    Sweet Thames, run softly, till I end my song.   90

' Ye gentle birds, the world's fair ornament,
And Heaven's glory, whom this happy hour
Doth lead unto your lovers' blissful bower,
Joy may you have, and gentle heart's content
Of your love's couplement ;   95

And let fair Venus, that is queen of love,
With her heart-quelling son upon you smile,
Whose smile, they say, hath virtue to remove
All love's dislike, and friendship's faulty guile
For ever to assoil.   100
Let endless peace your steadfast hearts accord,
And blessed plenty wait upon your board;
And let your bed with pleasures chaste abound,
That fruitful issue may to you afford
Which may your foes confound,   105
And make your joys redound
Upon your bridal day, which is not long:
    Sweet Thames, run softly, till I end my song.'

So ended she; and all the rest around
To her redoubled that her undersong,   110
Which said, their bridal day should not be long:
And gentle Echo from the neighbor ground
Their accents did resound.
So forth those joyous birds did pass along
Adown the Lee that to them murmured low,   115
As he would speak, but that he lacked a tongue,
Yet did by signs his glad affection show,
Making his stream run slow.
And all the fowl which in his flood did dwell
Gan flock about these twain that did excel   120
The rest so far as Cynthia doth shend
The lesser stars.   So they, enrangèd well,
Did on those two attend,
And their best service lend
Against their wedding-day, which was not long: 125
    Sweet Thames, run softly, till I end my song.

At length they all to merry London came,
To merry London, my most kindly nurse,
That to me gave this life's first native source,

Though from another place I take my name,   130
An house of ancient fame :
There when they came, whereas those bricky towers,
The which on Thames' broad agèd back do ride,
Where now the studious lawyers have their bowers
There whilom wont the Templar Knights to bide,   135
Till they decayed through pride :
Next whereunto there stands a stately place,   '
Where oft I gainèd gifts and goodly grace
Of that great lord which therein wont to dwell,
Whose want too well now feels my friendless case :   140
But ah ! here fits not well
Old woes, but joys, to tell
Against the bridal day, which is not long :
    Sweet Thames, run softly, till I end my song :

Yet therein now doth lodge a noble peer,   145
Great England's glory, and the world's wide wonder,
Whose dreadful name late through all Spain did thunder,
And Hercules' two pillars standing near
Did make to quake and fear :
Fair branch of honor, flower of chivalry !   150
That fillest England with thy triumphs' fame,
Joy have thou of thy noble victory,
And endless happiness of thine own name
That promiseth the same ;
That through thy prowess and victorious arms,   155
Thy country may be freed from foreign harms,
And great Eliza's glorious name may ring
Through all the world, filled with thy wide alarms,
Which some brave Muse may sing
To ages following   160
Upon the bridal day, which is not long :
    Sweet Thames, run softly, till I end my song.

From those high towers, this noble lord issuing,
Like radient Hesper when his golden hair
In th' ocean billows he hath bathèd fair,   165
Descended to the river's open viewing,
With a great train ensuing.
Above the rest were goodly to be seen
Two gentle knights of lovely face and feature,
Beseeming well the bower of any queen,   170
With gifts of wit and ornaments of nature
Fit for so goodly stature,
That like the twins of Jove they seemed in sight,
Which deck the baldrick of the heavens bright ;
They two, forth pacing to the river's side,   175
Received those two fair brides, their loves' delight ;
Which, at the appointed tide,
Each one did make his bride,
Against their bridal day, which is not long :
    Sweet Thames, run softly, till I end my song.   180

——•◦•——

BARNABE BARNES, *A Divine
Century of Spiritual Sonnets,*
1595.

THE TALENT.

GRACIOUS, Divine, and most Omnipotent !
Receive thy servant's talent in good part,
Which hid it not, but willing did convert
It to best use he could, when it was lent :
The sum — though slender, yet not all misspent —   5
Receive, dear God of grace, from cheerful heart
Of him that knows how merciful thou art,
And with what grace to contrite sinners bent.

I know my fault, I did not as I should ;
My sinful flesh against my soul rebelled ;   10
But since I did endeavor what I could,
Let not my little nothing be withheld
From thy rich treasuries of endless grace ;
But, for thy sake, let it procure a place.

———•◦•———

WILLIAM SHAKESPEARE, *The
Merchant of Venice,* 1596.

A SONG

THE WHILST BASSANIO COMMENTS ON THE CASKETS TO HIMSELF.

TELL me where is fancy bred,
Or in the heart or in the head ?
How begot, how nourishèd ?
    Reply, reply.

It is engendered in the eyes,   5
With gazing fed ; and fancy dies
In the cradle where it lies :
    Let us all ring fancy's knell ;
    I'll begin it, — Ding, dong, bell.
    Ding, dong, bell.   10

———•◦•———

From WILLIAM BARLEYS, *New
Book of Tabliture,* 1596.

SONNET.

THOSE eyes that set my fancy on a fire,
Those crispèd hairs that hold my heart in chains,
Those dainty hands which conquered my desire,
That wit which of my thoughts doth hold the reins :

Then Love be judge, what heart may there withstand 5
Such eyes, such head, such wit, and such a hand?
Those eyes for clearness doth the stars surpass,
Those hairs obscure the brightness of the sun,
Those hands more white than ever ivory was,
That wit even to the skies hath glory won. 10
O eyes that pierce the skies without remorse!
O hairs of night that wear a royal crown!
O hands that conquer more than Caesar's force!
O wit that turns huge kingdoms upside down!

From Nicholas Yonge's *Musica Transalpina*, Book *II.*, 1597.

MADRIGAL.

Brown is my love, but graceful;
And each renownèd whiteness,
Matched with thy lovely brown, loseth its brightness.

Fair is my love, but scornful;
Yet have I seen despisèd 5
Dainty white lilies, and sad flowers well prizèd.

William Shakespeare, *Sonnets*, 1609; written about 1598.

SONNETS.

XIX.

Devouring Time, blunt thou the lion's paws,
And make the earth devour her own sweet brood;
Pluck the keen teeth from the fierce tiger's jaws,
And burn the long-lived Phoenix in her blood;

Make glad and sorry seasons as thou fleets,   5
And do whate'er thou wilt, swift-footed Time,
To the wide world and all her fading sweets;
But I forbid thee one most heinous crime:
O, carve not with thy hours my love's fair brow,
Nor draw no lines there with thine antique pen;   10
Him in thy course untainted do allow
For beauty's pattern to succeeding men.
Yet, do thy worst, old Time: despite thy wrong,
My love shall in my verse ever live young.

XXIX.

WHEN, in disgrace with fortune and men's eyes,
I all alone beweep my outcast state,
And trouble deaf heaven with my bootless cries,
And look upon myself and curse my fate,
Wishing me like to one more rich in hope,   5
Featured like him, like him with friends possessed,
Desiring this man's art and that man's scope,
With what I most enjoy contented least;
Yet in these thoughts myself almost despising,
Haply I think on thee, and then my state,   10
Like to the lark at break of day arising
From sullen earth, sings hymns at heaven's gate;
For thy sweet love remembered such wealth brings
That then I scorn to change my state with kings.

XXXIII.

FULL many a glorious morning have I seen
Flatter the mountain-tops with sovereign eye,
Kissing with golden face the meadows green,
Gilding pale streams with heavenly alchemy;

Anon permit the basest clouds to ride 5
With ugly rack on his celestial face,
And from the forlorn world his visage hide,
Stealing unseen to west with this disgrace:
Even so my sun one early morn did shine
With all-triumphant splendor on my brow; 10
But out, alack! he was but one hour mine;
The region cloud hath masked him from me now.
Yet him for this my love no whit disdaineth;
Suns of the world may stain, when heaven's sun staineth.

LX.

LIKE as the waves make towards the pebbled shore,
So do our minutes hasten to their end;
Each changing place with that which goes before
In sequent toil all forwards do contend.
Nativity, once in the main of light, 5
Crawls to maturity, wherewith being crowned,
Crooked eclipses 'gainst his glory fight,
And Time that gave doth now his gift confound.
Time doth transfix the flourish set on youth
And delves the parallels in beauty's brow, 10
Feeds on the rarities of nature's truth,
And nothing stands but for his scythe to mow:
And yet to times in hope my verse shall stand,
Praising thy worth, despite his cruel hand.

LXXI.

No longer mourn for me when I am dead
Than you shall hear the surly sullen bell
Give warning to the world that I am fled
From this vile world, with vilest worms to dwell;

Nay, if you read this line, remember not   5
The hand that writ it; for I love you so
That I in your sweet thoughts would be forgot,
If thinking on me then should make you woe.
O, if, I say, you look upon this verse
When I perhaps compounded am with clay,   10
Do not so much as my poor name rehearse,
But let your love even with my life decay,
Lest the wise world should look into your moan,
And mock you with me after I am gone.

CVI.

WHEN in the chronicle of wasted time
I see descriptions of the fairest wights,
And beauty making beautiful old rime
In praise of ladies dead and lovely knights,
Then, in the blazon of sweet beauty's best,   5
Of hand, of foot, of lip, of eye, of brow,
I see their antique pen would have expressed
Even such a beauty as you master now.
So all their praises are but prophecies
Of this our time, all you prefiguring;   10
And, for they looked but with divining eyes,
They had not skill enough your worth to sing:
For we, which now behold these present days,
Have eyes to wonder, but lack tongues to praise.

CXVI.

LET me not to the marriage of true minds
Admit impediments.   Love is not love
Which alters when it alteration finds,
Or bends with the remover to remove:
O, no! it is an ever-fixèd mark   5
That looks on tempests and is never shaken;

It is the star to every wandering bark,
Whose worth's unknown, although his height be taken ;
Love's not Time's fool, though rosy lips and cheeks
Within his bending sickle's compass come ;   10
Love alters not with his brief hours and weeks,
But bears it out even to the edge of doom.
If this be error and upon me proved,
I never writ nor no man ever loved.

CXXX.

My mistress' eyes are nothing like the sun ;
Coral is far more red than her lips' red ;
If snow be white, why then her breasts are dun ;
If hairs be wires, black wires grow on her head.
I have seen roses damasked red and white,   5
But no such roses see I in her cheeks ;
And in some perfumes is there more delight
Than in the breath that from my mistress reeks.
I love to hear her speak, yet well I know
That music hath a far more pleasing sound ;   10
I grant I never saw a goddess go,
My mistress, when she walks, treads on the ground ;
And yet, by heaven, I think my love as rare
As any she belied with false compare.

———◄○►———

RICHARD BARNFIELD, *Poems: In Divers Humors*, 1598.

SONNET:

IN PRAISE OF MUSIC AND POETRY.

If music and sweet poetry agree,
As they must needs, the sister and the brother,
Then must the love be great 'twixt thee and me,
Because thou lov'st the one and I the other.

Dowland to thee is dear, whose heavenly touch   5
Upon the lute doth ravish human sense ;
Spenser to me, whose deep conceit is such,
As passing all conceit, needs no defence.
Thou lov'st to hear the sweet melodious sound
That Phœbus' lute, the queen of music, makes ;   10
And I in deep delight am chiefly drowned
Whenas himself to singing he betakes :
One god is god of both, as poets feign,
One knight loves both, and both in thee remain.

AN ODE.

As it fell upon a day,
In the merry month of May,
Sitting in a pleasant shade,
Which a grove of myrtles made,
Beasts did leap and birds did sing,   5
Trees did grow and plants did spring :
Everything did banish moan,
Save the nightingale alone.
She, poor bird, as all forlorn,
Leaned her breast up-till a thorn,   10
And there sung the dolefulst ditty,
That to hear it was great pity.
'Fie, fie, fie !' now would she cry ;
'Teru, teru !' by-and-by ;
That to hear her so complain   15
Scarce I could from tears refrain :
For her griefs so lively shown
Made me think upon mine own.
Ah, thought I, thou mourn'st in vain,
None takes pity on thy pain.   20
Senseless trees, they cannot hear thee ;
Ruthless bears, they will not cheer thee ;

King Pandion he is dead,
All thy friends are lapt in lead ;
All thy fellow birds do sing,   25
Careless of thy sorrowing.
Whilst as fickle Fortune smiled,
Thou and I were both beguiled.
Every one that flatters thee
Is no friend in misery :   30
Words are easy, like the wind ;
Faithful friends are hard to find ;
Every man will be thy friend,
Whilst thou hast wherewith to spend ;
But if store of crowns be scant,   35
No man will supply thy want.
If that one be prodigal,
Bountiful they will him call ;
And with such-like flattering,
'Pity but he were a king.'   40
If he be addict to vice,
Quickly him they will entice.
If to women he be bent,
They have at commandèment.
But if Fortune once do frown,   45
Then farewell his great renown :
They that fawned on him before,
Use his company no more.
He that is thy friend indeed,
He will help thee in thy need ;   50
If thou sorrow, he will weep ;
If thou wake, he cannot sleep :
Thus of every grief in heart
He with thee doth bear a part.
These are certain signs to know   55
Faithful friend from flatt'ring foe.

From GILES FARNABY'S *Canzonets*, 1598.

CANZONET.

THRICE blessèd be the giver
That gave sweet Love that golden quiver,
And live he long among the gods anointed
That made the arrow-heads sharp-pointed :
If either of them both had quailèd,　　　　5
She of my love and I of hers had failèd.

———•◦•———

From JOHN WILBYE'S *Madrigals*,
1598.

MADRIGAL.

LADY, when I behold the roses sprouting,
Which, clad in damask mantles, deck the arbors ;
And then behold your lips, where sweet love harbors ;
My eyes present me with a double doubting :
For viewing both alike, hardly my mind supposes,　　5
Whether the roses be your lips, or your lips the roses.

———•◦•———

GEORGE CHAPMAN, *Hero and
Leander*, 1598.

EPITHALAMION TERATOS.

COME, come, dear Night, Love's mart of kisses,
Sweet close of his ambitious line,
The fruitful summer of his blisses,
Love's glory doth in darkness shine.

O come, soft rest of cares, come, Night, 5
   Come naked Virtue's only tire,
The reapèd harvest of the light
   Bound up in sheaves of sacred fire.
      Love calls to war ;
        Sighs his alarms, 10
      Lips his swords are,
        The field his arms.

Come, Night, and lay thy velvet hand
   On glorious Day's outfacing face ;
And all thy crownèd flames command, 15
   For torches to our nuptial grace.
      Love calls to war ;
        Sighs his alarms,
      Lips his swords are,
        The field his arms. 20

No need have we of factious Day,
   To cast, in envy of thy peace,
Her balls of discord in thy way ;
   Here Beauty's day doth never cease ;
      Day is abstracted here, 25
      And varied in a triple sphere,
Hero, Alcmane, Mya, so outshine thee,
Ere thou come here, let Thetis thrice refine thee.
      Love calls to war ;
        Sighs his alarms, 30
      Lips his swords are,
        The field his arms.

MUNDAY and CHETTLE, *The
Death of Robert Earl of Hun-
tingdon*, acted 1598.

ROBIN HOOD'S DIRGE.

WEEP, weep, ye woodmen, wail,
  Your hands with sorrow wring ;
Your master Robin Hood lies dead,
  Therefore sigh as you sing.

Here lies his primer and his beads,   5
  His bent bow and his arrows keen,
His good sword and his holy cross :
  Now cast on flowers fresh and green.

And, as they fall, shed tears and say
  Well-a, well-a-day, well-a, well-a-day :   10
Thus cast ye flowers fresh, and sing,
  And on to Wakefield take your way.

———•◦•———

THOMAS DEKKER, *The Shoe-
makers' Holiday*, acted 1599.

THE SECOND THREE MEN'S SONG.

COLD's the wind, and wet's the rain,
  Saint Hugh be our good speed :
Ill is the weather that bringeth no gain,
  Nor helps good hearts in need.

Troll the bowl, the jolly nut brown bowl,   5
  And here, kind mate, to thee !
Let's sing a dirge for Saint Hugh's soul
  And down it merrily.

Down-a-down, hey, down-a-down,
Hey derry derry down-a-down !   10
　　Close with the tenor boy ;
Ho! well done, to me let come,
　　Ring compass, gentle joy.

Cold's the wind, and wet's the rain,
　　Saint Hugh be our good speed :   15
Ill is the weather that bringeth no gain,
　　Nor helps good hearts in need.

THOMAS DEKKER, *The Pleasant
Comedy of Patient Grissell,*
acted 1599.

O SWEET CONTENT.

ART thou poor, yet hast thou golden slumbers?
　　O sweet content !
Art thou rich, yet is thy mind perplexèd?
　　O punishment !
Dost thou laugh to see how fools are vexèd   5
To add to golden numbers, golden numbers?
O sweet content ! O sweet O sweet content !
　Work apace, apace, apace, apace ;
　Honest labor bears a lovely face ;
Then hey nonny nonny, hey nonny nonny !   10

Canst drink the waters of the crispèd spring?
　　O sweet content !
Swimm'st thou in wealth, yet sink'st in thine own tears?
　　O punishment !
Then he that patiently want's burden bears   15
No burden bears, but is a king, a king !
O sweet content ! O sweet O sweet content !

Work apace, apace, apace, apace ;
Honest labor bears a lovely face ;
Then hey nonny nonny, hey nonny nonny !   20

LULLABY.

GOLDEN slumbers kiss your eyes,
Smiles awake you when you rise.
Sleep, pretty wantons, do not cry,
And I will sing a lullaby :
Rock them, rock them, lullaby.   5

Care is heavy, therefore sleep you ;
You are care, and care must keep you.
Sleep, pretty wantons, do not cry,
And I will sing a lullaby :
Rock them, rock them, lullaby.   10

ROBERT DEVEREUX, Earl of
Essex, *Certain Verses (Ashm.
MS.)*, written about 1599.

A PASSION OF MY LORD OF ESSEX.

HAPPY were he could finish forth his fate
    In some unhaunted desert, most obscure
From all society, from love and hate
    Of worldly folk, there might he sleep secure ;
There wake again, and give God ever praise,   5
    Content with hips and haws and brambleberry,
In contemplation passing still his days,
    And change of holy thoughts to make him merry.
That when he dies, his tomb might be a bush,
Where harmless robin dwells with gentle thrush.   10

WILLIAM SHAKESPEARE, *As You
Like It*, acted 1599.

UNDER THE GREENWOOD TREE.

UNDER the greenwood tree
Who loves to lie with me,
  And turn his merry note
  Unto the sweet bird's throat,
Come hither, come hither, come hither: 5
    Here shall he see
    No enemy
But winter and rough weather.

Who doth ambition shun,
And loves to live i' the sun,   10
  Seeking the food he eats,
  And pleased with what he gets,
Come hither, come hither, come hither:
    Here shall he see
    No enemy   15
But winter and rough weather.

MAN'S INGRATITUDE.

BLOW, blow, thou winter wind,
Thou art not so unkind
    As man's ingratitude;
  Thy tooth is not so keen,
  Because thou art not seen,   5
    Although thy breath be rude.
Heigh-ho! sing heigh-ho! unto the green holly:
Most friendship is feigning, most loving mere folly:
    Then heigh-ho, the holly!
    This life is most jolly.   10

Freeze, freeze, thou bitter sky,
That dost not bite so nigh
     As benefits forgot:
Though thou the waters warp,
Thy sting is not so sharp   15
     As friend remembred not.
Heigh-ho! sing heigh-ho! unto the green holly:
Most friendship is feigning, most loving mere folly.
     Then heigh-ho, the holly!
     This life is most jolly.   20

IT WAS A LOVER AND HIS LASS.

It was a lover and his lass
     With a hey, and a ho, and a hey-nonino,
That o'er the green corn-field did pass
In the spring time, the only pretty ring time,
When birds do sing, hey ding a ding,   5
     Sweet lovers love the Spring.

Between the acres of the rye,
     With a hey, and a ho, and a hey-nonino,
These pretty country folks would lie,
In the spring time, the only pretty ring time,   10
When birds do sing, hey ding a ding,
     Sweet lovers love the Spring.

This carol they began that hour,
     With a hey, and a ho, and a hey-nonino,
How that a life was but a flower   15
In the spring time, the only pretty ring time,
When birds do sing, hey ding a ding,
     Sweet lovers love the Spring.

And therefore take the present time,
  With a hey, and a ho, and a hey-nonino,   20
For love is crownèd with the prime
In the spring time, the only pretty ring time,
When birds do sing, hey ding a ding,
  Sweet lovers love the Spring.

————◆◇◆————

JOHN DONNE, *Poems, with Elegies on the Author's Death,*
1633; written 1590–1600.

SONG.

Go and catch a falling star,
  Get with child a mandrake root,
Tell me where all past hours are,
  Or who cleft the Devil's foot ;
Teach me to hear mermaids singing,   5
Or to keep off envy's stinging,
      Or find
      What wind
Serves to advance an honest mind.

If thou be'st born to strange sights,   10
  Things invisible go see,
Ride ten thousand days and nights,
  Till age snow white hairs on thee.
Thou at thy return wilt tell me
All strange wonders that befell thee,   15
      And swear,
      Nowhere
Lives a woman true and fair.

If thou find'st one, let me know,
   Such a pilgrimage were sweet;   20
Yet do not, I would not go,
   Though at next door we should meet.
Though she were true when you met her,
And last till you write your letter,
            Yet she   25
            Will be
False, ere I come, to two or three.

LOVER'S INFINITENESS.

IF yet I have not all thy love,
Dear, I shall never have it all;
I cannot breathe one other sigh to move,
Nor can entreat one other tear to fall;
And all my treasure, which should purchase thee,   5
Sighs, tears, and oaths, and letters, I have spent;
   Yet no more can be due to me,
   Than at the bargain made was meant:
If, then, thy gift of love were partial,
That some to me, some should to others fall,   10
   Dear, I shall never have it all.

Or if then thou gavest me all,
All was but all which thou hadst then:
But if in thy heart since there be, or shall
New love created be by other men,   15
Which have their stocks entire, and can in tears,
In sighs, in oaths, in letters outbid me,
   This new love may beget new fears;
   For this love was not vowed by thee,
And yet it was, thy gift being general: 20
The ground, thy heart, is mine; whatever shall
   Grow there, dear, I should have it all.

Yet I would not have all yet;
He that hath all can have no more;
And since my love doth every day admit 25
New growth, thou shouldst have new rewards in store.
Thou canst not every day give me thy heart;
If thou canst give it, then thou never gav'st it:
Love's riddles are that, though thy heart depart,
It stays at home, and thou with losing sav'st it, 30
But we will love a way more liberal
Than changing hearts, — to join them; so we shall
Be one, and one another's All.

SONG.

SWEETEST love, I do not go
For weariness of thee,
Nor in hope the world can show
A fitter love for me;
But since that I 5
Must die at last, 'tis best
Thus to use myself in jest,
By feignèd deaths to die.

Yesternight the sun went hence,
And yet is here to-day; 10
He hath no desire nor sense,
Nor half so short a way.
Then fear not me,
But believe that I shall make
Hastier journeys, since I take 15
More wings and spurs than he.

O how feeble is man's power,
That, if good fortune fall,
Cannot add another hour,
Nor a lost hour recall. 20

But come bad chance,
And we join to it our strength,
And we teach it art and length,
Itself o'er us t' advance.

When thou sigh'st, thou sigh'st no wind,   25
But sigh'st my soul away;
When thou weep'st, unkindly kind,
My life's blood doth decay.
It cannot be
That thou lov'st me as thou say'st,   30
If in thine my life thou waste,
That art the best of me.

Let not thy divining heart
Forethink me any ill.
Destiny may take thy part   35
And may thy fears fulfil;
But think that we
Are but turned aside to sleep:
They who one another keep
Alive, ne'er parted be.   40

THE DREAM.

DEAR love, for nothing less than thee
Would I have broke this happy dream;
It was a theme
For reason, much too strong for fantasy.
Therefore thou wak'dst me wisely; yet   5
My dream thou brak'st not, but continu'd'st it:
Thou art so true, that thoughts of thee suffice
To make dreams truths, and fables histories.
Enter these arms, for since thou thought'st it best
Not to dream all my dream, let's do the rest.   10

As lightning or a taper's light,
Thine eyes, and not thy noise, waked me.
   Yet I thought thee
(For thou lov'st truth) an angel at first sight ;
But when I saw thou saw'st my heart,   15
And knew'st my thoughts, beyond an angel's art,
When thou knew'st what I dreamt, when thou knew'st when
Excess of joy would wake me, and cam'st then ;
I must confess, it could not choose but be
Profane to think thee anything but thee.   20

Coming and staying showed thee thee,
But rising makes me doubt, that now
   Thou art not thou.
That love is weak, where fear's as strong as he ;
'Tis not all spirit, pure and brave,   25
If mixture it of fear, shame, honor, have.
Perchance as torches, which must ready be,
Men light and put out, so thou dealst with me ;
Thou cam'st to kindle, go'st to come : then I
Will dream that hope again, but else would die. 30

THE MESSAGE.

Send home my long-strayed eyes to me,
Which, O, too long have dwelt on thee ;
But if there they have learned such ill,
  Such forc'd fashions
  And false passions,   5
   That they be
  Made by thee
Fit for no good sight, keep them still.

Send home my harmless heart again,
Which no unworthy thought could stain ; 10

But if it be taught by thine
    To make jestings
    Of protestings,
        And break both
        Word and oath,   15
Keep it, for then 'tis none of mine.

Yet send me back my heart and eyes,
That I may know and see thy lies,
And may laugh and joy when thou
        Art in anguish,   20
        And dost languish
            For some one
            That will none,
Or prove as false as thou dost now.

UPON PARTING FROM HIS MISTRESS.

As virtuous men pass mildly away,
    And whisper to their souls to go,
Whilst some of their sad friends do say
    Now his breath goes, and some say no ;

So let us melt, and make no noise,   5
    No tear-floods nor sigh-tempests move ;
'Twere profanation of our joys
    To tell the laity our love.

Moving of th' earth brings harms and fears,
    Men reckon what it did and meant ;   10
But trepidation of the spheres,
    Though greater far, is innocent.

Dull sublunary lovers' love,
    Whose soul is sense, cannot admit
Absence ; for that it doth remove   15
    Those things which elemented it.

But we, by a love so far refined
　That ourselves know not what it is,
Inter-assurèd of the mind,
　Care less, eyes, lips, and hands to miss. 20

Our two souls, therefore, which are one,
　Though I must go, endure not yet
A breach, but an expansiòn,
　Like gold to airy thinness beat.

If they be two, they are two so 25
　As stiff twin compasses are two ;
Thy soul, the fixed foot, makes no show
　To move, but doth if th' other do.

And though it in the centre sit,
　Yet when the other far doth roam, 30
It leans and hearkens after it.
　And grows erect as that comes home.

Such wilt thou be to me, who must,
　Like th' other foot, obliquely run :
Thy firmness makes my circle just, 35
　And makes me end where I begun.

LOVE'S DEITY.

I LONG to talk with some old lover's ghost,
　Who died before the god of love was born :
I cannot think that he, that then loved most, *
　Sunk so low as to love one which did scorn.
But since this god produced a destiny, 5
And that vice-nature, custom, lets it be,
I must love her that loves not me.

Sure they which made him god meant not so much,
    Nor he in his young godhead practised it ;
But when an even flame two hearts did touch,   10
    His office was indulgently to fit
Actives to passives ; correspondency
Only his subject was ; it cannot be
Love, if I love who loves not me.

But every modern god will now extend   15
    His vast prerogative as far as Jove ;
To rage, to lust, to write too, to commend,
    All is the purlieu of the god of love.
O were we wakened by this tyranny
To ungod this child again, it could not be   20
I should love her that loves not me.

Rebel and atheist, too, why murmur I,
    As though I felt the worst that Love could do ?
Love might make me leave loving, or might try
    A deeper plague, to make her love me too,   25
Which, since she loves before, I am loath to see ;
Falsehood is worse than hate ; and that must be,
If she whom I love should love me.

THE FUNERAL.

WHOEVER comes to shroud me, do not harm
        Nor question much
That subtle wreath of hair about mine arm ;
    The mystery, the sign, you must not touch,
        For 'tis my outward soul,   5
Viceroy to that which, unto heaven being gone,
        Will leave this to control
And keep these limbs, her provinces, from dissolution.

For if the sinewy thread my brain lets fall
    Through every part,   10
Can tie those parts, and make me one of all ;
The hairs, which upward grew and strength and art
    Have from a better brain,
Can better do it : except she meant that I
    By this should know my pain,   15
As prisoners then are manacled, when they're condemned
    to die.

Whate'er she meant by 't, bury it with me ;
    For since I am
Love's martyr, it might breed idolatry,
If into others' hands these relics came.   '   20
    As 'twas humility
T' afford to it all that a soul can do ;
    So 'tis some bravery,
That, since you would have none of me, I bury some of you.

———◆◆◆———

HENRY CONSTABLE, in *England's Helicon,* 1600.

DAMELUS' SONG TO HIS DIAPHENIA.

DIAPHENIA, like the daffadowndilly,
White as the sun, fair as the lily,
    Heigh ho, how I do love thee !
I do love thee as my lambs
Are belovèd of their dams ;   5
    How blest were I if thou wouldst prove me !

Diaphenia, like the spreading roses,
That in thy sweets all sweets encloses,
    Fair sweet, how I do love thee !

I do love thee as each flower   10
Loves the sun's life-giving power;
    For dead, thy breath to life might move me.

Diaphenia, like to all things blessèd
When all thy praises are expressèd,
    Dear joy, how I do love thee!   15
As the birds do love the Spring,
Or the bees their careful king:
    Then in requite, sweet virgin, love me.

TO HIS FLOCK.

FEED on, my flocks, securely,
Your shepherd watcheth surely;
Run about, my little lambs,
Skip and wanton with your dams,
    Your loving herd with care will tend ye.   5

Sport on, fair flocks, at pleasure,
Nip Vesta's flow'ring treasure;
I myself will duly hark,
When my watchful dog doth bark;
    From wolf and fox I will defend ye.   10

—◦◦◦—

NICHOLAS BRETON, in the same.

CORYDON'S SUPPLICATION TO PHYLLIS.

SWEET Phyllis, if a silly swain
    May sue to thee for grace,
See not thy loving shepherd slain
    With looking on thy face:

But think what power thou hast got 5
    Upon my flock and me,
Thou seest they now regard me not,
    But all do follow thee.
And if I have so far presumed
    With prying in thine eyes, 10
Yet let not comfort be consumed
    That in thy pity lies;
But as thou art that Phyllis fair,
    That fortune favor gives,
So let not love die in despair 15
    That in thy favor lives.
The deer do browse upon the briar,
    The birds do pick the cherries;
And will not Beauty grant Desire
    One handful of her berries? 20
If it be so that thou hast sworn
    That none shall look on thee,
Yet let me know thou dost not scorn
    To cast a look on me.
But if thy beauty make thee proud, 25
    Think then what is ordained;
The heavens have never yet allowed
    That love should be disdained.
Then lest the Fates that favor love
    Should curse thee for unkind, 30
Let me report for thy behoove
    The honor of thy mind;
Let Corydon with full consent
    Set down what he hath seen,
That Phyllida with Love's content 35
    Is sworn the shepherds' queen.

ANTHONY MUNDAY, in the same.

MONTANA THE SHEPHERD HIS LOVE TO AMINTA.

I SERVE Aminta, whiter than the snow,
    Straighter than cedar, brighter than the glass ;
More fine in trip than foot of running roe,
    More pleasant than the field of flow'ring grass ;
More gladsome to my withering joys that fade   5
Than winter's sun or summer's cooling shade.

Sweeter than swelling grape of ripest wine,
    Softer than feathers of the fairest swan ;
Smoother than jet, more stately than the pine,
    Fresher than poplar, smaller than my span ;   10
Clearer than Phœbus' fiery-pointed beam,
Or icy crust of crystal's frozen stream.

Yet is she curster than the bear by kind,
    And harder-hearted than the agèd oak ;
More glib than oil, more fickle than the wind,   15
    More stiff than steel, no sooner bent but broke.
Lo ! thus my service is a lasting sore,
Yet will I serve, although I die therefore.

TO COLIN CLOUT.

BEAUTY sat bathing by a spring,
    Where fairest shades did hide her,
The winds blew calm, the birds did sing,
    The cool streams ran beside her.
My wanton thoughts enticed mine eye   5
    To see what was forbidden,
But better memory said, fie,
    So vain desire was chidden.

Into a slumber then I fell,
  When fond imagination   10
Seemed to see, but could not tell
  Her feature or her fashion.
But even as babes in dreams do smile,
  And sometimes fall a-weeping,
So I awaked, as wise this while,   15
  As when I fell a-sleeping.

——•◦•——

EDMUND BOLTON, in the same.

A CANZON PASTORAL IN HONOR
OF HER MAJESTY.

ALAS! what pleasure, now the pleasant spring
    Hath given place
To harsh black frosts the sad ground covering,
    Can we, poor we, embrace,
When every bird on every branch can sing   5
    Naught but this note of woe, Alas?
Alas! this note of woe why should we sound?
With us, as May, September hath a prime;
Then, birds and branches, your Alas is fond,
Which call upon the absent summer-time.   10
    For did flowers make our May,
    Or the sunbeams your day,
When night and winter did the world embrace,
Well might you wail your ill and sing Alas.

Lo, matron-like the earth herself attires   15
    In habit grave;
Naked the fields are, bloomless are the briars,
    Yet we a summer have,
Who in our clime kindleth these living fires,
    Which blooms can on the briars save.   20

No ice doth crystallize the running brook,
No blast deflowers the flower-adornèd field.
Crystal is clear, but clearer is the look
Which to our climes these living fires doth yield.
    Winter, though everywhere,   25
    Hath no abiding here :
On brooks and briars she doth rule alone.
The sun which lights our world is always one.

A PALINODE.

As withereth the primrose by the river,
As fadeth summer's sun from gliding fountains,
As vanisheth the light-blown bubble ever,
As melteth snow upon the mossy mountains:
So melts, so vanisheth, so fades, so withers,   5
The rose, the shine, the bubble, and the snow,
Of praise, pomp, glory, joy, which short life gathers,
Fair praise, vain pomp, sweet glory, brittle joy.
The withered primrose by the mourning river,
The faded summer's sun from weeping fountains,   10
The light-blown bubble vanishèd for ever,
The molten snow upon the naked mountains,
    Are emblems that the treasures we uplay,
    Soon wither, vanish, fade, and melt away.

For as the snow, whose lawn did overspread .   15
Th' ambitious hills, which giant-like did threat
To pierce the heaven with their aspiring head,
Naked and bare doth leave their craggy seat ;
Whenas the bubble, which did empty fly,
The dalliance of the undiscernèd wind,   20
On whose calm rolling waves it did rely,
Hath shipwrack made, where it did dalliance find ;

And when the sunshine which dissolved the snow,
Colored the bubble with a pleasant vary,
And made the rathe and timely primrose grow,   25
Swarth clouds withdrawn, which longer time do tarry :
   O what is praise, pomp, glory, joy, but so
   As shine by fountains, bubbles, flowers, or snow?

         —◦◦—

From JOHN DOWLAND's *Second
Book of Songs or Airs,* 1600.

COME, SORROW, COME.

COME, ye heavy states of night,
Do my father's spirit right ;
Soundings baleful let me borrow,
Burthening my song with sorrow.
   Come, Sorrow, come ! her eyes that sings   5
   By thee are turnèd into springs.

Come, you virgins of the night,
That in dirges sad delight,
Choir my anthems : I do borrow
Gold nor pearl, but sounds of sorrow.   10
   Come, Sorrow, come ! her eyes that sings
   By thee are turnèd into springs.

I SAW MY LADY WEEP.

   I SAW my lady weep,
And Sorrow proud to be advancèd so
In those fair eyes where all perfections keep.
   Her face was full of woe :
But such a woe, believe me, as wins more hearts   5
Than Mirth can do with her enticing parts.

Sorrow was there made fair,
And passion wise ; tears a delightful thing ;
Silence beyond all speech, a wisdom rare ;
    She made her sighs to sing,   10
And all things with so sweet a sadness move
As made my heart at once both grieve and love.

    O fairer than aught else
The world can show, leave off in time to grieve.
Enough, enough : your joyful look excels ;   15
    Tears kill the heart, believe.
O strive not to be excellent in woe,
Which only breeds your beauty's overthrow.

————•◦•————

From THOMAS WEELKES' *Madrigals of Five and Six Parts*,
1600.

BEAUTY'S TRIUMPH.

LIKE two proud armies marching in the field,
Joining in thund'ring fight, each scorns to yield ;
So in my heart, your beauty and my reason,
One claims the crown, the other says 't is treason.
But O ! your beauty shineth as the sun ;   5
And dazzled reason yields as quite undone.

————•◦•————

From the *Oxford Music School
MS.;* author unknown, date
of writing uncertain.

MY HEART.

THOU sent'st to me a heart was sound,
    I took it to be thine ;
But when I saw it had a wound,
    I knew that heart was mine.

A bounty of a strange conceit,   5
　　To send mine own to me,
And send it in a worse estate
　　Than when it came to thee.

———◆◆———

BEN JONSON, *Cynthia's Revels,*
acted 1600.

ECHO'S DIRGE FOR NARCISSUS.

Slow, slow, fresh fount, keep time with my salt tears ;
　　Yet slower, yet, O faintly, gentle springs ;
List to the heavy part the music bears,
　　Woe weeps out her division when she sings.
　　　　Droop herbs and flowers,   5
　　　　Fall grief in showers,
　　　　Our beauties are not ours ;
　　　　　　O, I could still,
Like melting snow upon some craggy hill,
　　　　Drop, drop, drop, drop,   10
Since nature's pride is now a withered daffodil.

HYMN TO DIANA.

Queen and Huntress, chaste and fair,
　　Now the sun is laid to sleep,
Seated in thy silver chair,
　　State in wonted manner keep :
　　　　Hesperus entreats thy light,   5
　　　　Goddess excellently bright.

Earth, let not thy envious shade
　　Dare itself to interpose ;
Cynthia's shining orb was made
　　Heaven to clear when day did close :   10
　　　　Bless us then with wishèd sight,
　　　　Goddess excellently bright.

Lay thy bow of pearl apart
And thy crystal-shining quiver ;
Give unto the flying hart   15
  Space to breathe, how short soever :
  Thou that mak'st a day of night,
  Goddess excellently bright.
                                   •

BEN JONSON, *Poetaster*, 1601.

HIS SUPPOSED MISTRESS.

IF I freely can discover
What would please me in my lover,
  I would have her fair and witty,
  Savoring more of court than city ;
  A little proud, but full of pity ;   5
  Light and humorous in her toying ;
  Oft building hopes, and soon destroying ;
  Long, but sweet in the enjoying,
Neither too easy, nor too hard :
All extremes I would have barred.   10

She should be allowed her passions,
So they were but used as fashions ;
  Sometimes froward, and then frowning,
  Sometimes sickish, and then swowning,
  Every fit with change still crowning.   15
  Purely jealous I would have her;
  Then only constant when I crave her,
  'Tis a virtue should not save her.
Thus, nor her delicates would cloy me,
Neither her peevishness annoy me.   20

BEN JONSON, in *Divers Poetical Essays,* affixed to Chester's *Love's Martyr,* 1601.

EPODE.

Not to know vice at all, and keep true state,
    Is virtue, and not fate:
Next to that virtue is to know vice well,
    And her black spite expel.
Which to effect (since no breast is so sure,   5
    Or safe, but she'll procure
Some way of entrance) we must plant a guard
    Of thoughts to watch and ward
At th' eye and ear, the ports unto the mind,
    That no strange or unkind   10
Object arrive there, but the heart, our spy,
    Give knowledge instantly
To wakeful reason, our affections' king:
    Who, in th' examining,
Will quickly taste the treason, and commit   15
    Close, the close cause of it.
'Tis the securest policy we have,
    To make our sense our slave.
But this true course is not embraced by many:
    By many? scarce by any.   20
For either our affections do rebel,
    Or else the sentinel,
That should ring larum to the heart, doth sleep:
    Or some great thought doth keep
Back the intelligence, and falsely swears   25
    They're base and idle fears
Whereof the loyal conscience so complains.
    Thus, by these subtle trains,

Do several passións invade the mind,
   And strike our reason blind: 30
Of which usurping rank, some have thought love
   The first, as prone to move
Most frequent tumults, horrors, and unrests,
   In our inflaméd breasts:
But this doth from the cloud of error grow,   35
   Which thus we over-blow.
The thing they here call Love is blind Desire,
   Armed with bow, shafts, and fire;
Inconstant, like the sea, of whence 't is born,
   Rough, swelling, like a storm;   40
With whom who sails, rides on the surge of fear,
   And boils as if he were
In a continual tempest. Now, true Love
   No such effects doth prove;
That is an essence far more gentle, fine,   45
   Pure, perfect, nay, divine;
It is a golden chain let down from heaven,
   Whose links are bright and even,
That falls like sleep on lovers, and combines
   The soft and sweetest minds ·   50
In equal knots: this bears no brands nor darts,
   To murther different hearts,
But in a calm and godlike unity
   Preserves community.
O, who is he that in this peace enjoys   55
   Th' elixir of all joys?
A form more fresh than are the Eden bowers,
   And lasting as her flowers:
Richer than Time, and as Time's virtue rare:
   Sober, as saddest care;   60
A fixéd thought, an eye untaught to glance:
   Who, blest with such high chance,

Would, at suggestion of a steep desire,
    Cast himself from the spire
Of all his happiness? But soft, I hear   65
    Some vicious fool draw near,
That cries we dream, and swears there's no such thing
    As this chaste love we sing.
Peace, Luxury, thou art like one of those
    Who, being at sea, suppose,   70
Because they move, the continent doth so.
    No, Vice, we let thee know,
Though thy wild thoughts with sparrows' wings do fly,
    Turtles can chastely die.
And yet (in this t' express ourselves more clear)   75
    We do not number here
Such spirits as are only continent
    Because lust's means are spent ;
Or those who doubt the common mouth of fame,
    And for their place and name   80
Cannot so safely sin. Their chastity
    Is mere necessity.
Nor mean we those whom vows and conscience
    Have filled with abstinence :
Though we acknowledge, who can so abstain   85
    Makes a most blessèd gain ;
He that for love of goodness hateth ill
    Is more crown-worthy still
Than he, which for sin's penalty forbears :
    His heart sins, though he fears.   90
But we propose a person like our Dove,
    Grac'd with a Phœnix' love ;
A beauty of that clear and sparkling light,
    Would make a day of night,
And turn the blackest sorrows to bright joys :   95
    Whose od'rous breath destroys

All taste of bitterness, and makes the air
  As sweet as she is fair.
A body so harmoniously composed,
  As if nature disclosed   100
All her best symmetry in that one feature !
  O, so divine a creature,
Who could be false to? chiefly when he knows
  How only she bestows
The wealthy treasure of her love on him ;   105
  Making his fortunes swim
In the full flood of her admired perfection?
  What savage, brute affection
Would not be fearful to offend a dame
  Of this excelling frame?   110
Much more a noble and right generous mind
  To virtuous moods inclined,
That knows the weight of guilt: he will refrain
  From thoughts of such a strain ;
And to his sense object this sentence ever,   115
' Man may securely sin, but safely never.'

———◦◦◦———

THOMAS CAMPION, in PHILIP
ROSSETER'S *A Book of Airs,*
1601.

IN IMAGINE PERTRANSIT HOMO.

FOLLOW thy fair sun, unhappy shadow,
  Though thou be black as night,
  And she made all of light,
Yet follow thy fair sun, unhappy shadow.

Follow her whose light thy light depriveth ;   5
  Though here thou livest disgraced,
  And she in heaven is placed,
Yet follow her, whose light the world reviveth.

Follow those pure beams whose beauty burneth,
   That so have scorchèd thee,   10
   As thou still black must be
Till her kind beams thy black to brightness turneth.

Follow her, while yet her glory shineth:
   There comes a luckless night,
   That will dim all her light ;   15
. And this the black unhappy shade divineth.

Follow still, since so thy fates ordainèd ;
   The sun must have his shade,
   Till both at once do fade ;
The sun still proved, the shadow still disdainèd.   20

OF CORINNA'S SINGING.

WHEN to her lute Corinna sings,
Her voice revives the leaden strings,
And doth in highest notes appear
As any challenged echo clear:
But when she doth of mourning speak,   5
E'en with her sighs the strings do break.

And as her lute doth live or die,
Led by her passion, so must I :
For when of pleasure she doth sing,
My thoughts enjoy a sudden spring ;   10
But if she doth of sorrow speak,
E'en from my heart the strings do break.

THE CHALLENGE.

THOU art not fair, for all thy red and white,
   For all those rosy ornaments in thee ;
Thou art not sweet, though made of mere delight,
   Nor fair nor sweet, unless thou pity me.

I will not soothe thy fancies : thou shalt prove   5
That beauty is no beauty without love.

Yet love not me, nor seek thou to allure
  My thoughts with beauty, were it more divine .
Thy smiles and kisses I cannot endure,
  I'll not be wrapt up in those arms of thine :   10
Now show it, if thou be a woman right, —
Embrace, and kiss, and love me, in despite.

CONJURATION.

WHEN thou must home to shades of underground,
  And there arrived, a new admirèd guest,
The beauteous spirits do engirt thee round,
  White Iope, blithe Helen, and the rest,
To hear the stories of thy finished love   5
From that smooth tongue whose music hell can move ;

Then wilt thou speak of banqueting delights,
  Of masques and revels which sweet youth did make,
Of tourneys and great challenges of knights,
  And all these triumphs for thy beauty's sake :   10
When thou hast told these honors done to thee,
Then tell, O tell, how thou didst murder me.

———◦◦◦———

PHILIP ROSSETER, in the same.

ALL IS VANITY.

WHETHER men do laugh or weep,
Whether they do wake or sleep,
Whether they die young or old,
Whether they feel heat or cold ;
There is underneath the sun   5
Nothing in true earnest done.

All our pride is but a jest,
None are worst, and none are best,
Grief and joy, and hope and fear,
Play their pageants everywhere :   10
Vain opinion all doth sway,
And the world is but a play.

Powers above in clouds do sit,
Mocking our poor apish wit ;
That so lamely with such state   15
Their high glory imitate.
No ill can be felt but pain,
And that happy men disdain.

———•◦•———

From ROBERT JONES' *Second
Book of Songs and Airs,* 1601.

LOVE WINGED MY HOPES.

LOVE winged my hopes and taught me how to fly
Far from base earth, but not to mount too high :
    For true pleasure
    Lives in measure,
    Which if men forsake,   5
Blinded they into folly run and grief for pleasure take.

But my vain hopes, proud of their new-taught flight,
Enamoured sought to woo the sun's fair light,
    Whose rich brightness
    Moved their lightness   10
    To aspire so high
That, all scorched and consumed with fire, now drowned
   in woe they lie.

And none but Love their woeful hap did rue,
For Love did know that their desires were true ;
    Though Fate frownèd,   15
    And now drownèd
    They in sorrow dwell,
It was the purest light of heaven for whose fair love they
    fell.

—⸱◦⸱—

WILLIAM SHAKESPEARE, *Twelfth
Night,* about 1601.

O MISTRESS MINE, WHERE ARE YOU ROAMING?

O MISTRESS mine, where are you roaming?
O, stay and hear, your true love's coming,
    That can sing both high and low:
Trip no further, pretty sweeting,
Journeys end in lovers meeting,   5
    Every wise man's son doth know.

What is love? 't is not hereafter ;
Present mirth hath present laughter ;
    What 's to come is still unsure:
In delay there lies no plenty,   10
Then come kiss me, sweet and twenty,
    Youth's a stuff will not endure.

DIRGE OF LOVE.

COME away, come away, death,
And in sad cypress let me laid ;
Fly away, fly away, breath,
I am slain by a fair cruel maid.
    My shroud of white, stuck all with yew,   5
        O prepare it !
    My part of death, no one so true
        Did share it.

Not a flower, not a flower sweet
On my black coffin let there be strown ;   10
Not a friend, not a friend greet
My poor corpse, where my bones shall be thrown ;
A thousand thousand sighs to save,
    Lay me, O, where
Sad true lover never find my grave,   15
    To weep there!

————•◦•————

THOMAS MIDDLETON, *Blurt,*
Master Constable, 1601-02.

LIPS AND EYES.

LOVE for such a cherry lip
    Would be glad to pawn his arrows ;
Venus here to take a sip
    Would sell her doves and team of sparrows.
        But they shall not so ;   5
        Hey nonny, nonny no !
        None but I this lip must owe ;
        Hey nonny, nonny no !

Did Jove see this wanton eye,
    Ganymede must wait no longer ;   10
Phœbe here one night did lie,
    Would change her face and look much younger.
        But they shall not so ;
        Hey nonny, nonny no !
        None but I this lip must owe ;   15
        Hey nonny, nonny no !

THOMAS DEKKER, *The Noble
Spanish Soldier*, 1634; performed 1602 (?).

O, SORROW, SORROW.

O, SORROW, Sorrow, say where dost thou dwell?
    In the lowest room of hell.
    Art thou born of human race?
    No, no, I have a furier face.
    Art thou in city, town, or court?   5
    I to every place resort.
O, why into the world is Sorrow sent?
    Men afflicted best repent.
      What dost thou feed on?
      Broken sleep.   10
      What takest thou pleasure in?
      To weep,
To sigh, to sob, to pine, to groan,
To wring my hands, to sit alone.
O when, O when shall Sorrow quiet have?   15
    Never, never, never, never,
    Never till she finds a grave.

——◆——

NICHOLAS BRETON, *The Soul's
Harmony*, 1602.

SONNET.

THE SOUL'S HAVEN.

THE worldly prince doth in his sceptre hold
A kind of heaven in his authorities;
The wealthy miser in his mass of gold
Makes to his soul a kind of Paradise;

The epicure that eats and drinks all day,   5
Accounts no heaven but in his hellish routs ;
And she whose beauty seems a sunny day,
Makes up her heaven but in her baby's clouts.
But, my sweet God, I seek no prince's power,
No miser's wealth, nor beauty's fading gloss,   10
Which pamper sin, whose sweets are inward sour,
And sorry gains that breed the spirit's loss:
No, my dear Lord, let my heaven only be
In my love's service, but to live to thee.

———•◦•———

JOHN DONNE, in Davison's *Poetical Rhapsody*, 1602.

ODE.

*That time and absence proves
Rather helps than hurts to loves.*

ABSENCE, hear thou my protestation
    Against thy strength,
    Distance and length:
Do what thou canst for alteration,
    For hearts of truest mettle   5
Absence doth join, and time doth settle.

Who loves a mistress of such quality,
    He soon hath found
    Affection ground
Beyond time, place, and all mortality.   10
    To hearts that cannot vary
Absence is present, time doth tarry.

My senses want their outward motions,
  Which now within
    Reason doth win,   15
Redoubled in her secret notions:
  Like rich men that take pleasure
  In hiding more than handling treasure.

By absence this good means I gain,
  That I can catch her,   20
    Where none can watch her,
In some close corner of my brain:
  There I embrace and kiss her;
  And so I both enjoy and miss her.

——◦◦·——

JOSHUA SYLVESTER, in the same.

SONNET.

WERE I as base as is the lowly plain,
And you, my love, as high as heaven above,
Yet should the thoughts of me, your humble swain,
Ascend to heaven in honor of my love.
Were I as high as heaven above the plain,   5
And you, my love, as humble and as low
As are the deepest bottoms of the main,
Wheresoe'er you were, with you my love should go.
Were you the earth, dear love, and I the skies,
My love should shine on you like to the sun,   10
And look upon you with ten thousand eyes,
Till heaven waxed blind, and till the world were done.
Wheresoe'er I am, below, or else above you,
Wheresoe'er you are, my heart shall truly love you.

From the same, authors unknown.

MADRIGAL.

My love in her attire doth show her wit,
　It doth so well become her:
For every season she hath dressings fit,
　For winter, spring, and summer.
　No beauty she doth miss,　　　　　　　5
　When all her robes are on:
　But Beauty's self she is,
　When all her robes are gone.

IN PRAISE OF TWO.

Faustina hath the fairer face,
And Phyllida the feater grace;
　Both have mine eye enriched:
This sings full sweetly with her voice;
Her fingers make as sweet a noise:　　　　5
　Both have mine ear bewitched.
Ah me! sith Fates have so provided,
My heart, alas, must be divided.

—— ∙o∙ ——

Ben Jonson, *First Book of Epigrams,* 1616; written about
1602.

AN EPITAPH ON SALATHIEL PAVY,

A CHILD OF QUEEN ELIZABETH'S CHAPEL.

Weep with me all you that read
　This little story;
And know for whom a tear you shed
　Death's self is sorry.

'Twas a child that so did thrive   5
    In grace and feature,
As heaven and nature seemed to strive
    Which owned the creature.
Years he numbered scarce thirteen
    When Fates turned cruel,   10
Yet three filled zodiacs had he been
    The stage's jewel ;
And did act, what now we moan,
    Old men so duly,
As, sooth, the Parcæ thought him one,   15
    He played so truly.
So, by error to his fate
    They all consented ;
But viewing him since, alas too late,
    They have repented ;   20
And have sought to give new birth,
    In baths to steep him ;
But, being so much too good for earth,
    Heaven vows to keep him.

────◦◦◦────

WILLIAM SHAKESPEARE, *Hamlet*, 1603.

HOW SHOULD I YOUR TRUE LOVE KNOW?

How should I your true love know
    From another one ?
By his cockle hat and staff,
    And his sandal shoon.

He is dead, and gone, lady,   5
    He is dead and gone,
At his head a grass-green turf,
    At his heels a stone.

White his shroud as the mountain snow,
   Larded with sweet flowers,   10
Which bewept to the grave did go
   With true-love showers.

———◦●◦———

SIR WALTER RALEIGH, *Remains*,
1660; written about 1603.

HIS PILGRIMAGE.

GIVE me my scallop-shell of quiet,
   My staff of faith to walk upon,
My scrip of joy, immortal diet,
   My bottle of salvation,
My gown of glory, hope's true gage ;   5
And thus I'll take my pilgrimage.

Blood must be my body's balmer,
   No other balm will there be given ;
Whilst my soul, like quiet palmer,
   Travelleth towards the land of heaven ;   10
Over the silver mountains,
Where spring the nectar fountains :
     There will I kiss
     The bowl of bliss ;
And drink mine everlasting fill   15
Upon every milken hill :
My soul will be a-dry before ;
But after, it will thirst no more.
Then by that happy blestful day,
   More peaceful pilgrims I shall see,   20
That have cast off their rags of clay,
   And walk apparelled fresh like me.

I'll take them first
To quench their thirst
And taste of nectar suckets,   25
At those clear wells
Where sweetness dwells
Drawn up by saints in crystal buckets.

And when our bottles and all we
Are filled with immortality,   30
Then the blessed paths we'll travel,
Strowed with rubies thick as gravel ;
Ceilings of diamonds, sapphire floors,
High walls of coral, and pearly bowers.
From thence to heaven's bribeless hall,   35
Where no corrupted voices brawl ;
No conscience molten into gold,
No forged accuser bought or sold,
No cause deferred, no vain-spent journey ;
For there Christ is the King's Attorney,   40
Who pleads for all without degrees,
And he hath angels, but no fees.
And when the grand twelve-million jury
Of our sins, with direful fury,
'Gainst our souls black verdicts give,   45
Christ pleads his death, and then we live.

Be thou my speaker, taintless pleader,
Unblotted lawyer, true proceeder !
Thou giv'st salvation even for alms ;
Not with a bribèd lawyer's palms.   50
And this is mine eternal plea
To him that made heaven, earth, and sea,
That, since my flesh must die so soon,
And want a head to dine next noon,

Just at the stroke, when my veins start and spread, 55
Set on my soul an everlasting head.
Then am I ready, like a palmer fit ;
To tread those blest paths which before I writ.

———◆◆◆———

From JOHN DOWLAND'S *Third
and Last Book of Songs or
Airs,* 1603.

LULLABY.

WEEP you no more, sad fountains,
  What need you flow so fast?
Look how the snowy mountains
  Heaven's sun doth gently waste.
But my sun's heavenly eyes,   5
      View not your weeping,
      That now lies sleeping,
    Softly, now softly lies
      Sleeping.

Sleep is a reconciling,   10
  A rest that peace begets ;
Doth not the sun rise smiling
  When fair at ev'n he sets?
Rest you, then, rest sad eyes,
      Melt not in weeping,   15
      While she lies sleeping,
    Softly, now softly lies
      Sleeping.

From THOMAS BATESON'S *First
Set of English Madrigals,* 1604.

SONG OF THE MAY.

SISTER, awake ! close not your eyes,
   The day her light discloses,
And the bright morning doth arise
   Out of her bed of roses.

See, the clear sun, the world's bright eye,   5
   In at our window peeping:
Lo, how he blusheth to espy
   Us idle wenches sleeping.

Therefore, awake ! make haste, I say,
   And let us, without staying,   10
All in our gowns of green so gay
   Into the park a-maying.

———•◦•———

From THOMAS GREAVES' *Songs
of Sundry Kinds,* 1604.

MADRIGAL.

YE bubbling springs that gentle music makes
   To lovers' plaints with heart-sore throbs immixed,
Whenas my dear this way her pleasure takes,
   Tell her with tears how firm my love is fixed ;
And, Philomel, report my timorous fears,   5
And, Echo, sound my heigh-ho's in her ears :
But if she asks if I for love will die,
Tell her, ' Good faith, good faith, good faith, — not I.'

WILLIAM SHAKESPEARE, *Measure for Measure*, 1604.

SONG.

Take, O take those lips away,
That so sweetly were forsworn ;
And those eyes, the break of day,
Lights that do mislead the morn :
But my kisses bring again,   5
    Bring again,
Seals of love, but sealed in vain,
    Sealed in vain.

BEN JONSON, *The Forest*, 1616;
written 1605.

TO CELIA.

Drink to me only with thine eyes,
    And I will pledge with mine ;
Or leave a kiss but in the cup,
    And I'll not look for wine.
The thirst that from the soul doth rise   5
    Doth ask a drink divine ;
But might I of Jove's nectar sup,
    I would not change for thine.

I sent thee late a rosy wreath,
    Not so much honoring thee   10
As giving it a hope that there
    It could not withered be ;
But thou thereon didst only breathe
    And sent'st it back to me ;
Since when it grows, and smells, I swear,   15
    Not of itself, but thee.

From Tobias Hume's *The First
Part of Airs French, Polish,
and others together,* 1605.

IN LAUDEM AMORIS.

Fain would I change that note
To which fond love hath charmed me
Long long to sing by rote,
Fancying that that harmed me :
Yet when this thought doth come,   5
'Love is the perfect sum
        Of all delight,'
I have no other choice
Either for pen or voice
        To sing or write.   10

O Love ! they wrong thee much
That say thy sweet is bitter,
When thy rich fruit is such
As nothing can be sweeter.
Fair house of joy and bliss,   15
Where truest pleasure is,
        I do adore thee :
I know thee what thou art,
I serve thee with my heart,
        And fall before thee.   20

THOMAS HEYWOOD, *The Rape
of Lucrece*, 1608 ; acted about
1605 (?).

GOOD MORROW.

PACK, clouds, away, and welcome day,
   With night we banish sorrow ;
Sweet air blow soft, mount lark aloft,
   To give my love good-morrow.
Wings from the wind to please her mind,   5
   Notes from the lark I'll borrow ;
Bird, prune thy wing, nightingale, sing,
   To give my love good-morrow ;
      To give my love good-morrow,
      Notes from them both I'll borrow.   10

Wake from thy rest, robin-redbreast,
   Sing birds in every furrow ;
And from each bill let music shrill
   Give my fair love good-morrow.
Blackbird and thrush in every bush,   15
   Stare, linnet, and cock-sparrow,
You pretty elves, amongst yourselves
   Sing my fair love good-morrow ;
      To give my love good-morrow
      Sing birds in every furrow.   20

MICHAEL DRAYTON, *Certain Other Sonnets* in *Poems,* ed. 1605.

SONNET LXIII.

TO THE LADY L. S.

BRIGHT star of beauty, on whose eye-lids sit
A thousand nymph-like and enamoured graces,
The goddesses of memory and wit,
Which in due order take their several places ;
In whose dear bosom, sweet, delicious Love   5
Lays down his quiver, that he once did bear ;
Since he that blessed paradise did prove,
Forsook his mother's lap to sport him there.
Let others strive to entertain with words,
My soul is of another temper made ;   10
I hold it vile that vulgar wit affords,
Devouring time my faith shall not invade :
Still let my praise be honored thus by you,
Be you most worthy, whilst I be most true.

————•◦•————

MICHAEL DRAYTON, *Poems, Lyrics, and Pastoral,* 1605 (?).

ODE XII.

AGINCOURT.

TO MY FRIENDS THE CAMBER-BRITANS AND THEIR HARP.

FAIR stood the wind for France,
When we our sails advance,
And now to prove our chance
    Longer not tarry,

But put unto the main,   5
At Caux, the mouth of Seine,
With all his warlike train,
    Landed King Harry.

And taking many a fort,
Furnished in warlike sort,   10
Coming toward Agincourt
    In happy hour,
Skirmishing day by day
With those oppose his way,
Whereas the gen'ral lay   15
    With all his power:

Which in his height of pride,
As Henry to deride,
His ransom to provide
    Unto him sending;   20
Which he neglects the while,
As from a nation vile,
Yet with an angry smile,
    Their fall portending;

And, turning to his men,   25
Quoth famous Henry then,
'Though they to one be ten,
    Be not amazèd;
Yet have we well begun,
Battles so bravely won   30
Evermore to the sun
    By fame are raisèd.

'And for myself,' quoth he,
'This my full rest shall be,
England ne'er mourn for me,   35
    Nor more esteem me.

Victor I will remain,
Or on this earth be slain,
Never shall she sustain
    Loss to redeem me.   40

' Poyters and Cressy tell,
When most their pride did swell,
Under our swords they fell,
    No less our skill is
Than when our grandsire great,   45
Claiming the regal seat,
In many a warlike feat
    Lopp'd the French lilies.'

The Duke of York so dread,
The eager vaward led ;   50
With the main Henry sped,
    Amongst his henchmen.
Excester had the rear,
A braver man not there,
And now preparing were   55
    For the false Frenchmen,

And ready to be gone,
Armor on armor shone,
Drum unto drum did groan,
    To hear was wonder ;   60
That with the cries they make
The very earth did shake,
Trumpet to trumpet spake,
    Thunder to thunder.

Well it thine age became,   65
O noble Erpingham,
Thou didst the signal frame
    Unto the forces ;

When from a meadow by,
Like a storm suddenly,   70
The English archery
    Stuck the French horses.

The Spanish yew so strong,
Arrows a cloth-yard long,
That like to serpents stong,   75
    Piercing the wether ;
None from his death now starts,
But playing manly parts,
And like true English hearts
    Stuck close together.   80

When down their bows they threw,
And forth their bilbows drew,
And on the French they flew:
    No man was tardy ;
Arms from the shoulders sent,   85
Scalps to the teeth were rent,
Down the French peasants went,
    These were men hardy.

When now that noble king,
His broad sword brandishing,   90
Into the host did fling,
    As to o'erwhelm it ;
Who many a deep wound lent,
His arms with blood besprent,
And many a cruel dent   95
    Bruisèd his helmet.

Gloster, that duke so good,
Next of the royal blood,
For famous England stood,
    With his brave brother,   100

Clarence, in steel most bright,
That yet a maiden knight,
Yet in this furious fight
    Scarce such another.

Warwick in blood did wade,   105
Oxford the foes invade,
And cruel slaughter made,
    Still as they ran up ;
Suffolk his axe did ply,
Beaumont and Willoughby   110
Bare them right doughtily,
    Ferrers and Fanhope.

On happy Crispin day
Fought was this noble fray,
Which fame did not delay   115
    To England to carry ;
O when shall Englishmen,
With such acts fill a pen ?
Or England breed again
    Such a King Harry ?   120

—•◦•—

THOMAS CAMPION, in RICHARD
ALISON'S *An Hour's Recrea-*
tion in Music, 1606.

CHERRY RIPE.

THERE is a garden in her face,
    Where roses and white lilies grow ;
A heavenly paradise is that place,
    Wherein all pleasant fruits do flow ;
There cherries grow that none may buy,   5
Till 'Cherry-Ripe' themselves do cry.

Those cherries fairly do enclose
    Of orient pearl a double row,
Which when her lovely laughter shows,
    They look like rose-buds filled with snow: 10
Yet them no peer nor prince may buy,
Till 'Cherry-Ripe' themselves do cry.

Her eyes like angels watch them still;
    Her brows like bended bows do stand,
Threatening with piercing frowns to kill   15
    All that attempt with eye or hand
Those sacred cherries to come nigh
Till 'Cherry-Ripe' themselves do cry.

———•◦•———

From JOHN DANIEL'S *Songs for
the Lute, Viol and Voice*, 1606.

IF I COULD SHUT THE GATE AGAINST MY THOUGHTS.

IF I could shut the gate against my thoughts,
    And keep out sorrow from this room within,
Or memory could cancel all the notes
    Of my misdeeds, and I unthink my sin:
How free, how clear, how clean my soul should lie,   5
Discharged of such a loathsome company.

Or were there other rooms without my heart
    That did not to my conscience join so near,
Where I might lodge the thoughts of sin apart,
    That I might not their clam'rous crying hear;   10
What peace, what joy, what ease should I possess,
Freed from their horrors that my soul oppress.

But O my Saviour, who my refuge art,
  Let Thy dear mercies stand 'twixt them and me,
And be the wall to separate my heart   15
  So that I may at length repose me free ;
That peace, and joy, and rest may be within,
And I remain divided from my sin.

————◦◦————

JOHN DONNE, *Poems*, ed. 1635;
Holy Sonnets, written before
1607.

SONNET X.

DEATH, be not proud, though some have callèd thee
Mighty and dreadful, for thou art not so ;
For those whom thou think'st thou dost overthrow
Die not, poor Death ; nor yet canst thou kill me.
From rest and sleep, which but thy picture be,   5
Much pleasure, then from thee much more must flow :
And soonest our best men with thee do go,
Rest of their bones, and souls' delivery.
Thou art slave to Fate, chance, kings, and desperate men,
And dost with poison, war, and sickness dwell,   10
And poppy or charms can make us sleep as well,
And better than thy stroke ; why swell'st thou, then ?
One short sleep past, we wake eternally,
And Death shall be no more ; Death, thou shalt die.

From *The Fair Maid of the Exchange*, 1607; author unknown.

YE LITTLE BIRDS THAT SIT AND SING.

Ye little birds that sit and sing
    Amidst the shady valleys,
And see how Phyllis sweetly walks
    Within her garden-alleys ;
Go, pretty birds, about her bower ;   5
Sing, pretty birds, she may not lower;
Ah, me ! methinks I see her frown,
    Ye pretty wantons, warble.

Go, tell her through your chirping bills,
    As you by me are bidden,   10
To her is only known my love,
    Which from the world is hidden.
Go, pretty birds, and tell her so ;
See that your notes strain not too low,
For still, methinks, I see her frown,   15
    Ye pretty wantons, warble.

Go, tune your voices' harmony,
    And sing, I am her lover :
Strain loud and sweet, that every note
    With sweet content may move her :   20
And she that hath the sweetest voice,
Tell her I will not change my choice ;
Yet still, methinks, I see her frown,
    Ye pretty wantons, warble.

Oh, fly ! make haste ! see, see, she falls   25
    Into a pretty slumber ;
Sing round about her rosy bed,
    That waking she may wonder.

Say to her, 't is her lover true
That sendeth love to you, to you ;   30
And when you hear her kind reply,
Return with pleasant warblings.

———•◦•———

From THOMAS FORD'S *Music of*
Sundry Kinds, 1607.

LOVE'S STEADFASTNESS.

SINCE first I saw your face, I resolved to honor and renown
    ye,
If now I be disdained, I wish my heart had never known ye.
What? I that loved and you that liked, shall we begin to
    wrangle ?
No, no no, my heart is fast, and cannot disentangle.

If I admire or praise you too much, that fault you may
    forgive me,   5
Or if my hands had strayed but a touch, then justly might
    you leave me.
I asked you leave, you bade me love ; is 't now a time to
    chide me ?
No, no no, I'll love you still, what fortune e'er betide me.

The sun, whose beams most glorious are, rejecteth no
    beholder,
And your sweet beauty past compare made my poor eyes
    the bolder,   10
Where beauty moves, and wit delights, and signs of kind-
    ness bind me,
There, O there ! where'er I go, I'll leave my heart behind
    me.

JOHN WEBSTER, *Vittoria Corom-
bona*, 1612, acted 1607-8.

DIRGE.

CALL for the robin-redbreast and the wren,
Since o'er shady groves they hover,
And with leaves and flowers do cover
The friendless bodies of unburied men.
    Call unto his funeral dole   5
    The ant, the field-mouse, and the mole,
To rear him hillocks that shall keep him warm,
And, when gay tombs are robbed, sustain no harm;
But keep the wolf far thence, that's foe to men,
For with his nails he'll dig them up again.   10

———•◦•———

WILLIAM SHAKESPEARE, *Antony
and Cleopatra*, before 1608.

TO BACCHUS.

COME, thou monarch of the vine,
Plumpy Bacchus with pink eyne !
In thy vats our cares be drowned,
With thy grapes our hairs be crowned:
    Cup us till the world go round,   5
    Cup us till the world go round !

From ROBERT JONES' *Ultimum Vale, or Third Book of Airs*, 1608.

WHERE MY LADY KEEPS HER HEART.

SWEET Love, my only treasure,
   For service long unfeignèd,
   Wherein I naught have gainèd,
Vouchsafe this little pleasure,
   To tell me in what part   5
   My lady keeps her heart.

If in her hair so slender,
   Like golden nets entwinèd
   Which fire and art have finèd,
Her thrall my heart I render   10
   For ever to abide
   With locks so dainty tied.

If in her eyes she bind it,
   Wherein that fire was framèd
   By which it is enflamèd,   15
I dare not look to find it:
   I only wish it sight
   To see that pleasant light.

But if her breast have deignèd
   With kindness to receive it,   20
   I am content to leave it
Though death thereby were gainèd:
   Then, lady, take your own
   That lives by you alone.

WILLIAM SHAKESPEARE, *Cymbeline*, 1609.

HARK, HARK! THE LARK.

HARK, hark! the lark at heaven's gate sings,
    And Phœbus gins arise,
His steeds to water at those springs
    On chaliced flowers that lies;
And winking mary-buds begin   5
    To ope their golden eyes;
With everything that pretty is,
    My lady sweet, arise;
        Arise, arise.

DIRGE.

FEAR no more the heat o' the sun
    Nor the furious winters' rages;
Thou thy worldly task hast done,
    Home art gone, and ta'en thy wages:
Golden lads and girls all must,   5
As chimney-sweepers, come to dust.

Fear no more the frown o' the great,
    Thou art past the tyrant's stroke;
Care no more to clothe and eat;
    To thee the reed is as the oak: 10
The sceptre, learning, physic, must
All follow this, and come to dust.

Fear no more the lightning-flash,
    Nor the all-dreaded thunder-stone;
Fear not slander, censure rash;   15
    Thou hast finished joy and moan:
All lovers young, all lovers must
Consign to thee, and come to dust.

No exorciser harm thee !
Nor no witchcraft harm thee !   20
Ghost unlaid forbear thee !
Nothing ill come near thee !
Quiet consummation have,
And renownèd be thy grave.

——•◦•——

BEAUMONT and FLETCHER, *The
Maid's Tragedy*, 1619; produced about 1609.

ASPATIA'S SONG.

LAY a garland on my hearse
    Of the dismal yew;
Maidens, willow branches bear;
    Say, I died true.

My love was false, but I was firm   5
    From my hour of birth ;
Upon my buried body lie
    Lightly, gentle earth.

——•◦•——

From JOHN WILBYE'S *Second
Set of Madrigals*, 1609.

ALL IN NAUGHT.

I LIVE, and yet methinks I do not breathe ;
I thirst and drink, I drink and thirst again ;
I sleep and yet do dream I am awake ;
I hope for that I have ; I have and want :
I sing and sigh ; I love and hate at once.   5
    O, tell me, restless soul, what uncouth jar
    Doth cause in store such want, in peace such war?

RISPOSTA.

THERE is a jewel which no Indian mines
Can buy, no chymic art can counterfeit ;
It makes men rich in greatest poverty ;
Makes water wine, turns wooden cups to gold,
The homely whistle to sweet music's strain :   5
    Seldom it comes, to few from heaven sent,
    That much in little, all in naught, — content.

LOVE NOT ME FOR COMELY GRACE.

    LOVE not me for comely grace,
    .For my pleasing eye or face,
    Nor for any outward part :
    No, nor for a constant heart,
    For these may fail or turn to ill :   5
        So thou and I shall sever.
    Keep therefore a true woman's eye,
    And love me still, but know not why ;
    So hast thou the same reason still
        To doat upon me ever.   10

From THOMAS RAVENSCROFT'S
Deuteromelia, 1609.

THREE POOR MARINERS.

    WE be three poor mariners,
        Newly come from the seas ;
    We spend our lives in jeopardy,
        While others live at ease.

Shall we go dance the round. the round,   5
   Shall we go dance the round?
And he that is a bully boy
   Come pledge me on this ground.

We care not for those martial men
   That do our states disdain;   10
But we care for the merchant men
   Who do our states maintain:
To them we dance this round, around,
   To them we dance this round;
And he that is a bully boy   15
   Come pledge me on this ground.

⸱   —◦◦•—

BEN JONSON, *The Masque of
Queens,* 1609.

VIRTUE TRIUMPHANT.

WHO, Virtue, can thy power forget
That sees these live and triumph yet?
Th' Assyrian pomp, the Persian pride,
Greeks' glory and the Romans' died;
   And who yet imitate   5
Their noises, tarry the same fate.
Force greatness all the glorious ways
   You can, it soon decays;
   But so good fame shall never:
Her triumphs, as their causes, are forever.   10

BEN JONSON, *The Silent Woman,*
1609-10.

SIMPLEX MUNDITIIS.

STILL to be neat, still to be drest,
As you were going to a feast ;
Still to be powdered, still perfumed :
Lady, it is to be presumed,
Though art's hid causes are not found,   5
All is not sweet, all is not sound.

Give me a look, give me a face,
That makes simplicity a grace ;
Robes loosely flowing, hair as free :
Such sweet neglect more taketh me   10
Than all th' adulteries of art ;   •
They strike mine eyes, but not my heart.

————•◦•————

From ROBERT JONES' *The Muses'*
Garden of Delights, 1610.

THE WOES OF LOVE.

THE sea hath many thousand sands,
    The sun hath motes as many ;
The sky is full of stars, and love
    As full of woes as any :
Believe me, that do know the elf,   5
And make no trial by thyself.

It is in truth a pretty toy
    For babes to play withal ;
But O the honeys of our youth
    Are oft our age's gall !   10
Self-proof in time will make thee know
He was a prophet told thee so :

A prophet that, Cassandra-like,
    Tells truth without belief;
For headstrong youth will run his race,   15
    Although his goal be grief:
Love's martyr, when his heat is past,
Proves Care's confessor at the last.

UNCERTAINTY.

How many new years have grown old
    Since first your servant old was new;
How many long hours have I told
    Since first my love was vowed to you;
And yet, alas, she does not know   5
Whether her servant love or no.

How many walls as white as snow,
    And windows clear as any glass,
Have I conjured to tell you so,
    Which faithfully performèd was;   10
And yet you'll swear you do not know
Whether your servant love or no.

How often hath my pale, lean face,
    With true charàcters of my love,
Petitionèd to you for grace,   15
    Whom neither sighs nor tears can move;
O cruel, yet do you not know
Whether your servant love or no.

And wanting oft a better token,
    I have been fain to send my heart,   20
Which now your cold disdain hath broken,
    Nor can you heal't by any art:
O look upon't, and you shall know
Whether your servant love or no.

BEAUMONT and FLETCHER, *The
Knight of the Burning Pestle,*
1613; acted 1610.

LUCE'S DIRGE.

COME, you whose loves are dead,
   And, whiles I sing,
   Weep, and wring
Every hand, and every head
Bind with cypress and sad yew;   5
Ribbons black and candles blue
For him that was of men most true.

Come with heavy moaning,
   And on his grave   ·
   Let him have   10
Sacrifice of sighs and groaning;
Let him have fair flowèrs enow,
White and purple, green and yellow,
For him that was of men most true.

Samuel Daniel, *Tethys' Festival,* 1610.

EIDOLA.

ARE they shadows that we see?
   And can shadows pleasure give?
Pleasures only shadows be,
   Cast by bodies we conceive,
And are made the things we deem   5
In those figures which they seem.

But these pleasures vanish fast
  Which by shadows are expressed :
Pleasures are not, if they last,
  In their passing is their best :   10
Glory is most bright and gay
In a flash, and so away.

Feed apace then, greedy eyes,
  On the wonder you behold ;
Take it sudden as it flies,   15
  Though you take it not to hold :
When your eyes have done their part,
Thought must length it in the heart.

———•◦•———

WILLIAM SHAKESPEARE, *The Tempest*, 1611.

A SEA DIRGE.

FULL fathom five thy father lies,
  Of his bones are coral made,
Those are pearls that were his eyes :
  Nothing of him that doth fade,
But doth suffer a sea-change   5
Into something rich and strange.
Sea-nymphs hourly ring his knell :
  Ding-dong,
Hark ! now I hear them, ding-dong, bell.

ARIEL'S SONG.

WHERE the bee sucks, there suck I,
In a cowslip's bell I lie,
There I couch when owls do cry ;
On the bat's back I do fly

After summer merrily. 5
Merrily, merrily shall I live now
Under the blossom that hangs on the bough.

From WILLIAM BYRD's *Psalms,
Songs and Sonnets,* 1611.

THE HOME OF CONTENT.

In crystal towers and turrets richly set
  With glitt'ring gems that shine against the sun,
In regal rooms of jasper and of jet,
  Content of mind not always likes to won ;
But oftentimes it pleaseth her to stay 5
In simple cotes enclosed with walls of clay.

LOVE'S IMMORTALITY.

Crownèd with flowers I saw fair Amaryllis
  By Thyrsis sit, hard by a fount of crystal ;
And with her hand, more white than snow or lilies,
  On sand she wrote, 'My faith shall be immortal' :
And suddenly a storm of wind and weather 5
Blew all her faith and sand away together.

BEN JONSON, *The Forest,* 1616;
written about 1611.

WHY I WRITE NOT OF LOVE.

Some act of Love's bound to rehearse,
I thought to bind him in my verse :
Which when he felt, 'Away,' quoth he,
'Can poets hope to fetter me?

●

It is enough they once did get   5
Mars and my mother in their net :
I wear not these my wings in vain.'
With which he fled me ; and again
Into my rimes could ne'er be got
By any art : then wonder not   10
That since, my numbers are so cold,
When Love is fled, and I grow old.

SONG.

THAT WOMEN ARE BUT MEN'S SHADOWS.

FOLLOW a shadow, it still flies you,
    Seem to fly it, it will pursue ;
So court a mistress, she denies you,
    Let her alone, she will court you.
Say, are not women truly then   5
Styled but the shadows of us men ?

At morn and even, shades are longest ;
    At noon, they are short or none ;
So men at weakest, they are strongest,
    But grant us perfect, they're not known   10
Say, are not women truly then
Styled but the shadows of us men ?

―――◆―――

JOHN WEBSTER, *The Duchess
of Malfi,* 1623; acted about
1612.

DIRGE.

HARK, now everything is still,
The screech-owl and the whistler shrill
Call upon our dame aloud,
And bid her quickly don her shroud.

Much you had of land and rent ; 5
Your length in clay's now competent :
A long war disturbed your mind ;
Here your perfect peace is signed.
Of what is't fools make such vain keeping,
Sin their conception, their birth weeping, 10
Their life a general mist of error,
Their death a hideous storm of terror ?
Strew your hair with powders sweet,
Don clean linen, bathe your feet,
And — the foul fiend more to check — 15
A crucifix let bless your neck :
'Tis now full tide 'tween night and day ;
End your groan, and come away.

From *Wit Restored*, 1658 ; written about 1612 (?), author unknown.

PHILLADA FLOUTS ME.

O ! WHAT a pain is love,
　　How shall I bear it ?
She will inconstant prove,
　　I greatly fear it.
She so torments my mind, 5
　　That my strength faileth,
And wavers with the wind,
　　As a ship that saileth.
Please her the best I may,
She loves still to gainsay : 10
Alack and well a day !
　　Phillada flouts me.

All the fair yesterday,
  She did pass by me ;
She looked another way,   15
  And would not spy me.
. I wooed her for to dine,
  But could not get her.
Will had her to the wine, —
  He might intreat her.   20
With Daniel she did dance,
On me she looked askance.
O thrice unhappy chance !
  Phillada flouts me.

Fair maid be not so coy,   25
  Do not disdain me :
I am my mother's joy,
  Sweet, entertain me.
She'll give me when she dies
  All that is fitting,   30
Her poultry and her bees
  And her geese sitting.
A pair of mattress beds,
And a bag full of shreds.
And yet for all this goods,   35
  Phillada flouts me.

She hath a clout of mine
  Wrought with blue Coventry,
Which she keeps for a sign
  Of my fidelity.   40
But i' faith, if she flinch,
  She shall not wear it ;
To Tibb, my t'other wench,
  I mean to bear it.

And yet it grieves my heart,⁣ 45
So soon from her to part.
Death strikes me with his dart!
        Phillada flouts me.

Thou shalt eat curds and cream,
    All the year lasting; 50
And drink the crystal stream,
    Pleasant in tasting;
Whigge and whey whilst thou burst
    And ramble-berry;
Pie-lid and pasty-crust, 55
    Pears, plums and cherry.
Thy raiment shall be thin,
Made of a weaver's skin :
Yet all's not worth a pin,
        Phillada flouts me. 60

Fair maidens have a care,
    And in time take me;
I can have those as fair,
    If you forsake me.
For Doll, the dairy-maid, 65
    Laughed on me lately,
And wanton Winifred
    Favors me greatly.
One throws milk on my clothes,
T"other plays with my nose; 70
What wanton signs are those?
        Phillada flouts me.

I cannot work and sleep
    All at a season;
Love wounds my heart so deep, 75
    Without all reason.

I gin to pine away,
　With grief and sorrow,
Like to a fatted beast,
　Penned in a meadow.　　　　　　　　　80
I shall be dead, I fear,
　Within this thousand year ;
And all for very fear,
　Phillada flouts me.

———◦◦◦———

JOHN FLETCHER, *The Two Noble
Kinsmen*, 1634 ; written about
1612.

A BRIDAL SONG.

ROSES, their sharp spines being gone,
Not royal in their smells alone,
　But in their hue ;
Maiden pinks, of odor faint,
Daisies smell-less, yet most quaint,　　　　5
　And sweet thyme true ;

Primrose, first-born child of Ver,
Merry spring-time's harbinger,
　With her bells dim ;
Oxlips in their cradles growing,　　　　　10
Marigolds on deathbeds blowing,
　Larks'-heels trim —

All dear Nature's children sweet,
Lie 'fore bride and bridegroom's feet,
　Blessing their sense !　　　　　　　　15
Not an angel of the air,
Bird melodious, or bird fair,
　Be absent hence !

The crow, the slanderous cuckoo, nor
The boding raven, nor chough hoar   20
    Nor chattering pie,
May on our bride-house perch or sing,
Or with them any discord bring,
    But from it fly.

———•◦•———

From ORLANDO GIBBONS' *First
Set of Madrigals*, 1612.

FAIR IS THE ROSE.

FAIR is the rose, yet fades with heat or cold ;
Sweet are the violets, yet soon grow old ;
The lily's white, yet in one day 'tis done ;
White is the snow, yet melts against the sun :
So white, so sweet, was my fair mistress' face,   5
Yet altered quite in one short hour's space :
So short-lived beauty a vain gloss doth borrow,
Breathing delight to-day but none to-morrow.

———•◦•———

FRANCIS BEAUMONT, *The Masque
of the Inner Temple*, 1612-13.

SONG FOR A DANCE.

SHAKE off your heavy trance !
    And leap into a dance
Such as no mortals use to tread :
    Fit only for Apollo
To play to, for the moon to lead,   5
    And all the stars to follow !

THOMAS HEYWOOD, *Silver Age,*
before 1613.

PRAISE OF CERES.

WITH fair Ceres, Queen of Grain,
  The reapèd fields we roam,
Each country peasant, nymph and swain,
  Sing their harvest home ;
Whilst the Queen of Plenty hallows   5
Growing fields as well as fallows.

Echo, double all our lays,
  Make the champians sound
To the Queen of Harvest's praise,
  That sows and reaps our ground :   10
Ceres, Queen of Plenty, hallows
Growing fields as well as fallows.

JOHN FLETCHER, *The Captain,*
1647, acted before 1613.

WHAT IS LOVE?

TELL me, dearest, what is love ?
'Tis a lightning from above ;
'Tis an arrow, 'tis a fire,
'Tis a boy they call Desire.
        'Tis a grave,   5
        Gapes to have
Those poor fools that long to prove.

Tell me more, are women true ?
Yes, some are, and some as you.
Some are willing, some are strange,   10
Since you men first taught to change.

And till troth
Be in both,
All shall love, to love anew.

Tell me more yet, can they grieve? 15
Yes, and sicken sore, but live,
And be wise, and delay,
When you men are wise as they.
Then I see,
Faith will be, 20
Never till they both believe.

———◦◦•———

JOHN FLETCHER, *The Nice Valor*,
performed about 1013 (?).

MELANCHOLY.

HENCE, all you vain delights,
As short as are the nights
    Wherein you spend your folly :
There's naught in this life sweet
If man were wise to see't, 5
    But only melancholy,
    O sweetest melancholy !

Welcome folded arms and fixèd eyes,
A sigh that piercing mortifies,
A look that's fast'ned to the ground, 10
A tongue chained up without a sound.

Fountain heads, and pathless groves,
Places which pale passion loves ;
Moonlight walks, when all the fowls
Are warmly housed, save bats and owls ; 15

A midnight bell, a parting groan :
These are the sounds we feed upon.
Then stretch our bones in a still gloomy valley ;
Nothing 's so dainty sweet as lovely melancholy.

———•◦•———

WILLIAM SHAKESPEARE, *King
Henry VIII ;* acted 1613.

ORPHEUS.

ORPHEUS with his lute made trees,
And the mountain-tops that freeze,
　　Bow themselves when he did sing :
To his music plants and flowers
Ever sprung ; as the sun and showers　　　　5
　　There had made a lasting spring.

Everything that heard him play,
Even the billows of the sea,
　　Hung their heads and then lay by.
In sweet music is such art,　　　　　　10
Killing care and grief of heart
　　Fall asleep, or, hearing, die.

———•◦•———

THOMAS CAMPION, *Two Books
of Airs,* about 1613.

AWAKE, AWAKE! THOU HEAVY SPRITE.

AWAKE, awake ! thou heavy sprite
　　That sleep'st the deadly sleep of sin !
Rise now and walk the ways of light !
　　'Tis not too late yet to begin.
Seek heaven early, seek it late ;　　　　5
True Faith still finds an open gate.

Get up, get up, thou leaden man !
 Thy track to endless joy or pain,
Yields but the model of a span ;
 Yet burns out thy life's lamp in vain.   10
One minute bounds thy bane or bliss ;
Then watch and labor while time is.

SIC TRANSIT.

Come, cheerful day, part of my life to me :
 For while thou view'st me with thy fading light,
Part of my life doth still depart with thee,
 And I still onward haste to my last night.
Time's fatal wings do ever forward fly :   5
So every day we live a day we die.

But, O ye nights, ordained for barren rest,
 How are my days deprived of life in you,
When heavy sleep my soul hath dispossessed
 By feignèd death life sweetly to renew !   10
Part of my life in that you life deny :
So every day we live a day we die.

SAMUEL DANIEL, *Hymen's Triumph*, 1615 ; acted, 1613-14.

SONG OF THE FIRST CHORUS.

Love is a sickness full of woes,
 All remedies refusing ;
A plant that with most cutting grows,
 Most barren with best using.
  Why so ?   5
More we enjoy it, more it dies ;
If not enjoyed, it sighing cries,
  Heigh ho !

Love is a torment of the mind,
  A tempest everlasting ;   10
And Jove hath made it of a kind
  Not well, nor full, nor fasting.
      Why so ?
More we enjoy it, more it dies ;
If not enjoyed, it sighing cries,   15
      Heigh ho !

———◦∘◦———

Sɪʀ Hᴇɴʀʏ Wᴏᴛᴛᴏɴ, printed
with Overbury's *Wife and
Characters,* 1614.

THE CHARACTER OF A HAPPY LIFE.

How happy is he born and taught.
  That serveth not another's will ;
Whose armor is his honest thought
  And simple truth his utmost skill.

Whose passions not his masters are,   5
  Whose soul is still prepared for death,
Untied unto the world by care
  Of princes' grace, or vulgar breath ;

Who envieth none whom chance doth raise
  Or vice; who never understood   10
How deepest wounds are given by praise ;
  Nor rules of state, but rules of good ;

Who hath his life from rumors freed,
  Whose conscience is his strong retreat ;
Whose state can neither flatterers feed,   15
  Nor ruin make oppressors great ;

Who God doth late and early pray
　More of his grace than gifts to lend ;
And entertains the harmless day
　With a well-chosen book or friend.　　　20

This man is free from servile bands
　Of hope to rise, or fear to fall ;
Lord of himself, though not of lands,
　And having nothing, yet hath all.

———◦◦———

WILLIAM BROWNE, *The Inner
Temple Masque*, 1614–15.

SONG OF THE SIREN.

STEER hither, steer your wingèd pines,
　All beaten mariners,
Here lie love's undiscovered mines,
　A prey to passengers ;
Perfumes far sweeter than the best　　　5
Which make the Phoenix' urn and nest.
　　Fear not your ships,
Nor any to oppose you save our lips,
　　But come on shore,
Where no joy dies till love hath gotten more.　　10

For swelling waves, our panting breasts,
　Where never storms arise,
Exchange ; and be awhile our guests :
　For stars gaze on our eyes.
The compass Love shall hourly sing,　　　15
And, as he goes about the ring,
　　We will not miss
To tell each point he nameth with a kiss :
　　Then come on shore,
Where no joy dies till love hath gotten more.　　20

THE CHARM.

Son of Erebus and Night,
Hie away ; and aim thy flight,
Where consort none other fowl
Than the bat and sullen owl ;
Where upon thy limber grass   5
Poppy and mandragoras
With like simples not a few
Hang for ever drops of dew.
Where flows Lethe without coil
Softly like a stream of oil.   10
Hie thee thither, gentle Sleep :
With this Greek no longer keep.
Thrice I charge thee by my wand,
Thrice with moly from my hand
Do I touch Ulysses' eyes,   15
And with the jaspis: then arise
Sagest Greek.   .   .   .

GEORGE WITHER, *Fidelia*, 1615.

SHALL I, WASTING IN DESPAIR.

Shall I, wasting in despair,
Die because a woman's fair ?
Or make pale my cheeks with care
'Cause another's rosy are ?
Be she fairer than the day   5
Or the flow'ry meads in May —
   If she think not well of me
   What care I how fair she be ?

Shall my seely heart be pined
'Cause I see a woman kind;   10
Or a well disposèd nature
Joinèd with a lovely feature?
Be she meeker, kinder than
Turtle-dove or pelican,
    If she be not so to me   15
    What care I how kind she be?

Shall a woman's virtues move
Me to perish for her love?
Or her well deservings known
Make me quite forget mine own?   20
Be she with that goodness blest
Which may gain her name of Best;
    If she be not such to me,
    What care I how good she be?

'Cause her fortune seems too high,   25
Shall I play the fool and die?
She that bears a noble mind
If not outward helps she find,
Thinks what with them he would do,
That without them dares her woo;   30
    And unless that mind I see,
    What care I how great she be?

Great, or good, or kind, or fair,
I will ne'er the more despair;
If she love me, this believe,   35
I will die ere she shall grieve;
If she slight me when I woo,
I can scorn and let her go;
    For if she be not for me,
    What care I for whom she be?   40

FRANCIS BEAUMONT, *Poems*, ed.
1640; written before 1616.

THE INDIFFERENT.

NEVER more will I protest
To love a woman but in jest :
For as they cannot be true,
So to give each man his due,
 When the wooing fit is past,   5
 Their affection cannot last.

Therefore if I chance to meet
With a mistress fair and sweet,
She my service shall obtain,
Loving her for love again :   10
 Thus much liberty I crave
 Not to be a constant slave.

But when we have tried each other,
If she better like another,
Let her quickly change for me ;   15
Then to change am I as free.
 He or she that loves too long
 Sell their freedom for a song.

ON THE LIFE OF MAN.

LIKE to the falling of a star,
Or as the flights of eagles are,
Or like the fresh spring's gaudy hue,
Or silver drops of morning dew,
Or like the wind that chafes the flood, 5
Or bubbles which on water stood ;
Even such is man, whose borrowed light
Is straight called in and paid to-night.

The wind blows out, the bubble dies,
The spring entombed in autumn lies,   10
The dew 's dried up, the star is shot,
The flight is past, and man forgot.

Francis Beaumont, *Poems*, ed.
1653; written before 1616.

ON THE TOMBS IN WESTMINSTER ABBEY.

Mortality, behold and fear !
What a change of flesh is here !
Think how many royal bones
Sleep within this heap of stones ;
Here they lie, had realms and lands,   5
Who now want strength to stir their hands,
Where from their pulpits sealed with dust
They preach, ' In greatness is no trust.'
Here 's an acre sown indeed
With the richest, royall'st seed   10
That the earth did e'er suck in
Since the first man died for sin :
Here the bones of birth have cried,
'Though gods they were, as men they died !'
Here are sands, ignoble things,   15
Dropt from the ruined sides of kings :
Here 's a world of pomp and state
Buried in dust, once dead by fate.

JOHN FLETCHER, *The Bloody Brother*, acted about 1616.

DRINK TO-DAY, AND DROWN ALL SORROW.

DRINK to-day, and drown all sorrow,
You shall perhaps not do it to-morrow :
Best, while you have it, use your breath ;
There is no drinking after death.

Wine works the heart up, wakes the wit,   5
There is no cure 'gainst age but it :
It helps the head-ache, cough, and tisic,
And is for all diseases physic.

Then let us swill, boys, for our health ;
Who drinks well, loves the commonwealth.   10
And he that will to bed go sober
Falls with the leaf still in October.

JOHN FLETCHER, *Valentinian*, acted about 1616.

LOVE'S EMBLEMS.

Now the lusty spring is seen ;
    Golden yellow, gaudy blue,
    Daintily invite the view.
Everywhere on every green
Roses blushing as they blow,   5
    And enticing men to pull,
Lilies whiter than the snow   .
    Woodbines of sweet honey full :
    All love's emblems, and all cry,
    ' Ladies, if not plucked we die.'   10

Yet the lusty spring hath stayed ;
   Blushing red and purest white
   Daintily to love invite
Every woman, every maid.
Cherries kissing as they grow,   15
   And inviting men to taste,
Apples even ripe below,
   Winding gently to the waist :
     All love's emblems, and all cry,
     ' Ladies, if not plucked we die.'   20

CARE-CHARMING SLEEP.

CARE-CHARMING Sleep, thou easer of all woes,
Brother to Death, sweetly thyself dispose
On this afflicted prince ; fall like a cloud,
In gentle showers ; give nothing that is loud,
Or painful to his slumbers ; easy, light,   5
And as a purling stream, thou son of Night
Pass by his troubled senses ; sing his pain,
Like hollow murmuring wind or silver rain ;
Into this prince gently, O gently slide,
And kiss him into slumbers like a bride.   10

GOD LYÆUS, EVER YOUNG.

God Lyæus, ever young,
Ever honored, ever sung,
Stained with blood of lusty grapes,
In a thousand lusty shapes,
Dance upon the mazer's brim,   5
In the crimson liquor swim ;
From thy plenteous hand divine,
Let a river run with wine :
    God of youth, let this day here
    Enter neither care nor fear.   10

WILLIAM BROWNE, *Britannia's
Pastorals*, Book II, 1616.

WHAT WIGHT HE LOVED.

SHALL I tell you whom I love?
  Harken then awhile to me;
And if such a woman move,
  As I now shall versify,
Be assured, 'tis she or none   5
That I love, and love alone.

Nature did her so much right
  As she scorns the help of art;
In as many virtues dight
  As e'er yet embraced a heart: 10
So much good so truly tried,
Some for less were deified.

Wit she hath without desire
  To make known how much she hath;
And her anger flames no higher   15
  Than may fitly sweeten wrath.
Full of pity as may be,
Though, perhaps, not so to me.

Reason masters every sense,
  And her virtues grace her birth,   20
Lovely as all excellence,
  Modest in her most of mirth:
Likelihood enough to prove
Only worth could kindle love.

Such she is: and, if you know   25
  Such a one as I have sung,

Be she brown, or fair, or so
  That she be but somewhile young,
Be assured, 'tis she, or none
That I love, and love alone.   30

William Browne, *Poems from Lansdowne MS.* 777, printed 1815; date uncertain.

WELCOME, WELCOME, DO I SING.

Welcome, welcome, do I sing,
Far more welcome than the spring;
He that parteth from you never
Shall enjoy a spring forever.

Love, that to the voice is near,   5
  Breaking from your ivory pale,
Need not walk abroad to hear
  The delightful nightingale.
    Welcome, welcome, then I sing,
    Far more welcome than the spring;   10
    He that parteth from you never,
    Shall enjoy a spring forever.

Love, that looks still on your eyes,
  Though the winter have begun
To benumb our arteries,   15
  Shall not want the summer's sun.
    Welcome, welcome, etc.

Love, that still may see your cheeks,
  Where all rareness still reposes,   20
Is a fool, if e'er he seeks
  Other lilies, other roses.
    Welcome, welcome, etc.

Love, to whom your soft lip yields,
    And perceives your breath in kissing,   25
All the odors of the fields
    Never, never shall be missing.
        Welcome, welcome, etc.

Love, that question would anew
    What fair Eden was of old,   30
Let him rightly study you,
    And a brief of that behold.
        Welcome, welcome, then I sing,
        Far more welcome than the spring ;
        He that parteth from you never,   35
        Shall enjoy a spring forever.

                    A ROUND.

                        All.

Now that the spring hath filled our veins
    With kind and active fire,
And made green liv'ries for the plains,
    And every grove a choir ;

Sing we a song of merry glee,   5
    And Bacchus fill the bowl :
1. Then here's to thee ; 2. And thou to me
    And every thirsty soul.

Nor care, nor sorrow ere paid debt,
    Nor never shall do mine ;   10
I have no cradle going yet,
    Not I, by this good wine.

No wife at home to send for me,
    No hogs are in my ground,
No suit at law to pay a fee,   15
    Then round, old Jocky, round.

All.

Shear sheep that have them, cry we still,
 But see that no man scape
  To drink of the sherry,
   That makes us so merry,   20
 And plump as the lusty grape.

WILLIAM BROWNE, *Caelia, Sonnets,* from the same *MS.*

SONNET III.

FAIREST, when by the rules of palmistry
You took my hand to try if you could guess
By lines therein, if any wight there be
Ordained to make me know some happiness ;
I wished that those charàcters could explain,   5
Whom I will never wrong with hope to win ;
Or that by them a copy might be ta'en,
By you alone what thoughts I have within.
But since the hand of Nature did not set —
As providently loth to have it known —   10
The means to find that hidden alphabet,
Mine eyes shall be th' interpreters alone ;
By them conceive my thoughts, and tell me, fair,
If now you see her, that doth love me there?

WILLIAM BROWNE, *Visions,* from
the same.

SONNET VI.

DOWN in a valley, by a forest's side,
Near where the crystal Thames rolls on her waves,
I saw a mushroom stand in haughty pride,
As if the lilies grew to be his slaves ;

The gentle daisy, with her silver crown,   5
Worn in the breast of many a shepherd's lass,
The humble violet, that lowly down
Salutes the gay nymphs as they trimly pass :
Those, with a many more, methought, complained
That Nature should those needless things produce,   10
Which not alone the sun from others gained,
But turn it wholly to their proper use :
I could not choose but grieve, that Nature made
So glorious flowers to live in such a shade.

> WILLIAM BROWNE, from a *MS.*
> *in the Library of Salisbury*
> *Cathedral;* printed in 1894 ;
> date uncertain.

SONNET.

FOR her gait if she be walking,
    Be she sitting I desire her
    For her state's sake, and admire her
For her wit if she be talking :
    Gait and state and wit approve her ;   5
    For which all and each I love her.

Be she sullen, I commend her
    For a modest; be she merry
    For a kind one her prefer I :
Briefly everything doth lend her   10
    So much grace and so approve her
    That for everything I love her.

WILLIAM DRUMMOND, *Poems,
Amorous, Funeral, etc., Part I,*
1616.

SONNET.

TO THE NIGHTINGALE.

Dear chorister, who from those shadows sends,
Ere that the blushing morn dare shew her light,
Such sad lamenting strains, that night attends —
Become all ear — stars stay to hear thy plight ;
If one whose grief even reach of thought transcends,   5
Who ne'er — not in a dream — did taste delight,
May thee importune who like case pretends,
And seems to joy in woe, in woe's despite ;
Tell me, — so may thou fortune milder try
And long, long sing — for what thou thus complains,   10
Sith winter's gone and sun in dappled sky
Enamored smiles on woods and flowery plains ?
The bird, as if my questions did her move,
With trembling wings sighed forth, 'I love, I love !'

MADRIGALS.

SWEET ROSE, WHENCE IS THIS HUE?

Sweet rose, whence is this hue
    Which doth all hues excel ?
    Whence this most fragrant smell ?
And whence this form and gracing grace in you?
In fair Pæstana's fields perhaps you grew,   5
    Or Hybla's hills you bred,
Or odoriferous Enna's plains you fed,
Or Tmolus, or where boar young Adon slew ;

Or hath the Queen of Love you dyed of new
In that dear blood, which makes you look so red?   10
  No, none of those, but cause more high you blissed,
  My lady's breast you bore, her lips you kissed.

I FEAR NOT HENCEFORTH DEATH.

I FEAR not henceforth death,
Sith after this departure yet I breathe ;
  Let rocks, and seas, and wind
  Their highest treasons show ;
  Let sky and earth combined
Strive, if they can, to end my life and woe ;
Sith grief cannot, me nothing can o'erthrow :
  Or if that aught can cause my fatal lot,
  It will be when I hear I am forgot.

From the same, *Part II*, 1616.

SONNET.

THY head with flames, thy mantle bright with flow'rs,
Sweet Spring, thou turn'st with all thy goodly train ;
The zephyrs curl the green locks of the plain,
The clouds for joy in pearls weep down their show'rs.
Turn thou, sweet youth ? but ah ! my pleasant hours   5
And happy days with thee come not again ;
The sad memorials only of my pain
Do with thee turn, which turn my sweets in sours.
Thou art the same which still thou wert before,
Delicious, lusty, amiable, fair ;   10
But she, whose breath embalmed thy wholesome air,
Is gone ; nor gold, nor gems, can her restore.
Neglected virtue, seasons go and come,
While thine, forgot, lie closèd in a tomb.

MADRIGAL.

LIFE, A BUBBLE.

THIS Life, which seems so fair,
Is like a bubble blown up in the air
    By sporting children's breath,
    Who chase it everywhere
And strive who can most motion it bequeath :   5
And though it sometime seem of its own might,
Like to an eye of gold, to be fixed there,
And firm to hover in that empty height ;
That only is because it is so light.
But in that pomp it doth not long appear ;   10
For when 'tis most admirèd, in a thought,
Because it erst was naught, it turns to naught.

SONNET.

TO HIS LUTE.

MY lute, be as thou wert when thou did grow
With thy green mother in some shady grove,
When immelodious winds but made thee move,
And birds their ramage did on thee bestow.
Sith that dear voice which did thy sounds approve,   5
Which wont in such harmonious strains to flow,
Is reft from earth to tune those spheres above,
What art thou but a harbinger of woe?
Thy pleasing notes be pleasing notes no more,
But orphans' wailings to the fainting ear,   10
Each stroke a sigh, each sound draws forth a tear
For which be silent as in woods before,
Or if that any hand to touch thee deign,
Like widowed turtle, still her loss complain.

MADRIGAL.

My thoughts hold mortal strife ;
I do detest my life,
And with lamenting cries
Peace to my soul to bring
Oft call that prince which here doth monarchize.   5
But he grim grinning king,
Who caitiffs scorns, and doth the blest surprise,
Late having deck'd with beauty's rose his tomb,
Disdains to crop a weed, and will not come.

> WILLIAM DRUMMOND, *Madri-*
> *gals and Epigrams*, from the
> ed. 1656; date of writing un-
> certain.

PHYLLIS.

In petticoat of green,
Her hair about her eyne,
Phyllis beneath an oak
Sat milking her fair flock :
'Mongst that sweet-strainèd moisture, rare delight,   5
Her hand seemed milk, in milk it was so white.

————◆◆————

> BEN JONSON, *Epigrams*, 1616 ;
> date of writing unknown.

EPITAPH ON ELIZABETH L. H.

Wouldst thou hear what man can say
In a little ?   Reader, stay.
Underneath this stone doth lie
As much beauty as could die ;

Which in life did harbor give   5
To more virtue than doth live.
If at all she had a fault
Leave it buried in this vault.
One name was Elizabeth,
The other, let it sleep with death,   10
Fitter, where it died, to tell,
Than that it lived at all.   Farewell.

BEN JONSON, *The Devil is an
Ass,* 1631, acted 1616.

THE TRIUMPH OF CHARIS.

SEE the chariot at hand here of Love,
  Wherein my lady rideth !
Each that draws is a swan or a dove,
  And well the car Love guideth.
As she goes, all hearts do duty   5
    Unto her beauty ;
And, enamored, do wish, so they might
    But enjoy such a sight,
That they still were to run by her side,
Through swords, through seas, whither she would ride. 10

Do but look on her eyes, they do light
  All that Love's world compriseth !
Do but look on her hair, it is bright
  As Love's star when it riseth !
Do but mark, her forehead smoother   15
    Than words that soothe her !

And from her arched brows such a grace
　　Sheds itself through the face,
As alone there triumphs to the life
All the gain, all the good, of the elements' strife.　　20

Have you seen but a bright lily grow
　　Before rude hands have touched it?
Have you marked but the fall of snow
　　Before the soil hath smutched it?
Have you felt the wool o' the beaver?　　25
　　Or swan's down ever?
Or have smelt o' the bud o' the brier
　　Or the nard i' the fire?
Or have tasted the bag o' the bee?
O so white, O so soft, O so sweet is she!　　30

———◦◦◦———

BEN JONSON, *The Vision of De-light*, performed 1617.

SONG OF NIGHT.

BREAK, Fant'sy, from thy cave of cloud
　　And spread thy purple wings;
Now all thy figures are allowed,
　　And various shapes of things:
Create of airy forms a stream,　　5
It must have blood, but naught of fleam,
And though it be a waking dream,
　　Yet let it like an odor rise
　　　To all the senses here,
　　And fall like sleep upon their eyes　　10
　　　Or music in their ear.

THOMAS CAMPION, *Harleian*
MSS., before 1617.

SONNET.

THE CHARM.

THRICE toss those oaken ashes in the air,
And thrice three times tie up this true-love's knot ;
Thrice sit you down in this enchanted chair,
And murmur soft ' She will or she will not.'
Go burn these poisoned weeds in that blue fire,   5
This cypress gathered at a dead man's grave,
These screech owl's feathers, and this prickling briar,
That all thy thorny cares an end may have.
Then come, you fairies, dance with me a round :
Dance in a circle, let my love be center ;   10
Melodiously breathe out an enchanted sound,
Melt her hard heart, that some remorse may enter.
In vain are all the charms I can devise ;
She hath an art to break them with her eyes.

———◦◦◦———

THOMAS CAMPION, *The Third
Book of Airs,* about 1617.

NOW WINTER NIGHTS ENLARGE.

Now winter nights enlarge
   The number of their hours ;
And clouds their storms discharge
   Upon the airy towers.
Let now the chimneys blaze   5
   And cups o'erflow with wine,
Let well-tuned words amaze
   With harmony divine.

Now yellow waxen lights
  Shall wait on honey love, 10
While youthful revels, masques and courtly sights,
  Sleep's leaden spells remove.

This time doth well dispense
  With lovers' long discourse ;
Much speech hath some defence, 15
  Though beauty no remorse.
All do not all things well ;
  Some measures comely tread,
Some knotted riddles tell,
  Some poems smoothly read. 20
The summer hath his joys,
  And winter his delights ;
Though love and all his pleasures are but toys
  They shorten tedious nights.

SILLY BOY 'TIS FULL MOON YET.

SILLY boy ! 'tis full moon yet, thy night as day shines
    clearly ;
Had thy youth but wit to fear, thou couldst not love so
    dearly.
Shortly wilt thou mourn when all thy pleasures are
    bereavèd,
Little knows he how to love that never was deceivèd.

This is thy first maiden flame, that triumphs yet unstainèd ; 5
All is artless now you speak, not one word yet is feignèd ;
All is heaven that you behold, and all your thoughts are
    blessèd ;
But no spring can want his fall, each Troilus hath his
    Cressid.

Thy well-ordered locks ere long shall rudely hang neglected,
And thy lively pleasant cheer read grief on earth dejected ; 10
Much then wilt thou blame thy saint, that made thy heart
    so holy,
And with sighs confess, in love that too much faith is
folly.

Yet be just and constant still, Love may beget a wonder,
Not unlike a summer's frost, or winter's fatal thunder :
He that holds his sweetheart true unto his day of dying, 15
Lives, of all that ever breathed, most worthy the envying.

———•◦•———

THOMAS CAMPION, *Fourth Book
of Airs,* about 1617.

TRUE LOVE WILL YET BE FREE.

Turn all thy thoughts to eyes,
    Turn all thy hairs to ears,
Change all thy friends to spies,
    And all thy joys to fears ;
        True love will yet be free   5
        In spite of jealousy.

Turn darkness into day,
    Conjectures into truth,
Believe what th' envious say,
    Let age interpret youth :   10
        True love will yet be free
        In spite of jealousy.

Wrest every word and look,
    Rack every hidden thought,
Or fish with golden hook ;   15

True love cannot be caught :
For that will still be free
In spite of jealousy.

———❖———

SIR WALTER RALEIGH, printed
with his *Prerogative of Parlia-
ments*, 1628; written 1618.

EVEN SUCH IS TIME.

EVEN such is time, that takes on trust
  Our youth, our joys, our all we have,
And pays us but with‸earth and dust ;
  Who, in the dark and silent grave,
When we have wandered all our ways,   5
Shuts up the story of our days ;
But from this earth, this grave, this dust
My God shall raise me up, I trust !

———❖———

SIR WALTER RALEIGH (?) in
WALTON'S *Complete Angler*,
ed. 1653; date uncertain.

A FAREWELL TO THE VANITIES OF THE WORLD.

FAREWELL, ye gilded follies, pleasing troubles !
Farewell, ye honored rags, ye glorious bubbles !
Fame's but a hollow echo ; gold, pure clay ;
Honor, the darling but of one short day ;
Beauty — th' eye's idol — but a damasked skin ;   5
State, but a golden prison to live in
And torture free-born minds ; embroidered trains,
  but pageants for proud swelling veins :

And blood allied to greatness, is alone
Inherited, not purchased, nor our own :   10
Fame, honor, beauty, state, train, blood, and birth
Are but the fading blossoms of the earth.

I would be great, but that the sun doth still
Level his rays against the rising hill ;
I would be high, but see the proudest oak   15
Most subject to the rending thunder-stroke ;
I would be rich, but see men, too unkind,
Dig in the bowels of the richest mind ;
I would be wise, but that I often see
The fox suspected whilst the ass goes free ;   20
I would be fair, but see the fair and proud,
Like the bright sun, oft setting in a cloud ;
I would be poor, but know the humble grass
Still trampled on by each unworthy ass :
Rich, hated ; wise, suspected ; scorned, if poor ,   25
Great, feared ; fair, tempted ; high, still envied more ;
I have wished all, but now I wish for neither ;
Great, high, rich, wise, nor fair, poor I'll be rather.

Would the World now adopt me for her heir,
Would beauty's queen entitle me the fair,   30
Fame speak me Fortune's minion, could I vie
Angels with India, with a speaking eye
Command bare heads, bowed knees, strike Justice dumb
As well as blind and lame, or give a tongue
To stones by epitaphs, be called great master   35
In the loose rimes of every poetaster ;
Could I be more than any man that lives,
Great, fair, rich, wise, all in superlatives ;
Yet I more freely would these gifts resign,
Than ever Fortune would have made them mine ;   40
And hold one minute of this holy leisure
Beyond the riches of this empty pleasure.

Welcome, pure thoughts ! welcome, ye silent groves !
These guests, these courts, my soul most dearly loves :
Now the winged people of the sky shall sing   45
My cheerful anthems.to the gladsome spring ;
A pray'r-book now shall be my looking-glass,
In which I will adore sweet Virtue's face.
Here dwell no hateful looks, no palace cares,
No broken vows dwell here, nor pale-faced fears,   50
Then here I'll sit and sigh my hot love's folly,
And learn to affect an holy melancholy ;
And if contentment be a stranger then
I'll ne'er look for it, but in heaven, again.

From THOMAS BATESON'S *Second
Set of Madrigals*, 1618.

CAMELLA.

CAMELLA fair tripped o'er the plain,
    I followed quickly after ;
Have overtaken her I would fain,
    And kissed her when I caught her.
But hope being passed her to obtain,   5
    'Camella !' loud I call :
She answered me with great disdain,
    'I will not kiss at all.'

WILLING BONDAGE.

HER hair the net of golden wire,
    Wherein my heart, led by my wandering eyes
    So fast entangled is that in no wise
It can, nor will, again retire ;
    But rather will in that sweet bondage die   5
    Than break one hair to gain her liberty.

John Fletcher, *The Mad
Lover*, 1647 ; acted before
1618-19.

LOVE'S SACRIFICE.

Go, happy heart ! for thou shalt lie
Intombed in her for whom I die,
Example of her cruelty.

Tell her, if she chance to chide
Me for slowness, in her pride,   5
That it was for her I died.

If a tear escape her eye,
'Tis not for my memory,
But thy rites of obsequy.

The altar was my loving breast,   10
My heart the sacrificèd beast,
And I was myself the priest.

Your body was the sacred shrine,
Your cruel mind the power divine,
Pleased with hearts of men, not kine.   15

HYMN TO VENUS.

O, fair sweet goddess, Queen of loves,
Soft and gentle as thy doves,
Humble-eyed, and ever ruing
Those poor hearts their loves pursuing !
O, thou mother of delights,   5
Crowner of all happy nights,
Star of dear content and pleasure,
Of mutual loves and endless treasure !
Accept this sacrifice we bring,
Thou continual youth and spring ;   10
Grant this lady her desires,
And every hour we'll crown thy fires.

BEN JONSON, *Underwoods,*
1640; written before 1619.

A NYMPH'S PASSION.

I LOVE and he loves me again,
   Yet dare I not tell who ;
For if the nymphs should know my swain,
   I fear they'd love him too ;
     Yet if he be not known,   5
     The pleasure is as good as none,
For that's a narrow joy is but our own.

I'll tell, that if they be not glad,
   They may yet envy me ;
But then if I grow jealous mad   10
   And of them pitied be,
     It were a plague 'bove scorn ;
     And yet it cannot be forborne
Unless my heart would, as my thought be torn.

He is, if they can find him, fair   15
   And fresh and fragrant too,
As summer's sky or purgèd air,
   And looks as lilies do
     That are this morning blown :
     Yet, yet I doubt he is not known,   20
And fear much more that more of him be shown.

But he hath eyes so round and bright,
   As make away my doubt,
Where Love may all his torches light,
   Though Hate had put them out ;   25
     But then t' increase my fears
     What nymph soe'er his voice but hears
Will be my rival, though she have but ears.

I'll tell no more, and yet I love,
   And he loves me ; yet no   30
One unbecoming thought doth move
   From either heart I know ;
     But so exempt from blame
    As it would be to each a fame,
If love or fear would let me tell his name.   35

THE HOUR-GLASS.

Do but consider this small dust,
   Here running in the glass,
     By atoms moved ;
   Could you believe that this
     The body was   5
     Of one that loved ?
And in his mistress' flame playing like a fly
Turned to cinders by her eye ?
Yes, and in death, as life unblest
    To have 't expressed :   10
Even ashes of lovers find no rest.

THE DREAM.

Or scorn or pity on me take,
I must the true relation make,
   I am undone to-night ;
Love, in a subtile dream disguised,
   Hath both my heart and me surprised,   5
Whom never yet he durst attempt awake ;
   Nor will he tell me for whose sake
    He did me the delight
     Or spite ;

But leaves me to enquire   10
In all my wild desire
Of Sleep again who was his aid.
And Sleep ['s] so guilty and afraid
As since he dares not come within my sight.

> BEN JONSON, *The Sad Shepherd*,
> 1641; date of writing uncer-
> tain.

ÆGLAMOUR'S LAMENT.

HERE she was wont to go, and here, and here !
Just where those daisies, pinks, and violets grow :
The world may find the spring by following her ;
For other print her airy steps ne'er left :
Her treading would not bend a blade of grass,   5
Or shake the downy blow-ball from his stalk ;
But like the soft west-wind she shot along ;
And where she went, the flowers took thickest root
As she had sowed them with her odorous foot.

> MICHAEL DRAYTON, *Poems Col-
> lected, etc.*, folio ed. of 1619.

SONNET LXI.

SINCE there's no help, come let us kiss and part,
Nay I have done, you get no more of me ;
And I am glad, yea glad with all my heart,
That thus so cleanly I myself can free ;
Shake hands for ever, cancel all our vows,   5
And when we meet at any time again,
Be it not seen in either of our brows
That we one jot of former love retain.

Now at the last gasp of Love's latest breath,
When his pulse failing, Passion speechless lies,   10
When Faith is kneeling by his bed of death,
And Innocence is closing up his eyes :
Now if thou would'st, when all have given him over,
From death to life thou might'st him yet recover.

THE CRIER.

Good folk, for gold or hire,
But help me to a crier ;
For my poor heart is run astray
After two eyes that passed this way.
　　O yes, O yes, O yes,   5
　　If there be any man
　　In town or country can
　　Bring me my heart again,
　　I'll please him for his pain.
And by these marks I will you show   10
That only I this heart do owe :
　　It is a wounded heart,
　　Wherein yet sticks the dart ;
Every piece sore hurt throughout it ;
Faith and *troth* writ round about it.   15
It was a tame heart and a dear,
　　And never used to roam ;
But, having got this haunt, I fear
　　'T will hardly stay at home.
For God's sake, walking by the way,   20
　　If you my heart do see,
Either impound it for a stray,
　　Or send it back to me.

CANZONET.

TO HIS COY LOVE.

I PRAY thee leave, love me no more,
    Call home the heart you gave me,
I but in vain that saint adore,
    That can, but will not save me.
These poor half-kisses kill me quite   5
    Was ever man thus servèd?
Amidst an ocean of delight
    For pleasure to be stervèd.

Show me no more those snowy breasts,
    With azure riverets branchèd,   10
Where, whilst mine eye with plenty feasts,
    Yet is my thirst not staunchèd.
O, Tantalus! thy pains ne'er tell,
    By me thou art prevented;
'Tis nothing to be plagued in hell,   15
    But thus in heaven tormented!

Clip me no more in those dear arms,
    Nor thy life's comfort call me,
O these are but too powerful charms,
    And do but more enthrall me.   ·   20
But see how patient I am grown
    In all this coil about thee;
Come, nice thing, let thy heart alone,
    I cannot live without thee.

From THOMAS VAUTOR'S *Songs
of Divers Airs and Natures,*
1619.

SWEET SUFFOLK OWL.

SWEET Suffolk owl, so trimly dight
With feathers, like a lady bright,
Thou sing'st alone, sitting by night,
        Te whit, te whoo !
Thy note that forth so freely rolls,   5
With shrill command the mouse controls,
And sings a dirge for dying souls,
        Te whit, te whoo !

From MARTIN PEERSON'S *Private Music,* 1620.

LULLABY.

UPON my lap my sov'reign sits
    And sucks upon my breast ;
Meantime his love maintains my life
    And gives my sense her rest.
        Sing lullaby, my little boy,   5
        Sing lullaby, mine only joy.

When thou hast taken thy repast,
    Repose, my babe, on me ;
So may thy mother and thy nurse
    Thy cradle also be.   10
        Sing lullaby, my little boy,
        Sing lullaby, mine only joy.

I grieve that duty doth not work
　All that my wishing would,
Because I would not be to thee　　　　15
　But in the best I should.
　　Sing lullaby, my little boy,
　　Sing lullaby, mine only joy.

Yet as I am, and as I may,
　I must and will be thine,　　　　　20
Though all too little for thyself
　Vouchsafing to be mine.
　　Sing lullaby, my little boy,
　　Sing lullaby, mine only joy.

THE RETORT COURTEOUS.

'OPEN the door ! Who's there within ?
The fairest of thy mother's kin?
　O come, come, come abroad
And hear the shrill birds sing,
　The air with tunes that load.　　　5
It is too soon to go to rest,
The sun not midway yet to west:
　The day doth miss thee,
And will not part until it kiss thee.'

' Were I as fair as you pretend,　　10
Yet to an unknown seld-seen friend
　I dare not ope the door :
To hear the sweet birds sing
Oft proves a dangerous thing.
The sun may run his wonted race　　15
And yet not gaze on my poor face ;
　The day may miss me :
Therefore depart, you shall not kiss me.'

JOHN FLETCHER, *Women Pleased*,
1647; acted about 1620.

A WOMAN WILL HAVE HER WILL.

Question.

TELL me, what is that only thing
For which all women long;
Yet, having what they most desire,
To have it does them wrong?

Answer.

'Tis not to be chaste, nor fair, —   5
Such gifts malice may impair —
Richly trimmed, to walk and ride,
Or to wanton unespied ;
To preserve an honest name,
And so to give it up to fame ;   10
These are toys.   In good or ill
They desire to have their will ;
Yet, when they have it, they abuse it,
For they know not how to use it.

———◆——

From *Christ Church MS.*, printed
in 1888 ; date and author unknown.

A DIALOGUE.

'ART thou that she than whom no fairer is?
Art thou that she desire so strives to kiss ? '
'Say I am, how then?
Maids may not kiss
Such wanton-humored men.'   5

Art thou that she the world commends for wit?
Art thou so wise and mak'st no use of it?'
    'Say I am, how then?
    My wit doth teach me shun
    Such foolish, foolish men.'   10

        SIR HENRY WOTTON, in Michael
        Este's *Sixth Set of Books, etc.*,
        1624; written about 1620.

ON HIS MISTRESS, ELIZABETH OF BOHEMIA.

You meaner beauties of the night,
    That poorly satisfy our eyes
More by your number than your light,
    You common people of the skies,—
    What are you when the moon shall rise?   5

You curious chanters of the wood,
    That warble forth Dame Nature's lays,
Thinking your passions understood
    By your weak accents, what's your praise,
    When Philomel her voice shall raise?   10

You violets that first appear,
    By your pure purple mantles known
Like the proud virgins of the year,
    As if the spring were all your own.
    What are you when the rose is blown?   15

So, when my mistress shall be seen
    In form and beauty of her mind,
By virtue first, then choice, a queen,
    Tell me if she were not designed
    The eclipse and glory of her kind?   20

WILLIAM BROWNE, in Osborne's
*Memoirs of the Reign of King
James*, 1658; written after 1621.

EPITAPH.

ON THE COUNTESS OF PEMBROKE.

UNDERNEATH this sable hearse
Lies the subject of all verse,
Sidney's sister, Pembroke's mother :
Death, ere thou hast slain another,
Fair, and learned, and good as she,   5
Time shall throw a dart at thee.

Marble piles let no man raise
To her name : in after days,
Some kind woman born as she,
Reading this, like Niobe   10
Shall turn marble, and become
Both her mourner and her tomb.

GEORGE WITHER, *The Mistress
of Phil'arete*, 1622.

SONNET II.

HENCE AWAY, YOU SIRENS.

HENCE away, you Sirens, leave me,
And unclasp your wanton arms :
Sug'red words shall ne'er deceive me
Though you prove a thousand charms.
Fie, fie, forbear :   5
No common snare

Could ever my affection chain :
      Your painted baits
      And poor deceits
Are all bestowed on me in vain.   10

I'm no slave to such as you be :
Neither shall a snowy breast,
Wanton eye, or lip of ruby
      Ever rob me of my rest ;
            Go, go, display   15
            Your beauty's ray
To some o'ersoon enamored swain :
      Those common wiles
      Of sighs and smiles
Are all bestowed on me in vain.   20

I have elsewhere vowed a duty :
      Turn away your tempting eyes,
Show not me a naked beauty,
      Those impostures I despise ;
            My spirit loathes   25
            Where gaudy clothes
And feignèd oaths may love obtain :
      I love her so
      Whose look swears *no*,
That all your labors will be vain.   30

Can he prize the tainted posies
      Which on every breast are worn,
That may pluck the spotless roses
      From their never-touchèd thorn ?
            I can go rest   35
            On her sweet breast
That is the pride of Cynthia's train ;

Then stay your tongues,
Your mermaid songs
Are all bestowed on me in vain.   40

He's a fool that basely dallies
Where each peasant mates with him ;
Shall I haunt the throngèd vallies.
Whilst there 's noble hills to climb?
No, no, though clowns   45
Are scared with frowns,
I know the best can but disdain :
And those I'll prove,
So shall your love
Be all bestowed on me in vain.   50

Yet I would not deign embraces
With the greatest-fairest she,
If another shared those graces
Which had been bestowed on me.
I gave that one   55
My love, where none
Shall come to rob me of my gain.
Your fickle hearts
Makes tears, and arts
And all, bestowed on me in vain.   60

I do scorn to vow a duty
Where each lustful lad may woo ;
Give me her, whose sun-like beauty
Buzzards dare not soar unto :
She, she it is   65
Affords that bliss,
For which I would refuse no pain ;
But such as you.
Fond fools, adieu,
You seek to captive me in vain.   70

Proud she seemed in the beginning
And disdained my looking on,
But that coy one in the winning,
Proves a true one, being won.
    Whate'er betide   75
    She'll ne'er divide
The favor she to me shall deign ;
    But your fond love
    Will fickle prove,
And all that trust in you are vain.   80

Therefore know, when I enjoy one,
And for love employ my breath,
She I court shall be a coy one
Though I win her with my death.
    A favor there   85
    Few aim at dare ;
And if, perhaps, some lover plain ;
    She is not won
    Nor I undone
By placing of my love in vain.   90

Leave me, then, you Sirens, leave me,
Seek no more to work my harms,
Crafty wiles cannot deceive me,
 Who am proof against your charms :
    You labor may   95
    To lead astray
The heart that constant shall remain ;
    And I the while
    Will sit and smile
To see you spend your time in vain.   100

WILLIAM DRUMMOND, *Flowers
of Sion,* 1623.

SONNETS.

FOR THE MAGDALENE.

'THESE eyes, dear Lord, once brandons of desire,
Frail scouts betraying what they had to keep,
Which their own heart, then others set on fire,
Their trait'rous black before thee here out-weep ;
These locks, of blushing deeds the gilt attire,   5
Waves curling, wrackful shelves to shadow deep,
Rings wedding souls to sin's lethargic sleep,
To touch thy sacred feet do now aspire.
In seas of care behold a sinking bark,
By winds of sharp remorse unto thee driven,   10
O let me not be Ruin's aim'd-at mark !
My faults confessed, Lord, say they are forgiven.'
Thus sighed to Jesus the Bethanian fair,
His tear-wet feet still drying with her hair.

THE BOOK OF THE WORLD.

OF this fair volume which we World do name
If we the sheets and leaves could turn with care,
Of him who it corrects, and did it frame,
We clear might read the art and wisdom rare,
Find out his power which wildest powers doth tame,   5
His providence extending everywhere,
His justice which proud rebels doth not spare,
In every page, no period of the same :
But silly we, like foolish children, rest
Well pleased with colored vellum, leaves of gold,   10
Fair dangling ribbands, leaving what is best,
On the great Writer's sense ne'er taking hold :

Or if by chance we stay our minds on aught,
It is some picture in the margin wrought.

MADRIGAL.

THE WORLD, A HUNTING.

THIS world a hunting is,
The prey poor man, the Nimrod fierce is Death ;
His speedy greyhounds are
Lust, sickness, envy, care,
Strife that ne'er falls amiss,   5
With all those ills which haunt us while we breathe.
Now, if by chance we fly
Of these the eager chase,
Old Age with stealing pace
Casts on his nets, and there we panting die.   10

———•◦•———

FRANCIS BACON, from *Reliquiae
Wottonianae,* 1651 ; written
about 1625.

THE WORLD.

THE world's a bubble, and the life of man
    Less than a span ;
In his conception wretched, from the womb
    So to the tomb ;
Cursed from his cradle, and brought up to years   5
    With cares and fears.
Who then to frail mortality shall trust,
But limns on water, or but writes in dust.

Yet, whilst with sorrow here we live opprest,
    What life is best ?   10
Courts are but only superficial schools
    To dandle fools ;

The rural part is turned into a den
    Of savage men ;
And where's a city from foul vice so free,   15
But may be termed the worst of all the three ?

Domestic cares afflict the husband's bed,
    Or pains his head :
Those that live single, take it for a curse,
    Or do things worse :   20
These would have children: those that have them moan,
    Or wish them gone :
What is it, then, to have, or have no wife,
But single thraldom, or a double strife ?

Our own affections still at home to please   25
    Is a disease :
To cross the seas to any foreign soil,
    Peril and toil :
Wars with their noise affright us, when they cease,
    We are worse in peace ;   30
What then remains, but that we still should cry
For being born, or, being born, to die ?

———◦◦◦———

From *Christ Church MS.*, printed
in 1888; date and author unknown.

GUESTS.

YET if his majesty our sovereign lord
    Should of his own accord
    Friendly himself invite,
And say ' I'll be your guest to-morrow night,'
How should we stir ourselves, call and command   5
All hands to work ! 'Let no man idle stand.

Set me fine Spanish tables in the hall,
 See they be fitted all ;
 Let there be room to eat,
And order taken that there want no meat. 10
See every sconce and candlestick made bright,
That without tapers they may give a light.

Look to the presence : are the carpets spread,
 The dazie o'er the head,
 The cushions in the chairs, 15
And all the candles lighted on the stairs?
Perfume the chambers, and in any case
Let each man give attendance in his place.'

Thus if the king were coming would we do,
 And 'twere good reason too ; 20
 For 'tis a duteous thing
To show all honor to an earthly king,
And after all our travail and our cost,
So he be pleased, to think no labor lost.

But at the coming of the King of Heaven 25
 All's set at six and seven :
 We wallow in our sin,
Christ can not find a chamber in the inn.
We entertain him always like a stranger,
And, as at first, still lodge him in the manger. 30

NOTES.

NOTES.

1. George Gascoigne is the most considerable figure in English
poetry between Surrey and Sidney. A courtier, a soldier, and a poet,
his work is notable for his many trials of paths before him untrod by
English writers. See the editor's monograph on *Gascoigne*, *Publications
of the University of Pennsylvania*, *Series in Philology, Literature and
Archaeology*, II, No. 4. Gascoigne was step-father to Nicholas Breton,
whose literary career may have been determined by the older poet's
precept and example. Sir Walter Raleigh's earliest avowed verses, too,
are those prefixed to *The Steele Glas*. It is by this excellent satire that
Gascoigne is most deservedly remembered, although much of his verse
and prose is worthy of attention. The "novel" in the Italian manner,
from which this sonnet is taken, is the earliest specimen of its class
in English. The text is from Hazlitt's ed., 1869.

1 9. *Front.* Forehead.

1. *The Strange Passion.* *The Posies of George Gascoigne, Esquire*,
is the title of the second collected ed. of his works. The matter is
fancifully arranged under the headings : *Flowers, Herbs*, and *Weeds*.
This poem represents Gascoigne's love poetry at its best. Its fervor,
directness, smoothness, and somewhat excessive alliteration are all
characteristic of Gascoigne's poetry in general.

1 1. *Bale.* Sorrow.

2 7. *Lust.* Pleasure, delight ; cf. 19 1: "the light of human *lust*."

2 16. *Grutch.* Pain, grief ; a by-form of *grudge*.

2 28, 29. *Wray* and *bewray.* Reveal.

3. *Pilgrim to Pilgrim.* This poem is probably not Raleigh's. His
claim to it is based solely upon the initials "Sr. W. R." appended to a
MS. copy (*Rawl. 85*). The poem occurs in several versions, and was
very popular. It is quoted in *The Knight of the Burning Pestle* and in
Hans Beer-pot, his Invisible Comedy ; the second stanza may have suggested Ophelia's " How should I your true love know." (*Haml.* iv, 5,
23, see p. 128 of this volume.) The metres of the earlier years of
Elizabeth's reign are so overwhelmingly iambic, that this perfectly

metrical, if somewhat irregular, anapæstic movement comes like a surprise. Professor Gummere, of Haverford College, calls my attention to three epigrams — printed among the poems of Raleigh, ed. Hannah, p. 55 — all of them in more or less limping anapæsts, but not of this measure. It is quite possible that the tune to which these verses were sung may have affected the measure. See Chappell's *Old Engl. Popular Music*, I, 69. An interesting chapter on the relation of Elizabethan music to Elizabethan verse remains to be written. There is a large number of poems upon the pilgrimages to Walsingham (for which see the *Percy Folio MS.*, ed. 1868), several of them in the peculiar metre of this poem : —

> In the wracks of Walsingham
> Whom should I choose,
> But the queen of Walsingham,
> To be guide to my Muse?
> Then thou prince of Walsingham
> Grant me to frame
> Bitter plaints to rue thy wrong,
> Bitter woe for thy name.

4 26. *Now.* The MS. reads *no.*

4 27. *Love likes not the falling fruit.* Cf. " Let thy time of marriage be in thy young and strong years ; for, believe it, ever the young wife betrayeth the old husband, and she that had thee not in thy flower will despise thee in thy fall." Raleigh's *Instructions to his Son* (Bliss).

4 30. *Forgets.* MS., *forget.*

4 33. *Dureless.* That endures not.

4 36. *Toy.* Trifle. Cf. 151 7, 186 23, 199 11.

4 1. *Thomas Lodge* was son of a Lord Mayor of London, and, after many vicissitudes, attained distinction as a physician. As a writer he displays remarkable versatility ; romances, plays, satire, lyric, and occasional verse attesting this quality. The position, too, of Lodge among the dramatic predecessors of Shakespeare is one of great interest, but does not belong here. I take my text for Lodge from the reprints of the Hunterian Club : this poem from No. XXXV, 46. The original has no title. The first line of *Glaucus and Scilla*, the chief poem of the volume so entitled, fixes the date — of that poem at least — as prior to Lodge's departure from Cambridge, 1577 : —

> Walking alone — all lonely full of grief —
> Within a thicket near the Isis' flood, etc.

See also the author's dedication, in which he promises his friend a better poetical fare "next term."

Lament. According to Mr. Bullen (*Lyrics from Elizabethan Romances,* p. viii) this poem is "closely imitated from the opening stanzas of a longer poem of Philippe Desportes," beginning : —

> La terre, naguère glacée,
> Est ores de vert tapissée,
> Son sein est embelli de fleurs,
> L'air est encore amoureux d'elle,
> Le ciel rit de la voir si belle,
> Et moi j'en augmente mes pleurs.

Mr. Bullen adds : "It seems to me that whenever Lodge imitates Desportes, he greatly improves upon his model."

4 4. *Teen.* Grief, vexation.

5 11. *Where.* Whereas. ˙

5 1. *Perigot and Willie's Roundelay.* As the diction of *The Shepherds' Calendar* is intentionally archaic, and indeed artificially so, I have here reproduced the original in spelling and punctuation, following Dr. Sommer's *Photographic Facsimile* of the original ed. of 1579. It is likely that either *Hobbinol's Ditty in Praise of Eliza,* in *April,* or the beautiful *Lament for Dido,* of *November,* would better have represented the *Calendar.* But both are long, and Spenser is represented with full spread sail in the *Prothalamion,* p. 76, below. This roundelay was afterwards reprinted in *England's Helicon.*

"*It fell upon.* Perigot maketh his song in praise of his love, to whom Willy answereth every under verse." E. K.'s *Glosse* upon the *Calendar.* With this note it becomes unnecessary to print the names Perigot and Willy in alternation throughout the poem, as in the original.

5 3. *Shrieve.* Shrive, confess sinners.

5 4. *Gynneth.* Begins.

5 8. *Spill.* Perish.

6 10. *Bellibone. Belle et bonne,* a compound, the reverse of the more usual *Bonibell* of the next verse.

6 14. *Gray is greete.* Grey denotes weeping or mourning.

6 15. *Saye.* A strong coarse stuff, like serge.

6 18. *Chapëlet.* Trisyllabic.

6 22. *Seely.* Innocent, cf. 7 65 and 169 9.

6 23. *Wood.* Mad.

6 27. *Rovde.* Took a chance, or roving shot at. Cf. "At marks full forty score they used to prick and *rove.*" *Polyolbion,* Song xxvi.

6 35. *Lightsome levin.* Brilliant lightning.

6 38. *Moonëlight.* Trisyllabic.

7 43. *Gryde.* " Pearced," explains E. K.

7 44. *Wexen.* Wax, grow.

7 45. *Kaunch.* Wrench.

7 52. *Carelesse.* Collier reads *cureless*, a tempting emendation.

7 53. *Bale.* Cf. 1 1.

7 55. *Thilk.* The ilk, the same.

7 56. *You may buye gold*, etc. A proverb.

7 61. *Gracelesse griefe.* A grief that comes from not obtaining her grace or favor.

7 64. *Priefe.* Proof.

" Nothing can be prettier in its way than this little song. It has that true lyrical quality which forces us to chant the words to a melody suggested by themselves." (Collier.) On the metrical freedom of this Roundelay, see *Introduction*, § 2.

Although well known, one of the earliest critical utterances on Spenser may well find a place here : " This place have I purposely reserved for one, who if not only, yet in my judgment principally, deserveth the title of the rightest English Poet that ever I read : that is the author of the *Shepherds' Calendar*, intituled to the worthy gentleman, Master Philip Sidney, whether it was Master Sp. or what rare scholar in Pembroke Hall soever, because himself and his friends, for what reason I know not would not reveal it, I force not greatly to set down : sorry I am that I can not find none other with whom I might couple him in this catalogue in his rare gift of poetry." (W. Webbe, *A Defense of English Poetry*, 1586.)

8 1. *Come hither.* This poem is quoted in part by Puttenham (*Art of English Poesy*, 1589, written about 1580) as an instance of "*antipophora* or figure of response," and there mentioned as Oxford's (ed. Haselwood, I, 172). It was very popular, appearing in Breton's *Bower of Delight*, 1591 and 1597, and in Deloney's *Garland of Goodwill*, 1596. Cf. with this the same author's *The Judgment of Desire*, in *The Paradise of Dainty Devises*, ed. Brydges, p. 69. It is variously entitled.

Gascoigne calls the verse of this poem, here divided in printing, " the commonest sort of verse which we use nowadays (viz: the long verse of twelve and fourteen syllables), I know not certainly how to name it, unless I should say that it doth consist of Poulter's measure, which giveth twelve for one dozen and fourteen for another." (*Certain Notes of Instruction concerning the Making of Verse or Rime in English*, ed. Arber, p. 39.)

I follow Dr. Grosart's text, which purports to be that of the earliest MS. (*Rawl. MS. 15*). This editor finds "an atmosphere of graciousness and culture that is grateful about the verses of this Earl." (*Fuller Worthies' Miscellanies*, IV, 11.) Oxford is ramblingly described by Mr. Saintsbury as "Sidney's enemy (which he might be if he chose), and apparently a coxcomb (which is less pardonable), but a charming writer of verse." (*A History of Elizabethan Literature*, p. 127.) Oxford was Lord High Chamberlain in 1588.

8 4. *Fond.* Foolish. Cf. 19 5, 41 11, 62 13.

8 8. *Self-Conceit.* Probably here equal to *very imagination* rather than in the ordinary modern sense.

9 27. I insert *the* to make the metre agree with that of the corresponding line in the preceding stanza. Another reading gives: "Whom dost thou think to be thy foe."

9 34. *Make.* Mate. Cf. 32 35.

No one who would know Sidney should neglect the reading of Greville's tribute to their early friendship, usually entitled *The Life of the Renowned Sir Philip Sidney.* "Indeed he was a true model of worth ; a man fit for conquest, plantation [*i.e.*, colonizing], reformation, or what action soever is greatest and hardest amongst men: withal such a lover of mankind and goodness, that whoever had any real parts, in him found comfort, participation, and protection to the uttermost of his power : like Zephyrus he giving life where he grew." (*Works of Fulke Greville, Lord Brooke*, ed. Grosart, IV, 37.)

9. *Wooing Stuff.* In the absence of any external evidence, I prefer to place this poem in lighter vein before the strong, pure notes of *Astrophel and Stella.* I follow Dr. Grosart's text for Sidney. The title is not in the MS.

9 8. *Use.* Be accustomed to, to make a practice of.

9 10. *Learns.* This verb was commonly employed with a personal object in Elizabethan English. Cf. "The red plague rid you For learning me your language," *Tempest*, i, 2, 365 ; and see Abbott's *Shakespearian Grammar*, § 291.

10 22. *In question.* This line reads in the MS.: "In question? nay, 'uds-foot, she loves thee than." The oath is ugly in itself and destructive of the metre. I therefore omit it with Ellis and Linton.

10 22. *Than.* A common by-form of *then*, as *then* of *than* (*quam*). These variations are in this book reduced to modern spelling, except where the older form is necessary to preserve the rime.

10. *My true love hath my heart.* I prefer to give this little poem in the form in which it first appeared in print, in Puttenham's *Art of English Poesy* (ed. Arber, p. 233), where it is quoted as an illustration of "*Epimone* or the love-burden." In the next year it appeared in

sonnet form in the *Arcadia.* This version adds the following lines to those of the text, transferring the refrain to the close:

> His heart his wound receivèd from my sight,
> My heart was wounded with his wounded heart;
> For as from me on him his hurt did light,
> So still methought in me his hurt did smart:
> Both equal hurt, in this change sought our bliss,
> My true-love hath my heart and I have his.

Dr. Grosart considers both forms Sidney's own. (Introd. to *The Shepherds' Calendar,* in his ed. of Spenser, IV, p. xxxvi.)

ll 3. *Sense.* Probably here plural, the final *s* not being pronounced — nor in this case even written — for euphony's sake. See *Sh. Gram.,* § 471 and the numerous examples there given. Cf. also a possible instance, 160 15.

ll 13. *Sprite.* Spirit. These forms are interchangeable in Elizabethan English. Cf. v. 4 of this sonnet, above.

11. *Astrophel and Stella.* The chronology of *Astrophel and Stella* seems beyond accurate solution. I content myself with an upward limit, as in the cases of Donne and the *Sonnets* of Shakespeare. Stella became Lady Rich in March, 1581, by our calendar. It is doubtful if a sonnet of the series was written after the close of that year. Sidney himself was married in January, 1583. For a discussion of the biographical particulars underlying the writing of this sonnet sequence, the reader should consult Dr. Grosart's *Introduction, Poems of Sidney,* 1877. Mr. F. T. Palgrave thus concludes a discerning note on Sidney in the last edition of his *Golden Treasury of English Lyrics:* "In a certain depth and chivalry of feeling — in the rare and noble quality of disinterestedness (to put it in one word),— he has no superior, hardly perhaps an equal, amongst our poets; and after or beside Shakespeare's *Sonnets,* his *Astrophel and Stella* .. offers the most intense and powerful picture of the passion of love in the whole range of our poetry." (Ed. 1892, p. 351.)

11. *First Song.* The readings of this song are various and may be seen in Dr. Grosart's *Sidney,* I, 151. I have followed this editor in preferring the (!) to the (?), as the successive outbursts of each stanza seem to me rather rapturous exclamations than mere interrogations.

ll 3. *All song of praise is due* seems better than the reading *be due.*

ll 5. *Marry state with pleasure.* Combine dignity with vivacity. Cf. 178 3.

ll 8. *Forgat all measure, i.e.,* when heaven made her. (Grosart.)

12 10. *Staineth.* Stains by comparison. (Grosart.) Cf. 41 4.

12 13. *The feet, whose step all sweetness planteth.* Cf. below the concluding lines of *Aglamour's Lament*, p. 194 : —

> And where she went, the flowers took thickest root
> As she had sowed them with her odorous foot.

12 17. *Doth patience nourish.* The passage is obscure, if not corrupt. Grosart reads and defends the variant of some of the early edd. *passions nourish.* Professor Kittredge reminds me that patience, with constancy, secrecy and obedience, was one of the conventional virtues of the chivalric lover (cf. Chaucer's *Troilus*, iii, 21), and hence an appropriate feeling for the lady to inspire.

12 22. *Long-dead beauty with increase reneweth,* i.e., reincarnates, so to say, and enhances in her person the charms of beauties long since dead. Cf. in this vol. Daniel's sonnet on p. 48 and Shakespeare's on p. 86.

12 24. *Rueth.* Sorrows, laments.

12 25. *Loosest fastest tieth.* Possibly intentionally difficult of utterance to symbolize the thought.

12 32. *Not miracles, etc.* Miracles are not wonders.

13 1. *With how sad steps.* "The first perfectly charming sonnet in the English language," declares Mr. Saintsbury. (*Elizabethan Literature*, p. 102.) Cf. a fine sonnet of Charles Best, printed in Davison's *Poetical Rhapsody* (ed. Nicolas, p. 184): —

A SONNET OF THE MOON.

> Look how the pale Queen of the silent night
> Doth cause the ocean to attend upon her,
> And he as long as she is in his sight,
> With his full tide is ready her to honor :
> But when the silver waggon of the Moon
> Is mounted up so high he cannot follow,
> The sea calls home his crystal waves to moan,
> And with low ebb doth manifest his sorrow.
> So you, that are the sovereign of my heart,
> Have all my joys attending on your will ;
> My joys low ebbing when you do depart,
> When you return, their tide my heart doth fill.
> So as you come, and as you do depart,
> Joys ebb and flow within my tender heart.

13 5. *Long-with-love-acquainted.* Sidney, like Shakespeare, is fond of compound words ; and in his *Defence of Poesy* (ed. Cook, *Athenæum*

Press Series, p. 55), considers English "particularly happy in compositions of two or three words together, . . . which is one of the greatest
beauties can be in language." Cf. *chamber-melody*, 14 4 ; *safe-left*, 14 6;
false-seeming, 15 15. See also *Sh. Gram.*, §§ 428–435. In lyrical composition compound words are not so frequent as in the drama or in satire. In
this collection there are scarcely four score, none of them compounded
of more than two words, excepting the one which forms the heading of
this note. Some of the noun compounds are : *morning-grey*, 38 7;
care-charmer, 50 1; *bride-house*, 161 22 ; adjectives : *sweet-breathing*, 76 2 ;
heart-quelling, 79 97; *flower-adorned*, 110 22; *humble-eyed*, 191 3; adverbs:
ill-adventred, 50 6; *seld-seen*, 198 11; verbs : *over-blow*, 116 36 ; *out-weep*,
205 4. Bold and otherwise notable compounds are Donne's *long-strayed*
eyes, 101 1, and *vice-nature*, 103 6 ; Jonson's *crown-worthy*, 117 68 ;
Lodge's *morn-waking* birds, 59 3 ; Drummond's *sweet-strained* moisture,
182 5 ; and Wither's *greatest-fairest*, 203 52.

13 8.   *Descries.*   Shows, discloses.

13 10.   *Wit.*   Mind, understanding.   Cf. 13 2, 14 12, 16 38, 178 4, 186 2.

13. 14.   Do they call ungratefulness a virtue there ?

13.   *Come Sleep!*   Cf. Daniel's *Care-charmer Sleep*, p. 50 below, and
the note there.

13 4.   *Indifferent.*   Impartial.

13 5.   *Prease.*   Press, throng : the spelling of the original preserved
for the rime.

13 10.   *Deaf of noise and blind of light.*   *Of* is the earlier reading.
To seems, as Dr. Grosart puts it, "the countess' or the editors' im-
provement."

13 11.   *A rosy garland.*   *Rosy*, "as the garland of silence (*sub rosa*),"
comments Dr. Grosart, and refers to an interesting use of the word *rose*
in the *Epistle* prefixed to the *Arcadia*, ed. 1593. Speaking of those who
carp at the author's works, the editor writes : "To us, say they, the
pastures are not pleasant : and as for the flowers, such as we light on
we take no delight in, but the greater part grow not within our reach.
Poor souls ! what talk they of flowers ? They are *roses* [*i.e.*, allusions
about which silence had better be kept], not flowers, must do them
good."

13 12.   *In right.*   In modern English, *by right* or *of right*.   See *Sh.
Gram.*, § 163.

14 1.   *High way, since you my chief Parnassus be.*   Since my path to
fame is the military high way, not the poet's *gradus ad Parnassum.*

14 2.   *My Muse . . tempers her words.*   Cf. the familiar lines of the
opening speech of *Richard III*, i, 1, 10 : —

And now instead of mounting barbed steeds
To fright the souls of fearful adversaries,
He capers nimbly in a lady's chamber
To the lascivious pleasing of a lute.

14 6. *Safe-left.* Cf. 13 5.

14 8. *Thanks and wishes, wishing thankfully.* Playing with words
was the besetting sin of Elizabethan authors from Shakespeare himself,
whose puns and double meanings are notorious, to jesters like Tarlton
and professional jugglers with words, like Nashe, in his prose. Cf. in
this volume: Breton's "The *heaven* of *heavens* with *heavenly* power
preserve thee," 66 11; Davison's "Which *presence* still *presented*, *Absence*
hath not *absented*," 75 42–43; Shakespeare's "Love is not love which
alters when it *alteration* finds, Or bends with the *remover* to *remove*,"
86 2–4; Jonson's "*Close* the *close* cause of it," 115 16. For puns and
plays upon the meaning of a single word, see 78 67 and 180 8.

14 9. *Still.* Ever, continuously, always. This is the usual Elizabethan meaning of the word. See Abbott's *Shakespearian Grammar*,
§ 69, and cf. 25 18, 28 33, 181 14, 187 13, 188 17, etc.; on p. 143 23 the
word occurs in its modern sense.

14 12. *Lot.* More in the original sense of *chance* than in the sense
we are accustomed to give the word in modern English.

14 14. "*Hundreds of years!*" exclaims Mr. Ruskin, "you think that
a mistake? No, it is the very rapture of love. A lover like this does
not believe his mistress can grow old, or die." (*Fors Clavigera*, vol. III,
p. 6, Lecture XXXV.)

14 9. *Ne.* Nor. This form was already archaic in Sidney's time.
It was employed by Spenser and Watson, the latter, in a limited sense,
a poet of Sidney's school. Cf. 23 18.

14 11. *Without.* Unless.

14 12. *Wit.* Cf. 13 10.

"Sidney's sonnets — I speak of the best of them — are among the
very best of their sort. They fall below the plain moral dignity, the
sanctity, the high yet modest spirit of self-approval, of Milton, in his
compositions of a similar structure. . . . [But] the sonnets which we
oftenest call to mind of Milton were the compositions of his maturest
years. Those of Sidney . . . were written in the very heyday of his
blood. They are stuck full of amorous fancies — far-fetched conceits,
befitting his occupation: for true love thinks no labor to send out
thoughts upon vast, and more than Indian voyages, to bring home rich
pearls, outlandish wealth, gums, jewels, spicery, to sacrifice in self-
depreciating similitudes, as shadows of true amiabilities in the beloved.

We must be lovers — or at least the cooling touch of time, the *circum
praecordia frigus* must not so have damped our faculties, as to take
away our recollection that we were once so — before we cån duly appre-
ciate the glorious vanities and graceful hyperboles of the passion. The
images which lie before our feet (though by some accounted the only
natural) are least natural for the high Sidnean love to express its fancies
by." (*Last Essays of Elia, Some Sonnets of Sir Philip Sidney, Works
of Lamb*, ed. Talfourd, II, 232.)

15. *A Dirge.* Dr. Grosart (*Sidney*, II, 4) conjectures that this
dirge was written upon the marriage of Stella. There is no evidence,
however, to show that it was ever connected with the *Astrophel and
Stella* collection.

15 8. *Franzy.* Frenzy. Cf. 10 22.

15 15. *False-seeming holy.* Perhaps false-seeming-holy, *i.e.*, hypocrisy.

15 21. *Trentals.* From Late Latin, *trigintalia.* Services lasting
thirty days, in which thirty masses were said for the repose of the dead.

15 23–26. *Sir Wrong*, etc. Injustice ordains that the marble of my
mistress' heart shall be the tomb of love, inscribed with this epitaph :
Her eyes, etc.

16. *Fulke Greville*, afterwards Lord Brooke, held no mean place in
the favor of Elizabeth, nor "for any short term," says Naunton. "He
had the longest lease and the smoothest time without rub, of any of her
favorites. . . . He was a brave gentleman, and honorably descended.
. . . Neither illiterate ; for . . . there are of his now extant some
fragments of his poem, and of those times, which do interest him in the
Muses, and which shews the Queen's election had ever a noble conduct,
and its motions more of virtue and judgment, than of fancy." (*Fragmenta Regalia*, ed. Arber, p. 50.)

The words of the general title of Greville's works, ed. 1633, " written
in his youth and familiar exercises with Sir Philip Sidney," are sufficient
to justify the position which I give the selections in this volume.
Greville must have begun writing at an early age ; if the poem attributed
to him in the *Paradise of Dainty Devises* be his — which is doubtful —
as early as 1576. *Cælica* exhibits very decidedly, it seems to me, a
deepening maturity of mind, and may have been written through a
series of years. The text is from Dr. Grosart's *Greville, Fuller
Worthies*, 1870 ; the titles of the first three poems are those of the
original edition.

16 3. *Fires.* Dissyllabic. Cf. 21 13.

16 7–8. *Strong nature, etc.* Just as verses 11–14 answer the question of vv. 9–10, so these verses reply to the question: *Are you afraid,*

they (your eyes) show me too much pleasure? The answer, with its ellipses supplied, may be given somewhat thus: That is an idle fear: for all hope of pleasure (*i.e.*, in the reward of my love to you) is dead and buried. Yet *strong, i.e.,* compulsive and uncontrollable, *nature* forces me to *deck* with admiring and lover-like speeches — as a grave with flowers — *the grave wherein it* (*i.e.*, dead pleasure) *lies ;* using these admiring speeches not, as you may wrongly suppose, because I regard myself as your hopeful lover, but because impelled by your *Excellence,* which is such that it *can never be expressed in measure.*

16 14. *Star-gazers only multiply desires.* Those whose lowliness removes them far from the possibility of becoming partakers in Cynthia's (that is, the Queen's) love, only multiply their own desires of the unattainable by contemplating her star-like glory.

17 3. *In the chimneys . . . wrought.* Cf. 152 7–10.

17 20. *O'erwatched with.* Out-watched by.

17 21. *Ever.* I read for *even.*

17 24. *Vulcan's brothers.* Perhaps those that emulate Vulcan in their attempt to entrap lovers. *Fine nets,* evidently suggested by a recollection of the net in which Vulcan caught Mars and Venus, and possibly here a figure for the wiles by which the lover was rendered jealous and parted from his mistress. My colleague, Professor Gudeman, suggests that *Vulcan's brothers* stands for lovers in general, placed as was Vulcan with respect to Mars and Venus. The allusion is certainly far from clear.

17 28. *Wit.* Cf. 13 10 and the references there.

17 29. *Leave.* Cease. Cf. 51 6.

18 7. *Abuse.* Deceive.

18 9. *Yet who this language,* etc. Yet whoever speaks to the people of things as they actually are destroys the rule of prevalent opinion, and breaks the idol which the senses worship, *i.e.,* the appearances of things. This is a typical ' difficulty ' of Greville, due to pregnancy of thought and excessive condensity of expression. Cf. 16 14, 18 9–14 and 19 5.

18 3. *Be distasted.* Disgusted, out of temper with.

18 6. *Lustings.* Longings, desires.

18 9–14. *Then man,* etc. Man is here exhorted to endure himself, that is, to practice Stoicism ; or to forsake himself and turn to heaven, that is, accept the Christian solution. I am indebted for this note to Professor Kittredge.

19 1. *Whenas.* When. Cf. 30 8, 38 11.

19 1. *Lust.* Cf. 2 7.

19 5.　*Fond.*　Foolish.　Cf. 8 4.

19 5.　*Then fond desires,* etc. *I.e.,* Then the folly of those that fear
death only because it ends life is shown in their vain longing for life,
that they may amend the past. The difficulty consists in making "fond
desires" stand first for the folly of those that fear, and secondly for the
folly of vainly wishing. In the first, "desires" is misleading; in the
second, superfluous.

19 8.　*Eternal glass.*　Cf. *2 Corinthians,* iii, 18.

19 11.　*Living men.*　*I.e.,* those now enjoying the eternal life.

19 11.　*How he left his breath.*　How could he come to die without
once having thought of his end. The contrast in this poem lies between
the dying mortal with his longings for the continuance of an earthly
life and the blessed, *living men,* who wonder how a man could consent
to live to his end without thought of death. Professor Kittredge suggests an alternative explanation for the phrase heading this note: "Did
he make a good or a bad end?" in which case we have the same contrast between the dying mortal and the blessed, "who so despise mortal
life in comparison with immortality (which they are enjoying) that they
really consider, in connection with that mortal life, only *one* moment, —
and that the moment of dissolution."

Charles Lamb's remark on Greville's work is well known : "Whether
we look into his plays or his most passionate love-poems, we shall find
all frozen and made stiff with intellect." (*Specimens of English Dramatic Poets,* ed. 1835, I, p. 316.) Less known, but not less excellent, is
the following from *The Muses' Library,* 1737, quoted by Dr. Grosart
(*Greville,* II, vi): "Perhaps few men that dealt in poetry had more
learning or real wisdom than this nobleman ; and yet his style is sometimes so dark and mysterious, I mean it appears so to me, that one
would imagine that he chose rather to conceal than illustrate his meaning : at other times, his wit breaks out with an uncommon brightness,
and shines, I had almost said without an equal. 'Tis the same thing
with his poetry : sometimes so harsh and uncouth, as if he had no ear
for music ; at others, so smooth and harmonious, as if he was master
of all its powers." It is not Donne, but Greville, that is the Elizabethan
Browning. For substantiation of this I would recommend a comparative
reading of *Alaham* and *Sordello.*

19.　*Apelles' Song.*　The songs of Lyly's plays, bearing the titles
here given, appeared first in print in the collected edition of his works
by Blount, 1632 ; the authorship is not certain, although it is highly
probable that they are Lyly's, as it was no unusual custom to excise
the songs of a play in putting it to press. Mr. Bullen, after praising the

"fairy lightness" of Lyly's lyrics, calls our attention to the fact that they were "written at a time when our English lyrists were doubtfully feeling their way." (*Lyrics from the Dramatists*, p. vii.) Notwithstanding the labors of Arber, Landmann, and others, John Lyly, the Euphuist, is still an author much misunderstood. Euphuism was in Lyly but one phase of a genius admirably light, agile, and alert. Little is known of his life, except that he danced attendance upon the court and was disappointed in his ambition to become Master of the Revels. See especially his two witty petitions to the Queen, published by Professor Arber in his *Introduction* to *Euphues*, p. 9.

20. *George Peele.* In presence of the delicacy and beauty of such songs as these, it is difficult to believe Peele the reprobate that he is often described. However miserable or degraded the later part of his life may have been, it is certain that he began his dramatic career in no small estimation at court, the play from which these songs are taken having been performed before the Queen. It is probable that Peele died when no more than thirty, one of the several whose untimely fall made way for the mightier Shakespeare.

20 10. *Bene.* Cf. 21 7, and *Sh. Gram.*, § 332.

20 11. *Roundelay.* See p. 5, and *Introduction*, § 2.

20 27. *Can.* Here in its original sense of *have knowledge* or *skill.* Cf. the v. above for the more usual modern sense, 38 1 and 65 14; see also *Sh. Gram.*, § 307.

21 13. *Prayers.* Words of this class are usually dissyllabic, *e.g.*: *fire*, 16 3; *flowers*, 74 20, 92 8; *power*, 43 10, 107 5; *hour*, 137 12, 161 6. Occasionally, however, they are contracted to a monosyllable: *bower*, 30 33. See *Sh. Gram.*, § 480.

21 3. *Sleep with velvet hand.* Cf. Chapman's "Night . . . lay thy velvet hand," 91 13.

22 10. Note how the omission of the unaccented syllable, which ordinarily begins each line, brings precisely the rhetorical stress required upon the word *such*.

22 11. I read *be* for *by* with Bullen.

22 14. I read *mock* for *mockes* with the same editor.

22 1. *Shag-hair.* See *Sh. Gram.*, § 433, p. 320, and cf. 13 5, 22 13.

22 6. *Wanton.* The restriction of this word to an objectionable sense is of modern growth. It is here equivalent to our playful use of the word *rogue* or *rascal.* Cf. 29 9 and 30, where the word is used as a term of endearment.

22 7 14. *These headed are with golden blisses,* etc. Cf. Ovid, *Metamorphoses*, i. 466: —

Eque sagittifera prompsit duo tela pharetra
Diversorum operum ; fugat hoc, facit illud amorem.
Quod fecit auratum est, et cuspide fulget acuta,
Quod fugat obtusum est et sub arundine plumbum.

22 12. *Trance.* Fit of abstraction.

22 13. *Buss.* Kiss.

22 14. *Untruss.* Literally to untie the points or laces by which the breeches were held, or to loosen the girdle, hence to give relief. A natural exclamation from the smitten clown, who thinks that death alone can relieve him.

23. *Thomas Watson* appears to have been an unusually accomplished man. He was a competent scholar, translating much from Latin and from contemporary Italian and French poets, having been associated with Dr. Byrd in the publication of the earliest madrigals in English. His own poetry is in Latin and English ; and his association was chiefly with the court circles of Sidney and Oxford, and the poets Spenser, Lyly, and Peele. He "was highly valued among ingenious men," says Anthony à Wood, but was all but lost to our literature until Professor Arber restored "his name in golden letters to the great Bead-Roll of the acknowledged Poets of Great Britain." (*Arber's Reprints, Watson*, p. 3.) It may be surmised that others besides his contemporaries have overestimated Watson.

23 1. *If Jove himself.* This poem was subsequently reprinted with a few verbal changes in *England's Helicon*, and there entitled *The Shepherd's Resolution in Love.*

23 4. *Wight.* Being, mortal. Cf. 177 3.

23 18. *Ne.* Cf. 14 9.

23 1. *Resolved to dust.* Each of the poems of Watson's *Passionate Century* is preceded by a brief explanation, after the manner of E. K.'s *Glosse* upon the *Shepherds' Calendar*. The last twenty sonnets, so-called, are written under the motto, "My Love is Past," and the prefatory note to this one is as follows : —

"The author faineth here, that Love, essaying with his brand to fire the heart of some lady, on whom it would not work, immediately, to try whether the old virtue of it were extinguished or no, applied it unto his own breast, and thereby foolishly consumed himself. This invention hath some relation unto the *Epitaph of Love*, written by M. Girolimo Parabosco : —

In cenere giace qui sepolto Amore,
Colpa di quella, che morir mi face, etc."

Watson is at much pains that the reader may believe his "passions" "but supposed"; and this, with his learned gloss, has not a little destroyed their effect.

23 4. *Doubting.* Fearing lest, being in doubt whether.

23 5. *His.* Here the neuter form of the possessive, since superseded by *its.* See *Sh. Gram.*, § 228.

23 5. *Gan.* Cf. 147 2, 160 77.

24 7. *In sooth, no force.* No matter for that, indeed. *Lust.* Desire, wish.

24 14. *Illing.* Harming, injuring. Used also by Sylvester in his translation of Du Bartas.

24 17. *Here lieth Love*, etc. Note the inversion, an affectation of classic construction.

24. *A Handful of Pleasant Delights.* This collection, "a song book rather than a book of poetry," is supposed to have appeared first as early as 1566, having been licensed in 1561. No ed. earlier than that of 1584 is extant, however. This has been reprinted by the Spenser Society, 1871, and by Mr. Arber in his *English Scholar's Library*, No. 3, 1878. Of Clement Robinson nothing is known; he may have been the author of some of the selections as well as the editor, as in the case of Grimald. As to the poem of the text, the Stationers' Register exhibits that a ballad, entitled *A fayne would I have a godly thing to show unto my ladye*, was registered July 22, 1566. This may have been an earlier form of our selection, or the latter may be a parody. I make no apology for including these verses under the circumstances.

24 7. *Make adventure* was the term applied to the undertaking of any business venture or speculation; whence *adventurer* was applied to merchants of importance, or capitalists, as we should term them.

24 12. *Lacks.* Cf. 25 26.

25 16. *Gazes be not geason.* It is not uncommon to see people looking about. *Geason.* Scarce, unusual.

25 18. *Still.* Always. Cf. 14 9.

25 26. *Silk wives.* The original reads *silkye wiues.*

25 26. *What lack ye?* The familiar cry of tradesmen to passers by.

25 30. *Cheap.* Cheapside; also a general term for any market, or marketplace. Cf. Eastcheap.

25 32. *On a heap.* See *Sh. Gram.*, § 180.

25 35. *Gravers of the golden shows.* Goldsmiths, whose shops were amongst the richest and most conspicuous.

25 37. *Sempsters that sews.* The third person plural of the verb in *-s* is common in Elizabethan English. It is perhaps here intentionally colloquial. See *Sh. Gram.*, § 333, and cf. 65 36, 125 1 and 132 1.

25 3s. *Let me.* Hinder me, prevent me.

25 42. *Than.* Then. Cf. 10 22.

26 46. *Willing.* Will, intent.

26. *Robert Greene.* The author of *A Groatsworth of Wit* is ⬦
assuredly too well known to require here any repetition of the sad
details of youth and talents thrown away. Whoever would know this
remarkable career should not fail to consult Professor Storojenko's
study and Professor Brown's *An Early Rival of Shakespeare,* both
reprinted, the latter in part, by Dr. Grosart. The text is from the
Huth Library, Greene.

26. *Doralicia's Ditty.* Cf. a superficial resemblance, in the earlier
parts, between this poem and a poem signed " M. T." in *The Paradise
of Dainty Devises,* beginning : —

> The sturdy rock for all his strength,
> By raging seas is rent in twain ;
> The marble stone is pierced, at length,
> With little drops of drizzling rain.

26 9. *Alate.* The origin of these forms in a preposition, *on,* is
noticed by Ben Jonson in his Grammar. "*A* hath also the force of
governing before a noun." (Ed. Cunningham, III, 450.)

26 13. *Hap.* Outcome, fulfilment ; more usually *fortune, lot,* 122 13.

27. *Lament. Verses of Praise and Joy upon Her Majesty's preserva-
tion, whereunto is annexed Tychborne's Lamentation written in the Tower
with his own hand and an answer to the same.* 1586. So runs the title
of the tract in which this poem first occurred (*Collectanea Anglo-Poetica
X,* 337). It was frequently republished in the song-books of the day,
and also appears in *Reliquiae Wottonianae.* Tychborne, a young man
of good family, was one of Babington's fellow-conspirators against the
life of Elizabeth. He was executed in 1586.

27. *Nicholas Breton* seems to have been the earliest of that class of
Elizabethan writers somewhat vaguely called the pamphleteers; writing
incessantly and unequally verse, prose, it mattered little what ; frequently in debt and trouble ; facile, ready, ever fertile. It is surprising
what really good work was sometimes done under such conditions.
Even now, far from all the works of Breton have been collected. His
very popularity, which was great amongst his contemporaries, has contributed to make his works of great scarcity. There is a naturalness,
an easy flow, and gaiety, a tenderness and purity about Breton that
ought to restore him to fame. For an interesting account of him, see
Mr. Bullen's *Introduction* to his *Lyrics from Elizabethan Romances,* p.
xix sqq., also Dr. Grosart's *Memorial Introduction, Breton.*

27. *Olden Love-Making.* First reprinted by Dr. Grosart (*Chertsey Worthies' Library, Breton, Daffodils and Primroses,* p. 19) from a MS. in the possession of F. W. Cosens, Esq., of London. The MS. also contains poems on the death of Sidney, and may therefore be assigned to a date soon after 1586. Mr. Bullen, who quotes this poem in the *Introduction* to his *Lyrics from Elizabethan Romances,* remarks upon it as follows: "There can be no harm in quoting here one little poem, a description of love-making in the happy days of pastoral simplicity, when girls did not look for costly presents (rings, chains, etc.) from their lovers, but were content with a row of pins or an empty purse, — the days when truth was on every shepherd's tongue and maids had not learned to dissemble. Whether there ever was such a time, since our first parents were driven out of Paradise, we need not stop to enquire. The old poets loved to talk about it."

28 19. *Sunny beam.* Text apparently corrupt.

29. *Rosalind's Madrigal.* "A charming picture in the purest style of the late Italian Renaissance," says Mr. Palgrave. For the form of the Madrigal, see *Introduction,* p. liv.

29 5–8. Notice the rhetorical force of the repeated rime, and cf. Lodge's success in the same device, p. 60.

29 9. *Wanton.* Cf. 22 6.

29 15. *If so.* If.

30 33. *Bower.* A private chamber, boudoir.

30 34. *I like of thee.* I am pleased with thee. Cf. "You have been bolder in my house Than I could well like of." Middleton, *A Chaste Maid in Cheapside,* v. 2.

30 36. *Play thee.* Cf. *Sh. Gram.,* § 296.

30 1. *Rosalind's Description.* "Readers who have visited Italy," says Mr. Palgrave, "will be reminded of more than one picture by this gorgeous Vision of Beauty, equally sublime and pure in its Paradisaical naturalness. Lodge wrote it on a voyage to 'the Islands of Terceras and the Canaries'; and he seems to have caught, in those southern seas, no small portion of the qualities which marked the almost contemporary Art of Venice, — the glory and the glow of Veronese, or Titian, or Tintoret, when he most resembles Titian, and all but surpasses him." (*Golden Treasury of English Lyrics,* p. 351.)

30 1–3. *Like to the clear . . . is her hair. The clear* (clearness) *in highest sphere* is the empyrean or sphere of pure fire, which was outermost and next to the *primum mobile* in the old cosmography, not the crystalline sphere as explained by Mr. Palgrave. The passage then means: Her hair is of the selfsame color as the brightness (the clear)

of the empyrean. The difficulty of the passage consists in the tautology, or possibly the double construction, involved in saying *like to* and *of selfsame*, of the same color like to the empyreal brightness. I am indebted to Professor Kittredge for this note.

30 7. *Refining heaven by every wink.* Making heaven seem more beautiful whenever she opens her eyes or gives a glance, because heaven is bright and blue, like them.

30 8. *Whenas.* When. Cf. 59 17, 88 12, 110 19.

30 13. *Shroud.* Here used for any covering.

30 18. *Within which bounds she balm encloses.* Note the alliteration of this line.

31 37. *In her sight. In*, or as we should say *at* or *by* the sight of her, *i.e.*, when they behold her perfections.

31 41. *Nymphs.* Marriageable girls.

31 43. *For her fair there is fairer none.* Compared with her beauty there is none more beautiful. The use of an adjective, *fair*, where we should employ a noun is a familiar Elizabethan idiom. Cf. *clear* above, 30 1. Mr. Palgrave prefers to read : *"for a fair there's fairer none:* If you desire a beauty, there is none more beautiful than Rosaline."

31 1. *Down a down.* Cf. the following close imitation of the metre and spirit of this poem, sometimes attributed to Raleigh (Oxford ed. of his works, VIII, 705) : —

> Hey down a down did Dian sing
> Amongst her virgins sitting,
> Than love there is no vainer thing,
> For maidens most unfitting
> And so think I with a down, down, derry, etc.

The metrical parallel continues throughout the poem.

32 7-10. *When Love was first begot*, etc. Thus paraphrased : "When Love was first begotten, and, by the will of the Creator, was given to mankind as a part of his earthly lot in order to fill up the measure of his joy in life," then, *devoid of all deceit*, etc.

32 13. *Conceit.* Thought, idea, conception. Cf. 88 7.

32 29. *False semblance.* Hyprocrisy. One of the allegorical personages made famous by the *Roman de la Rose.*

32 33. *Makes.* I read *makes* with Bullen for *made* of the original ed.

32 35. *Make.* Mate. Cf. 9 34.

33 1. *If women could be fair.* This poem is ascribed to Oxford in Rawl. MS. 85, fol. 16; it exists in various versions. I have followed the text of Dr. Grosart in his *Fuller Worthies' Miscellanies*, IV, with

the one or two variations noted from the less vigorous version contained in Byrd's *Psalms, Sonnets and Songs.*

33 1. *Fond.* Foolish. Cf. 8 4.

33 2. *Still.* Ever. Cf. 14 9.

33 6. *Laugh.* For *muse,* according to the version of Byrd.

33 9. *Haggards.* Wild or untrained hawks.

33 13. *Our sport.* For *disport.* I read with Byrd's version.

33 15. *Lure.* An artificial or other decoy used to recall the hawk to its perch on the fist. Cf. 70 13.

34 1. *Fair is my love.* Cf. with the first stanza a madrigal in Morley's *First Book of Madrigals,* 1594 : —

> April is in my mistress' face,
> And July in her eyes hath place ;
> Within her bosom is September,
> But in her heart a cold December.

Oliphant (*Musa Madrigalesca,* p. 74) surmises that both are translations from a foreign original.

34 17, 18. *My harvest in the grass bears grain* and *The rock will wear,* etc., are proverbs. With the latter cf. the familiar *Gutta cavat lapidem non vi sed saepe cadendo* and 26 1–2.

34 1. *Ah, were she pitiful.* This poem is found on the back of the title of some of the latest eds. of *Pandosto.* Dyce prints it from the ed. of 1694 (*Greene and Peele,* p. 294). Collier conjectures that it may have been taken from the earliest, now non-extant, ed. of *Pandosto.* There is nothing, however, to prove the existence of any ed. earlier than that of 1588. "The lines are written by Dorastus in praise of Faunia ; the characters of which correspond to Florizel and Perdita " in Shakespeare's *Winter's Tale.*

35 8. *There is.* These words are supplied by Dyce.

35 9. *So as.* In modern English *such as.* See *Sh. Gram.,* § 145.

35 12. *Cankered bower.* The *canker* is the dog-rose. Cf. *1 Hen. IV,* i, 3, 176: "To put down Richard, that sweet lovely rose, and plant this thorn, this canker, Bolingbroke." *Bower* is conjectured for *flower,* which repeats the rime above. (*The Gentleman's Magazine,* March, 1833, p. 218.)

35 1. *Some say Love.* Note in this poem Greene's skillful handling of the repeated words, and compare this with the management of the refrain of *Doron's Description of Samela,* p. 37. Greene's phrasing too in these short measures is remarkable for its freedom and success.

36 3. *Sower.* Sour.

36 1. *Wanton.* Frolicsome creature. Used here as at 29 9 as a term of endearment. Cf. *wag* below, *v.* 3 and a modern use of the words *rogue, rascal,* etc.

36 7. *I was woe.* This idiom for the earlier *woe is (to) me* is of very early origin, well before Chaucer. As the sense of the inflection was weakened, *woe* came to be considered as a predicate. Cf. *Sh. Gram.,* § 230.

37 13. *Stint.* Stop, cease.

37 15. *By course.* In a stream. Cf. "The people . . . by numbers swarm to us." *3 Hen. VI,* iv, 2, 2, and *Sh. Gram.,* § 145.

37 28. *Bliss.* Bless, with which it was early confused. Cf. the Middle English verbs, *blissen, blissien, blissen,* and 180 11.

37 1. *Weed.* A garment of any kind.

37 5. *Arethusa Fount.* This is the emendation of Walker; the original edd. read *Arethusa faint.*

38 7. *Morning-grey.* Cf. 13 5.

38 8. *Glister.* Glitter, glow. Cf. 76 4.

38 11. *Whenas.* When. Cf. 30 8.

38 11. *Brightness . . . move.* Cf. 45 12. A misagreement far less frequent than the plural subject followed by a verb in *-s,* for which cf. 25 37.

38 19. *Bravest.* Gayest, most beautiful.

38 19-21. *Venus . . . Juno . . . Pallas.* A revision of the judgment of Paris, by which his award was taken from the fortunate goddess and bestowed upon the adored one, was a frequent device of Elizabethan poetical flattery. Peele's *Arraignment of Paris* is a dramatic amplification of it, and it was used still earlier, in 1577, by Gascoigne in a satirical poem entitled *The Grief of Joy.* In each of these cases it was the peerless perfections of "the nymph Eliza" which demanded this reversal of the decrees of the gods.

38 20. *Show.* Pomp, august appearance, state.

38 22. *Wit.* Cf. 13 10.

38 10. *Buxom.* Here in much its modern meaning. Cf. Bardolph's *buxom valor,* which has been variously explained as 'obedient' and 'sturdy.' *Hen. V,* iii, 6, 28.

39 1. *Philon, the Shepherd, his Song.* The authorship of this beautiful song is absolutely unknown; it was reprinted in *England's Helicon.* Dr. Byrd "was senior chorister of St. Paul's in 1554; he is conjectured to have been born in 1538. From 1563 to 1569 he was organist of Lincoln Cathedral. He and Tallis were granted a patent, which must have proved fairly lucrative, for the printing of music and

the vending of music-paper. In later life he appears to have become a convert to Romanism." He died in 1623. (Oliphant.)

40 21. *Was leapt.* *To be* for *to have* is still in use with certain verbs of motion. In Elizabethan English this use was more general. See *Sh. Gram.*, § 295.

41 4. *Stains all faces, i.e.*, by comparison ; cf. 12 10.

41 7. *Touched does melt.* Cf. 35 6.

41 11. *Fond.* Cf. 8 4, 19 5.

41 3. *As brightly shine, Aurora's face*, etc. In modern idiom *so brightly shine that Aurora's face.*

41 12. *Bed.* Couch of state.

42 12. *Neat.* Spruce, finical in dress. Cf. " Still to be *neat*," 151 1.

42 1. *Polyhymnia, a Description of a Triumph at Tilt* was reprinted by Dyce from a copy in the Library of the University of Edinburgh presented by William Drummond (Dyce's ed. of *Peele*, p. 565). I quote the following from Oliphant's condensation of Sir W. Segar's account of *Honors, Military and Civil*, 1602. (Nichol's *Progresses of Queen Elizabeth*, III, 60 ; Oliphant, *Mus. Madr.*, p. 157.) " Certain yearly Triumphs were solemnized in memory of the applause of Her Majesty's subjects at the day of her most happy accession to the crown of England, which triumphs were first begun and occasioned by the right virtuous and honorable Sir Henry Lea, master of Her Highness' armory ; who of his great zeal and desire to eternize the glory of her Majesty's court in the beginning of her reign, voluntarily vowed, — unless infirmity, age or other accident did impeach him, — during his life to present himself at the tilt, armed, the day aforesaid, yearly ; there to perform in honor of her sacred Majesty the promise he formerly made. The worthy knight, however, feeling himself at length overtaken with old age, and being desirous of resigning his championship, did on the 17th of Nov. 1590, present himself, together with the Earl of Cumberland unto her Highness under her gallery window in the Tilt yard at Westminster, where at that time her Majesty did sit, accompanied . . . by many ladies and the chiefest nobility. Her majesty beholding these armed knights coming towards her, did suddenly hear a music so sweet and secret, as everyone thereat greatly marvelled. The music aforsaid was accompanied with these verses, pronounced and sung by Mr. Hale, her Majesty's servant, a gentleman in that art excellent. . . . After other ceremonies Sir Henry Lea disarmed himself, and kneeling upon his knees presented the Earl of Cumberland ; humbly beseeching that she would receive him for her knight, to continue the yearly exercise aforesaid. Her Majesty having accepted the offer, this aged knight armed

the earl, and mounted him upon his horse. That being done, he put upon his own person a side-coat of black velvet and covered his head in lieu of an helmet with a button-cap of the country fashion." The assignment of the song to Essex in a *Masque at Greenwich* (Arber's *English Garner,* IV, 45) is clearly wrong. The poem is undoubtedly Peele's. It was reprinted by Dowland in 1597.

43 7. *His helmet now shall make a hive for bees.* Cf. Geoffrey Whitney's *Choice of Emblems,* 1586 : —

> The helmet strong that did his head defend,
> Behold for hive of bees in quiet serve, etc. (Bullen.)

Thackeray has applied these lines most fittingly to Colonel Newcome's retirement as a pensioner. (*The Newcomes,* chap. 76.)

43 10. *Prayers.* Dissyllabic here, as frequently. Cf. 21 13.

43 18. *Beadsman.* Here one who prays for another, rather than one who is supported upon alms.

43. I have followed Dyce in general as to the dates of Shakespeare's plays.

43 1. *Winter.* Regarding the concluding song of this play as made up, as it really is, of two companion pieces, the one on Spring, the other on Winter, I do not depart from my plan of including only entire poems in printing only the latter.

43 9. *Keel the pot.* Cool by ladling to prevent boiling over. (Malone.)

43 11. *Saw.* A story, long tale, here; rather than a maxim as in " wise *saws* and modern instances."

44 14. *Crabs.* Wild apples.

44. *Thomas Dekker.* The known events in the life of Dekker exhibit little more than successive debt, imprisonment, and advances from Henslowe on promised work. Well may Mr. Fleay exclaim in his *Biographical Chronicle* of Dekker's : "the saddest story in all this book." Mr. Fleay — to whom all students of our dramatic literature owe a great debt, vexatious as his contradictions are at times — assigns the writing of the earliest version of *Fortunatus,* in which he includes the portions containing the lyrics of the text (*i.e.,* Act i, Sc. 1–6), to 1590, by reason of the many allusions to Lyly and his imitators. The play was revived in 1596, again in 1599, and printed in 1600.

44 2. *Alack.* Sometimes explained as a by-form of *alas;* more probably *ah !* + *lack,* failure.

45. *The Shepherd's Wife's Song.* Professor Brown of Canterbury College, Christ Church, New Zealand, uses these words of the "lyrical cry" of Robert Greene: "[Here was a man], wild with the feverish

life of an actor, yet penning songs that breathe in every line of rest, like
that beautiful one . . . beginning : 'Sweet are the thoughts that savor
of content ' (see p. 47), . . . oblivious to the graces of his most virtuous
wife, for the blandishments of 'a sorry ragged quean,' and yet capable
of uttering the most lyrical eulogy of rustic married life, *The Shepherd's
Wife's Song."* (*An Early Rival of Shakespeare*, Grosart's *Greene*,
I, xlix.)

46 28. *Affects.* Affections, feelings. Cf. " I hope I shall not need
to urge the sacred purity of our *affects."* *The Case is Altered*, i, 3, 15.

46 36. *Spill.* Spoil, destroy. Cf. 5 8.

46 37. *Snort their fill.* It is probable that this expression conveyed
no objectionable meaning to Elizabethan readers. Cf. 66 46, 77 55.

46 42. *Tide or sithe.* Both of these words here signify time. *Tide* was
commonly substituted by the Puritans for *mass*, in such words as Chris-
tide ; cf. 81 177. *Sithe* was originally a journey, hence a time, occasion.

47. *Content.* Cf. with this poem Barnes' beautiful sonnet, p. 56, and
Dekker's song, p. 93.

47 9. *Grees.* Agrees.

47 10. *Consort.* Agreement in the musical sense of producing
harmony. *Mean.* The middle part in three-part music ; sometimes
alto, sometimes *tenor*. Here with a play on the ordinary sense (*aurea
mediocritas*).

47 10. *Mirth and modest fare.* With Linton I read *modest* for
music's fare, which is unintelligible, and a misprint probably due to the
word *music* immediately above.

47. This *Honorable Entertainment* was "given to the Queen's
Majesty in Progress at Elvetham in Hampshire, by the Right Honorable
the Earl of Hertford." The song is therein entitled *The Ploughman's
Song;* I have preferred the title in *England's Helicon*.

47 3. *With a troop*, etc. I follow the reading of Dr. Grosart in this
and the following three lines ; this he derives from the *Cosens MS.*

47 4. *Forth the wood.* *Forth* is here a preposition. Cf. "*forth* thy
father's house," *i.e.*, out of the house. *M. N. D.*, i, 1, 162.

48 23. *Abuse.* Deceive, beguile.

48. *Samuel Daniel* enjoyed a great reputation in his day, especially
at Court, where as a member of the Queen's (*i.e.*, Anne, the Queen of
James I) household, he held various offices, for a time rivaling Jonson
as court writer of Masques. Daniel attempted tragedy in the style of
Seneca. and the pastoral drama in imitation of Guarini, as well as narrative and lyric verse, whilst his answer to Campion's attack on English
rime exhibits sensible ideas and a graceful prose style.

48 1. *Restore thy tresses.* This sonnet was one of twenty-seven sonnets of Daniel, which were published, without his consent and during
his absence abroad, by Thomas Nashe with *Sonnets after Astrophel.* I
have followed Daniel's own later revision, that of 1623, as in Dr.
Grosart's ed.   Jonson, who regarded Daniel with jealousy from his
preferment at Court, ridicules this sonnet in *Cynthia's Revels*, v, 4, thus:
" You that tell your mistress her beauty is all composed of thefts ; her
hair stole from Apollo's goldy locks ; her white and red, lilies and
roses stolen out of Paradise ; her eyes two stars plucked out of the
skies ; her nose the gnomon of Love's dial, that tells you how the clock
of your heart goes." etc.

48 4. *Remove.* Send back.

48 9. *Her.* Here dative. Cf. *Sh. Gram.*, § 220.

49. *Delia.* There were three early editions of *Delia*, two in 1592
and one in 1594, all under the author's supervision.   Daniel, like Drayton, was much given to revising his works, not always for the best.
The position of Daniel as a sonneteer is interesting, as he was the first
to follow the work of Sidney.   See on this subject especially an interesting article entitled : *Wie weit geht die Abhängigkeit Shakespeare's von
Daniel als Lyriker?* by Dr. Hermann Isaac, *Sh. Jahrbuch*, XVII, 165.

49 14. *Whilst that.*   Note the addition of the conjunctional affix,
that. Sh. Gram., § 287.

49 2. *Refresh.* Refreshing.   Other cases of nouns formed from verbs
without suffix are *flourish*, 49 5, 51 21, 85 9 ; *shine*, 58 6 ; *remove*, 70 4.

49 3. *But till.* Only until.

49 5. *Flourish.* Blossom, perfect growth.   A favorite word with
Daniel.   Cf. 51 21 ; used also by *Shakespeare*, 85 9.

50 11. *And that in beauty.*   The ed. of 1594 exhibits this reading :

> When time has made a passport of thy fears,
> Dated in age, the kalends of our death,
> But ah ! no more ! this hath been often told,
> And women grieve to think they must grow old.

50. *Care-charmer Sleep.*   This is one of a series of "tournament
sonnets," as Mr. Saintsbury aptly calls them, sonnets written on a theme
already practiced, and in emulation of former achievements.   Professor
Cook of Yale has pointed out that this sonnet of Daniel's is second in
a series celebrating the same subject, beginning with Sidney's sonnet,
p. 13, and going through Southwell, Griffin, Drummond, and Fletcher,
to 1619.   He has also shown that the sources of all are ultimately to
be found in Seneca, Ovid, and the so-called Orphic Hymn to Sleep ; and

further, in Spenser, Ariosto, Politian, and Chaucer. See *Mod. Lang. Notes*, IV, 8, 229; and V, 1, 11. See also a note in Main's *English Sonnets*, p. 253.

50 6. *Shipwrack.* The usual form. Cf. 110 22.

50 6. *Ill-adventred.* Ill-adventured.

50. *An Ode.* This poem appeared in the first authorized ed. of *Delia*, 1592.

50 3. *Reports.* Answers or echoes back to.

51 11. *Bereaven.* Taken away by violence, a by-form of bereaved formed on the analogy of the strong verbs.

Lowell instances " well-languaged Daniel," as he was called by William Browne, to show "that the artistic value of choice and noble diction was quite as well understood in his day as in ours." He adds of Daniel : " His poetic style is mainly as modern as that of Tennyson." *Shakespeare Once More, Prose Works*, III, 11, and *ibid.*, IV, 280.

51. *Thomas Nashe.* To those who know Thomas Nashe only as a not over successful playwright, the master of vigorous contemporary colloquial English, the rough and ready controversialist, gifted with inexhaustible Rabelaisian humor and a terrible mastery of the language of Billingsgate, it may be a surprise to find him likewise a sweet and fervent lyrist.

51 3. *Less than in a day.* In less than a day.

51 6. *Leav'st to appear.* Ceasest to appear.

52 8. *Dispersed.* Scattered.

52 5. *The palm.* Flowers and branches in general. It was a common practice of the day so to decorate houses.

52 2. *Fond.* Foolish. Cf. 9 33. *Toys.* Trifles. Cf. 4 36.

52 6. *Lord have mercy on us.* Not an unusual refrain in the songs of the day. See Chappell, *Early Engl. Popular Music*, I, 74. Professor Kittredge informs me that "this inscription, with a cross, was officially put on the doors of infected houses"; and refers me to R. West's poem *To the pious memory of my dear Brother-in-law, Mr. Thomas Randolph :* " The titles of their satires fright some more than *Lord have mercy* writ upon a door."

53 25. *Earth holds ope her gate.* The grave.

53 26. *The bells.* Funeral bells, perhaps also those rung by the attendants of the dead-cart, calling on all to bring out their dead.

52 31–33. *Hell's executioner*, the plague; *vain art*, physic or medicine.

52 32. *For to hear.* The double preposition before the infinitive, now a vulgarism, was good usage in Nashe's day, and before and after. as in Herrick. See *Sh. Gram.*, § 152.

53 39. *Earth but a player's stage.* Cf. 121 12. Also the familiar passage of *As You Like It*, ii, 7, 139; Chapman's *Bussy D'Ambois*, i, 1; Jonson's *The New Inn*, i, 1; and verses prefixed to Heywood's *Apology for Actors.*

I quote the following words of Mr. Bullen on these poems of Nashe: "The songs of *Summer's Last Will and Testament* are of a sombre turn. We have, it is true, the delicious verses in praise of Spring. . . . But when the play was produced it was sickly autumn and the plague was stalking through the land.

> 'Short days, sharp days, long nights come on apace:
> Ah, who shall hide us from the winter's face?
> Cold doth increase, the sickness will not cease,
> And here we lie, God knows, with little ease.'

Very vividly does Nashe depict the feeling of forlorn hopelessness caused by the dolorous advent of the dreaded pestilence. His address to the fading summer, 'Go not yet hence, bright soul of the sad year,' is no empty rhetorical appeal, but a solemn supplication; and those pathetic stanzas, 'Adieu, farewell earth's bliss,' must have had strange significance at a time when on every side the death bells were tolling." (*Introd., Lyrics from Elizabethan Dramatists*, p. ix.)

54 5. *Gan.* This tense of the verb *gin* was commonly employed with an infinitive in Middle English as equal to *did.* Cf. 23 5.

54 12. *Perfit.* Perfect. An older form. See below, v. 16.

54 20. *Grees.* Agrees.

54 21. *Folded.* Interlocked.

55 1. *The Solitary Shepherd's Song.* "In imitation of Martelli, having the right nature of an Italian melancholy," are Lodge's own prefatory words. (*Hunterian Club* ed. of *Margarite*, p. 78.) For another of Lodge's imitations, see 4 1. The story, *A Margarite of America*, was written while Lodge was with Cavendish in the Straits of Magellan, and may possibly be esteemed by those who consider the accidental place of writing, rather than language and nationality, as the criterion of the literature of a country, the earliest specimen of 'American Literature.'

55 12. *Whenas.* When. Cf. 30 8.

56. *Barnabe Barnes*, was the son of a bishop, an Oxford man, and much traveled abroad. As the friend of Gabriel Harvey, he was traduced by Thomas Nashe. He is widely known for his erotic sequence of sonnets and other Italian forms, *Parthenophil and Parthenope.* Professor Dowden rates him above Watson: *The Academy*, Sept. 2, 1876.

56 3. *Which.* Note the use of *which* here and in verses 6 and 12 for the modern *who*. Cf. 81 3 and *Sh. Gram.*, § 265.

57. *Come live with me.* Marlowe was dead before Lyly's practice of writing original songs for dramas became popular. Considering his marvelous passion and the surpassing lyrical excellence of certain passages of his plays, it is surprising that Marlowe should have left behind him no more than this solitary specimen of his mastery over the shorter lyric. I have given the version of *England's Helicon ;* in *The Passionate Pilgrim* the fourth and sixth stanzas do not appear, nor is the author's name given. In the second ed. of Walton's *Complete Angler*, 1653, the following stanza is inserted before the last : —

> Thy silver dishes for thy meat,
> As precious as the gods do eat,
> Shall on an ivory table be
> Prepared each day for thee and me.

This poem enjoyed great popularity and inspired a number of imitations and answers. Cf. 'If all the world and love were young,' attributed to Sir Walter Raleigh, and 'Come live with me and be my dear,' both published in *England's Helicon ;* Donne's *The Bait ;* and Herrick's ' Live love with me and thou shalt' see.' I quote the first of these : —

THE NYMPH'S REPLY TO THE SHEPHERD.

> If all the world and love were young,
> And truth in every shepherd's tongue,
> These pretty pleasures might me move
> To live with thee and be thy love.
>
> Time drives the flocks from field to fold,
> When rivers rage and rocks grow cold ;
> And Philomel becometh dumb ;
> The rest complains of cares to come.
>
> The flowers do fade, and wanton fields
> To wayward winter reckoning yields ;
> A honey tongue, a heart of gall
> Is fancy's spring, but sorrow's fall.
>
> Thy gowns, thy shoes, thy beds of roses,
> Thy cap, thy kirtle, and thy posies
> Soon break, soon wither, soon forgotten,
> In folly ripe, in reason rotten.

Thy belt of straw and ivy-buds,
Thy coral clasps and amber studs,
All these in me no means can move
To come to thee and be thy love.

But could youth last, and love still breed.
Had joys no date, nor age no need,
Then these delights my mind might move
To live with thee and be thy love.

58. *Sonnets.* That two poems of such different forms and so far removed from the quatorzain should be called sonnets, is an illustration of the looseness with which that term was often employed. The title of the first is that given in Ward's *English Poets.*

58 1. *Gilds.* The original reads *guides*, an evident misprint, gui[l]des. This is Bullen's emendation.

58 5. *Bower.* Cf. 30 33, and also 21 13 note.

58 10. *Firm.* Make firm, strengthen. Almost any noun could be converted into a verb in Elizabethan English without the addition of a suffix. Cf. *deads*, 58 10, *spark*, 64 4, *ungod*, 104 20, *length*, 154 10. See *Sh. Gram.*, § 290.

59. *To Phyllis.* This poem has been assigned to Sir Edward Dyer with a steady perversity which is surprising. Ward prints it as Dyer's, *Engl. Poets*, 1, 378, and Mr. Andrew Lang more recently says : " The young English Muse is like Sir Edward Dyer's *Phyllis, the Fair Shepherdess*," quoting the first four lines of this poem immediately after. (*Introduction to Elizabethan Songs in Honor of Love and Beauty*, 1893, p. xxx.) The mistake has arisen from the fact that when this poem was reprinted in *England's Helicon*, seven years after its appearance in *Phyllis honored with Pastoral Sonnets*, the initials "S. E. D." were ignorantly subscribed to it. The poem is in the best style of Lodge, and it may be suspected that not a little of the reputation of Sir Edward has depended upon this mistake.

59 4. *For to.* Cf. 53 32.

59 5. *Prime-feathered.* Perhaps blossoming early in the spring.

59 11. *Desart.* A common Elizabethan form. Cf. 60 15, 66 9.

59 17. *Whenas.* Cf. 88 12, 110 19.

59 18. *Deads one.* Not an unusual verb in this age ; cf. 58 10 and Chapman, *Ody.* xviii : " With many an ill hath numbed and *deaded* me."

59 19. *Nill.* Ne will, will not. " Lodge's love poems have an exquisite delicacy and grace : they breathe a tenderer and truer passion than we find in any of his contemporaries. His sonnets are loose and straggling, lighter and less compactly built than Constable's or Daniel's;

but they have a wonderful charm of sweet fancy and unaffected tenderness. . . . There is a seeming artlessness in Lodge's sonnets, a winning directness, that constitutes a great part of their charm. They seem to be uttered through a clear and pure medium, straight from the heart itself." William Minto, *Characteristics of English Poets*, p. 259.

60. *The Phœnix' Nest* was edited by one 'R. S. of the Inner Temple,' whose identity seems undiscoverable. Mr. Bullen informs us that many of the best poems of this collection were republished in *England's Helicon*.

60 1. *Accurst be Love.* Notice the effect of the repeated rimes, an effect dependent upon the fact that not one of them is forced. Cf. *Now what is Love*, on the next page, where the device is less successful because more forced and longer sustained. The same device, used for musical effect rather than for emphasis, will be found in Nashe's *Spring*, above, p. 52.

61. *Now what is Love.* As *The Phœnix' Nest* is inaccessible to me except in selection, I have been compelled to follow Mr. Bullen in the following note : "This poem originally appeared in *The Phœnix' Nest*, 1593 ; it is also printed (in form of a dialogue) in *England's Helicon*, 1600, and Davison's *Poetical Rhapsody*, 1602. It is ascribed to Raleigh in a MS. list of Davison's." (*Lyrics from Elizabethan Song Books*, p. 191 f.) Mr. Bullen likewise refers to Hannah's ed. of Raleigh. I can find this poem in neither Mr. Bullen's ed. of *England's Helicon*, nor in Nicolas' ed. of the *Rhapsody*, moreover neither the older nor the newer ed. of Hannah's *Raleigh* mentions it so far as I can discover. The poem does occur in Robert Jones' *Second Book*, 1601 (see Bullen, *ibid.*, p. 89), and also in Heywood's *Rape of Lucrece*, 1609. I notice that Mr. Gosse appears recently to have accepted it as Heywood's. (*The Jacobean Poets*, p. 121.) This seems highly improbable. In the absence of proofs I have no opinion to offer. The somewhat antiquated language, especially the *sauncing bell*, seems to suggest an early date, however.

61 4. *Sauncing bell.* Saints'-bell ; the little bell that called to prayers. (Bullen.)

61 13. *Sain.* Sayen. Cf. 20 10, 51 11 ; an archaic form at this date, common in the old ballads ; *e.g.*, *The Battle of Otterburn*, stanza 46. Here falsely used as an imperative. Cf. v. 18 below where the use as an infinitive is correct.

62 26. *Go.* Walk ; cf. 87 11.

62 29. *Proves.* This verb was frequently employed intransitively. See *Sh. Gram.*, § 293.

62 30. *Trow.* Believe, think.

62. *Amoretti.* Dr. Grosart, whose text and whose assignment of the date I follow, writes thus : "Always tender and chivalrous, almost always beautiful, here and there perhaps on a level with Petrarch's ordinary vein, — these sonnets leave upon the mind a more thoroughly pleasing picture of the poet himself than he gives elsewhere. . . . The pastoral disguise is less marked ; and if the gracious and fantastic con-ventionalities of the love-sonnet, which he shares with a thousand other writers, throw a veil which blunts the outline of natural expression, yet the note of genuine feeling, — hardly, perhaps, rising to the authentic tone of absolute passion, — is audible throughout." (See Dr. Grosart's *Spenser*, IV, lxxxvii.)

62 6-8. *She may entangle,* etc. Cf. Bateson's *Song* on p. 190.

62 13. *Fondness.* Cf. 8 4.

63 7. *Rare.* Rarified.

63 10. *Mote.* Must, generally employed in the subjunctive.

63 12. *Eke.* Also, likewise.

63 13. *Sith.* Since ; a form often employed by Spenser; see also Drummond's frequent use of it, 179 11, 12 ; 180 2, 7 ; and 181 5; and Jonson, 127 7.

63 9. *Spill.* Destroy. Cf. 5 8.

63 12. *Salve.* Cure, apply a remedy to.

63 14. *Bower.* Cf. 30 33 and 58 10.

64 1. *Hairs.* The original eds. read *heares,* which I have modern-ized for the sake of intelligibility.

64 4. *Does spark.* Sparkle. Cf. 58 10, 154 18.

64 10. *The gate with pearls.* Cf. Gascoigne's use of the same familiar image: "two rocks, bedecked with pearls of price." 1 8.

64 12. *Sprite.* Cf. 11 13.

64. *The Arbor of Amorous Devises: wherein young gentlemen may read many pleasant fancies and fine devices, and thereon meditate divers sweet conceits to court the love of fair ladies and gentlewomen, 1597,* so runs Breton's title. The title was entered in the Stationers' Register, *delights* standing for *devices,* in Jan. 1593-94. But one copy of this work is extant.

64 3. *Doubt.* Fear. *Dole.* Misfortune.

64 4. *Unhappy chief.* Unfortunate above all. *Chief* = chiefly.

64 5. *Lap.* Wrap.

64 9. *Wit.* Cf. 13 10.

64 12. Note the personal use of the verb *ail.*

65 13. *Wretch.* Cf. the use of this word as a term of endearment with *wanton,* similarly employed, 36 1.

65 14. *Can.* Cf. 20 27.

65 22. *Right well.* Formerly good usage. Cf. 65 37 below, and 110 111.

65 36. *Words hath.* Cf. 25 37.

65 37. *Right glad.* See above, 65 22, and cf. the expression *right honorable.*

65 39. *Rascal.* Here in the obsolete, technical sense employed in hunting, the *rascal* being an inferior deer or other beast, unfit for the chase.

65 40. *Of blood and bone.* In blood and bone. An antiquated expression found in the Middle English metrical romances.

66 46. *Wail my fill.* Cf. 46 37, 77 55.

66. *A Sonnet.* Although of considerable subtlety of construction, this "sonnet" is carried off so artlessly and sincerely that it seems to me the perfection of the light, fantastic rapture of an Elizabethan lover. Cf. the *Sonnet* of Barley's *New Book of Tabliture*, below, p. 82.

66 1–2. *Those eyes,* etc. Cf. Hood's lines:

> We thought her dying when she slept,
> And sleeping when she died.

Breton delights to juggle with words, to invert them, distribute and rearrange them, *e.g.*:

> Say that I should say, I love ye?
> Would you say, 'tis but a saying?
> But if love in prayers move ye,
> Will you not be moved with praying?

66 15. *Amaze.* Bewilder, perplex.

67. *A Pastoral.* This poem also appears in *England's Helicon.* Mr. Palgrave considers this "a stronger and finer piece of work than any known to be his [Breton's]." After some, perhaps considerable, reading of Breton's poetry, I cannot subscribe to this, but would place Breton beside Greene and Lodge in this lighter pastoral mode.

67 1. *On a hill,* etc. The charming particularity of these two stanzas as to trifles might teach the lesser pre-Raphaelites somewhat.

67 11. *Did despite.* Did an act of injury to; more usually, cast despite on.

68. *Robert Southwell* was educated at the Jesuit College at Douay, and sent back to England as a missionary, like his fellow-priests, Parsons and Campion. He was apprehended in 1592, imprisoned, racked, and at last hanged for a traitor in 1595. He appears to have been a man

of high principle and much amiability. His works, which must have been written some years before their publication, were exceedingly popular.

"Never must be forgotten *St. Peter's Complaint*," writes Bolton (*Hypercritica*, Haselwood's *Ancient Critical Essays*, II, 250), "and those other serious poems, said to be Father Southwell's; the English whereof as it is most proper, so the sharpness and light of the wit is very rare in them."

68 1. *Where wards.* This has been repeatedly misprinted *words*.

68 6. *When sun is set.* Southwell omits the definite article more frequently than many of his contemporaries. Cf. 68 7, 14, 24 ; 70 9.

68 7. *Seely.* Innocent, harmless. Cf. 6 22.

68 16. *Fearful. I.e.*, full of fear, timorous ; not, as now, terrible to others. Cf. 69 5.

68 18. *Mushrumps.* Mushrooms. Both forms were common in Southwell's day. Marlowe uses the former in *Edward II*, i, 4; Browne the latter, 177 3.

68 19. *In Aman's pomp. Esther,* chap. 4. The forms Aman and Mardocheus, for Haman and Mordecai, are those of the Vulgate, the Bible, of course, which Southwell read.

68 21. *Dives' feast. Luke,* xvi, 19–31.

69. *The Burning Babe.* Jonson told Drummond that, "so he had written that piece of his [Southwell's], *The Burning Babe*, he would have been content to destroy many of his." (*Notes of Ben Jonson's Conversations with William Drummond, Sh. Soc. Publ.*, 1842, p. 13.)

69 5. *Fearful.* Cf. 68 16.

69 14. *Fry.* Here simply to *burn*, conveying to the Elizabethan no such sense as it now conveys.

70. *Mæoniae, or certain excellent Poems and Spiritual Hymns, omitted in the last impression of Peter's Complaint ; being needful thereunto to be annexed, as being both divine and witty. All composed by R. S.:* so runs the title of this work.

70 4. *Remove.* Removal. Cf. 46 28, 49 2, 51 21, 58 6.

70 5. *Haled.* Hauled.

70 9. *When inward eye.* Cf. 68 6.

70 11. *Jesses.* The short strap, usually of leather, fastened about the leg of a hawk used in falconry and continually worn. (*Century Dic'y.*)

70 13. *Trains to Pleasure's lure.* "To train" was the usual term in falconry for drawing or enticing the hawk back to the fist. "The lure" was the decoy. Cf. 33 15.

70 19–20. *Foes senses are*, etc. Our senses are foes to the lessons of virtue; they draw our understanding to the fulfillment of their desires.

70 22. *Bents.* Propensities, dispositions.

71 29–31. *Dame Pleasure's drugs. Drugs* seems here, from the following verse = comfits. *Gin*, a trap or snare of any kind.

71. *Henry Chettle* was a publisher as well as a pamphleteer and playwright. It was he that edited *Greene's Groatsworth of Wit* in 1592, and shortly after apologized handsomely to Shakespeare, in *Kind-Heart's Dream*, for the slighting allusions of the former tract.

71 2. *Beguile ye. Ye* and *you*, earlier distinguished as the nominative and objective cases, were generally confused by writers of this age. Cf. 144 1 and *Sh. Gram.*, § 236.

71 8. *Wag.* Here, as often, used humorously for a rogue, a mad fellow.

71 11. *Witty.* Clever, intellectually able.

72. *Francis Davison* was the eldest son of William Davison, the unfortunate privy councillor and secretary of state of Queen Elizabeth, disgraced for carrying her warrant for the execution of Mary Stuart to the Council. Francis was educated at Gray's Inn, where a Masque of his was performed in 1594. Davison and his father were adherents of the Earl of Essex and lost all chance of political preferment with his fall. Young Francis seems to have made little of the law, and in 1602, turned his attention to publishing the poetry he had written and collected. There is no trace of him after the year 1608, when the will of his father was probated He is supposed, however, to have lived until about 1618. Sir Nicholas Harris Nicolas has collected the data about Davison in his ed. of the *Rhapsody*, pp. i–lxii. Mr. Bullen confesses that he has nothing to add. (Bullen's ed. of the *Rhapsody*, I, p. ix.)

72. *Madrigal.* I have referred this poem and the two following, undoubted works of Davison, to 1595–96, on the authority of the poet's words in 1602: "Mine own [poems] were made, most of them, six or seven years since, at idle times, as I journeyed up and down during my travels." *To the Reader*, Preface to the *Poetical Rhapsody*, ed. Nicolas, p. vii, as above. Mr. Bullen informs us that this poem is a translation from the Italian, *Delle Rime di Luigi Groto, Cieco d'Hadria, nuovamente ristampate*, etc., 1592, p. 63. (Bullen's ed. of the *Rhapsody*, II, 185.)

72 9. *Sets not a fly.* Wagers or stakes not a fly or small stake, and hence *cares not* a fly.

73. *Dispraise of Love.* This "ode" was subsequently reprinted in *England's Helicon*, ed. 1614, and there subscribed 'Ignoto.' I see no

reason for depriving Davison of the authorship of it; as it is not only
in his manner, but occurs, with the two poems above, in a section of
the *Poetical Rhapsody*, entitled *Sonnets, Odes, Elegies and Epigrams* by
Francis and Walter Davison. This Walter was the third son of William
Davison. The poetical gift of the family seems to have extended to
still another brother, Christopher, who appears as the translator of
several psalms towards the end of the collection.

73 7. *An happy life.* Ironical of course, and a better reading than
Unhappy life of some edd.

74. *My only star.* This poem is thus entitled in the ed. of 1602 :
*Ode, being deprived of her sweet looks, words, gestures, by his absence in
Italy, he desires her to write unto him.*

74 8. *That all his thoughts.* Cf. Sidney's ' Only in you my song
begins and endeth,' 11 4.

74 15. *Still.* Ever. Cf. 14 9.

75 26. *Lines.* Letter. Cf. v. 53 below.

75 37–40. *Your sweet voice . . . far distant places.* Some of this
" ode " reads not unlike Donne, who may well have affected so facile a
genius as Davison.

75 38. *Weeds.* Cf. 37 1.

75 42–43. *Which presence . . . absented.* It was next to impossible
for the alert Elizabethan mind to resist these verbal quibbles. See 14 8
note.

76. *Prothalamion or a spousal verse made by Edm. Spenser in honor
of the double marriage of the two honorable and virtuous ladies, the Lady
Elizabeth and the Lady Katherine Somerset, daughters to the right honorable the Earl of Worcester and espoused to the two worthy gentlemen
M. Henry Gilford and M. William Peter, Esquires :* so runs the title of
this poem, which was printed privately for the families concerned.

76 2. *Play A gentle spirit. Spirit* is here the object of the verb
play.

76 3. *Delay.* Temper, mitigate. (Todd.)

76 4. *Glister.* Glitter. Cf. 38 8.

76 12. *Rutty.* Full of roots, rooty, is the explanation of Collier,
with a reference to Chapman's " rutty sides " of a hill. (*Iliad*, xvii, 654.)
Professor Kittredge, however, suggests the simpler explanation, " full
of hollows, gullies, tracks (as it were ' ruts ') worn by the rains."

76 12. *The which.* See *Sh. Gram.*, § 270.

76 15. *Bowers.* Cf. 30 33.

76 16. *Paramours.* Lovers ; the word was seldom used in the derog-
atory modern sense at this time.

76 17. *Is not long.* Is not far hence.

76 25. *Entrailed.* Interwoven.

76 26. *Flasket.* A long, shallow basket.

76 27. *Featcously.* Neatly, nimbly. Cf. 127 2.

77 33. *Vermeil.* A favorite word with Spenser.

77 38. *Lee.* The river of that name, a tributary of the Thames at Greenwich; mentioned also below, v. 115.

77 48. *To them.* In comparison to them.

77 55. *Eftsoons.* Soon after, before long.

77 55. *Their fill.* Cf. 46 37.

77 60. *Them seemed.* It seemed to them. Note the use of the old dative. Cf. 48 9.

78 67. *Bred of summer's heat.* A punning allusion to the surname of the Ladies Somerset. See the note on *Prothalamion*, p. 76 and note, 14 8.

78 75. *Sense.* Possibly here plural as above, 11 3.

78 95. *Couplement.* Union, marriage.

79 100. *Assoil.* Remove, set free.

79 110. *Undersong.* Burden, refrain; cf. *Shep. Cal., Aug.*, 128.

79 121. *Shend.* Injure by outshining. Cf. the use of *stain*, 12 10.

79 128. *My most kindly nurse.* This little autobiographical 'aside' is managed most deftly, and is precious from a poet so allegorical, if not enigmatic, in his allusions as Spenser.

80 135. *Whilom.* Once, at one time. The *-om* is here a dative plural termination used adverbially. *Sh. Gram.*, § 137.

80 145. *A noble peer, Great England's glory.* Robert Devereux, Earl of Essex, in August, 1596, just returned, the hero of the expedition against Spain, in which Cadiz was captured by Essex personally and the Spanish navy badly crippled.

81 166. *To the river's open viewing.* To the open or uninterrupted view of the river.

81 169. *Feature.* Shape, form.

81 174. *Baldrick.* Belt. Here the belt or circle of the zodiac.

81 177. *Tide.* Time. Cf. 46 42.

81. *The Talent.* "The quaint, solemn beauty of *The Talent*," remarks Mr. Waddington, editor of *English Sonnets by Poets of the Past*, p. 225, "might have added another leaf to the wreaths that encircle the brows of Donne and George Herbert."

81 3. *Which.* Cf. Barnes' use of *which* for *who* above, 56 3, 6, 10.

82. *Tell me where.* In *Notes and Queries*, Ser. IV, XII, 304, the following parallel is noted: " For as by Basill the Scorpion is engendred, and by the meanes of the same hearb destroyed : so love which by time

and fancie is bred in an idle head, is by time and fancie banished from the heart." Lyly, *Euphues*, 1579, ed. Arber, p. 298. This song has been referred (*Quarterly Rev.*, CXXXIV, 124) to an Italian original of Jacopo da Lentino, beginning:

> Amore è un desio, che vien dal core.

82 1. *Fancy.* Love.

82 2. *Or in the heart or in the head.* Like *whether . . . whether*, an Elizabethan idiom of frequent occurrence. See *Sh. Gram.*, § 136.

82 5. *Eyes.* It is possible that the true reading is *eye* to rime with *reply* above, and that the mistake has arisen through a kind of attraction to the succeeding rimes.

82. *Barley's New Book of Tabliture* is extremely rare. It is not mentioned by Rimbault or Oliphant. *Tabliture* means writing in score.

82 1. *Those eyes that set.* It will be noticed that the construction of this sonnet is quite a piece of artifice. The four words *eyes*, *hairs*, *hands* and *wit* are spread out, as it were, successively, each briefly characterized, and then gathered back into one in the question : *Then Love be judge*, etc. These words are again spread forth in the same order, with a characterization, and lastly each is apostrophized. See the same method, even more complicated, in Breton's sonnet, p. 66.

83 5. *What heart may there withstand.* Bullen reads *may therewith stand.*

83 7. *Doth.* Cf. 25 37.

83 11–14. *O eyes that pierce.* Mr. Bullen especially praises the last lines of this sonnet as representative of "the great Elizabethan style." *Lyrics from Elizabethan Song Books*, revised ed., p. xxiv.

83 12. *That wear a royal crown.* It has been inferred that this sonnet may have been originally addressed to Elizabeth (*Percy Soc. Pub.*, XIII, 37); but assuredly the Queen's auburn locks could not be designated "hairs of night."

83. *Brown is my love.* The titles of Yonge's two collections show that the words as well as the music were originally Italian.

83. *Shakespeare, Sonnets.* "Upon the sonnets," says Mr. Swinburne, "such a preposterous pyramid of presumptuous commentary has long since been reared by the Cimmerian speculation and Bœotian 'brain-sweat' of sciolists and scholiasts, that no modest man will hope, and no wise man will desire, to add to the structure or subtract from it one single brick of proof or disproof, theorem or theory." (*A Study of Shakespeare*, p. 62.) Without raising the question of modesty or wisdom, we may agree with several authorities (of whom Dowden and

Fleay are among the latest) that few, if any, of Shakespeare's sonnets were written before 1592 or 1593, that Daniel was probably Shakespeare's master in this form of poetry, and that the greater number, as published in the ed. of 1609, were in existence when Meres, in 1598, mentioned "Shakespeare's sugared sonnets amongst his private friends." As to the autobiographic nature of this species of the Elizabethan lyric, the reader is referred to the Introduction of this volume. Mr. Fleay finds a greater number of parallels between the sonnets of Shakespeare and Drayton than between the sequences of any other two Elizabethan sonneteers. (See his *Biographical Chronicle of the English Drama, s. v.*) See also Dr. Isaac's paper on the indebtedness of Shakespeare to Daniel, note on *Delia*, p. 49 above.

83 XIX 1. *Devouring Time.* Cf. Barnes' sonnet dedicatory to the Earl of Northumberland (Arber's *Garner*, v, 483) :

> Your thrice noble house : which shall outwear
> Devouring time itself.

See also *L. L. L.*, i, 1, 4.

84 5. *Fleets.* For *fleetest.* There are a number of these cases of the second person singular in *-ts* in Shakespeare, which may be explained on the score of euphony, with a possible influence of the northern inflection of this person and number in *-s*. Cf. Drummond's use of this latter, 179 10 and 181 1, and see *Sh. Gram.*, § 340 and the examples there.

84 XXIX 5-9. *Wishing me like*, etc. "The modesty evinced in the wishes for the features and faculties of other persons has, in such a man especially, been deservedly admired ; and the pause and the change of tone, full of triumphant emotion, at the words, ' Haply I think on thee,' produce the utmost effect of masterliness in art from the perfection of the feeling." (Leigh Hunt, *The Book of the Sonnet*, I, 156.)

84 12. *Sings hymns.* Cf. the song in *Cymbeline*, p. 147 below, and Lyly's *Alexander and Campaspe*, v, 1.

84 13-14. Cf. Drummond, quoted by Main, *English Sonnets*, p. 285 :

> From this so high transcending rapture springs
> That I, all else defaced, not envy kings.

84 XXXIII 2. *Flatter the mountain tops.* Leigh Hunt says that he is not sure that he has "not extracted this sonnet solely on account of the magnificent second line." (*The Book of the Sonnet*, p. 162.) "Loftily beautiful " are the words which he elsewhere applies to the first two lines.

84 4. *Gilding pale streams.* Cf. *King John*, iii, 1, 77–80:

> The glorious sun
> Stays in its course and plays the alchemist,
> Turning with splendor of his precious eye
> The meagre cloddy earth to glittering gold.
>   (*Shakespeare's Sonnets*, ed. Dowden.)

85 6. *Rack.* "The winds in the upper region (which move the clouds above, which we call rack, and are not perceived below) pass without noise." (Bacon, *Sylva Sylvarum*, cent. ii, § 115, quoted in Clark and Wright's *Haml.*, ii, 2, 469.)

85 12. *Region cloud.* See note above. Region = sky (as often).

85 14. *Stain.* The play upon the two meanings of the word is apparent. Cf. 12 10, 41 4, 57 6.

85 LX 5. *Nativity, once in the main of light.* "When a star has risen and entered on the full stream of light" is Palgrave's explanation of this astrological term.

85 7. *Crooked eclipses.* "Formerly, periods of eclipse, especially of the moon, were held to be peculiarly unpropitious for the conception or execution of lawful, and favorable to evil enterprises." (Main.)

85 9. *Flourish.* Blossom, perfect growth. Cf. 49 5, 51 21.

85 10. *Delves the parallels in beauty's brow.* Cf. Sh.'s *Son.* ii :

> When forty winters shall besiege thy brow
> And dig deep trenches in thy beauty's field.

85 LXXI 1. *No longer mourn*, etc. "It is not easy," exclaims Leigh Hunt, "to call to mind anything more . . . deeply and affectingly beautiful." And further down of the lines beginning: *For I love you so :* "All the tears, tenderness, and generosity of the truest love are in that passage." (*The Book of the Sonnet*, p. 77.)

86 6. *Writ.* Wrote. Cf. 87 14.

86 8. *On me.* Of me or about me. See *Sh. Gram.*, § 181.

86 CVI 2. *Wights.* Mortals, beings, cf. 23 4, 177 3.

86 7. *Antique pen.* Cf. 84 10.

86 8. *Master.* Possess as a master; cf. *Hen. V*, ii, 4, 137 (Dowden).

86 9. *So all their praises*, etc. Cf. Constable's *Sonnets from Todd's MS.*, vii (not *Diana* as Professor Dowden has it) :

> Miracle of the world, I never will deny
> That former poets praise the beauty of their days;
> But all those beauties were but figures of thy praise,
> And all those poets did of thee but prophesy.

86 13. *We, which.* Cf. 56 3.

86 CXVI 1. *Let me not to the marriage of true minds.* " It would be difficult to cite a finer passage of moral poetry than this description of the master passion. How true and how ennobling to our nature! We at once recognize in it the abstraction of that conception which has found a dwelling and a name in the familiar forms of Desdemona, Juliet, Imogen, Cordelia, of Romeo and of Othello too." (Dowden, as above, p. 160.)

86 2. *Impediments.* This word, which Hunt considers "very prosaic," Professor Dowden explains as the technical term of the marriage ceremony of the *Book of Common Prayer*.

86 2-3. *Love is not love which alters.* Cf. *Lear*, i, 1, 241.

86 4. *With the remover to remove.* Cf. Son. xxv, 13, 14; and see note 14 8.

86 5-6. *An ever-fixed mark.* Cf. *Coriolanus*, v, 3, 74 :

> Like a great sea-mark, standing in every flaw,
> And saving those that eye thee.

87 7. *The star . . . whose worth's unknown although his height be taken.* " As the star, over and above what can be ascertained concerning it for our guidance at sea, has unknowable occult virtue and influence, so love beside its power of guiding us, has incalculable potencies."

87 9. *Time's fool.* The sport of Time ; and cf. *1 Hen. IV*, v, 4, 81. This note and several preceding it I owe to Professor Dowden's excellent ed. of the *Sonnets of Shakespeare*.

87 11. *His brief hours.* I.e., Time's brief hours.

87 CXXX 1. *My mistress' eye.* With this sonnet cf. the large class of contemporary poems which abound in rapturous comparisons, Spenser's *Amoretti*, ix and xv, Sidney's *Sonnets*, ix, and Lodge's *Phyllis*, viii, pp. 62-64, 11-14, 59.

87 11. *Go.* Walk. Cf. 62 26.

87. *Richard Barnfield* was an Oxford man and friend to Thomas Watson. He appears to have given up authorship early, in 1605, and to have retired to the life of a country gentleman. Interest attaches to Barnfield by reason of the long-standing confusion of some of his poems with Shakespeare's. In 1599 a piratical publisher, W. Jaggard, included both of the poems of the text in a collection entitled *The Passionate Pilgrim*, placing on the title-page the words, "by William Shakespeare." The poems are undoubtedly Barnfield's. A *résumé* of the arguments on this topic will be found in Arber's reprint of Barn-

field's *Poems*, pp. xix onward. *Poems in Divers Humors* was appended
to the same author's *Encomion of Lady Pecunia*.

88 5. *Dowland.* See note on p. 111.

88 7. *Conceit.* Thought, invention. Cf. 32 13.

88 12. *Whenas.* When. Cf. 59 17, 110 19.

88. *As it fell upon a day.* In *England's Helicon* this "ode" appears
truncated at v. 28 with the addition of two verses for conclusion :

> Even so, poor bird, like thee,
> None alive will pity me.

Mr. Swinburne calls Barnfield "our first-born Keats," probably in allusion to his proficiency in the heptasyllabic trochaics of this poem, a
favorite measure with Keats. (See *A Study of Shakespeare*, p. 65.)

88 10. *Up-till.* Up against.

88 17. *So lively.* In so lively a manner. This word, historically an
adverb, has come to be used only as an adjective.

89 23. *King Pandion*, in the ancient story, was father to Philomela.

89 24. *Lapt in lead.* In allusion to the ancient custom of rolling or
lapping the dead in a sheet of lead.

89 27. *Whilst as.* Whilst that, or simply whilst.

89 41. *Addict.* Addicted.

Mr. Arber (*Barnfield*, p. xxiii) finds the chief characteristics of Barnfield in "his abundant vocabulary," and his "constant strain after
novelty": no very distinguishing traits these for his day.

90. *Giles Farnaby* flourished towards the close of Elizabeth's reign,
arranging much for the virginals. His musical style is described as
florid like that of Dr. Bull. (*Dic. Nat. Biog., s. v.*) The full title of his
work runs: *Canzonets to four voices, with a song in eight parts.*

90. *John Wilbye* is called the "first of madrigal writers" by Oliphant
(*Mus. Madr.*, p. 174); the term is apparently applied to his skill as a
composer, not to priority in time. The work from which these verses
have been taken was Wilbye's *First Set of Madrigals;* he published a
Second Set in 1609. Both have been reprinted in score by the Musical
Antiquarian Society.

90 1. *Lady when I behold.* These lines are translated from an Italian
original (Oliphant). Lodge had translated them less successfully five
years earlier in his *The Life and Death of William Longbeard* (ed. Hunterian Club, p. 21):

> When I admire the rose
> That nature makes repose
> In you the best of many,
> More fair and blest than any,

And see how curious art
Hath deckèd every part;
I think with doubtful view
Whether you be the rose, or the rose is you.

90 5. *Hardly.* With difficulty.

90. *George Chapman*, despite the genuine force and genius that must always secure him a high place among the great names of his age, discloses in his works, to a surprising degree, the confusion of imagery, the prolixity of thought and the tedious diffuseness, if beauty, of expression which characterized the poetic school of his youth and the later, lesser Spenserians. Well may Mr. Swinburne, who has written judiciously and eloquently of Chapman (*On George Chapman's Poetical and Dramatic Works*, prefixed to the *Works of Chapman*, London, 1875), say: "He enters the serene temples and handles the holy vessels of Hellenic art with the stride and the grasp of a high-handed and high-minded barbarian." On the other hand Chapman's moral power and his deep and manifold learning court a comparison with Jonson, although the older poet more frequently runs into curious and intricate pedantry, and never wholly acquired by his long and intimate contact with the classics, as did Jonson, a clear and unquestionable English style. "The name of Chapman," says Mr. Swinburne in the same essay, p. lix, "should always be held great; yet must it always at first recall the names of greater men. For one who thinks of him as the author of his best play or his loftiest lines of gnomic verse, a score will at once remember him as the translator of Homer or the continuator of Marlowe."

90. *Epithalamion Teratos.* Mr. Fleay thinks that Chapman's continuation of Marlowe's *Hero and Leander* was written as early as 1594-5 (*The English Drama*, I, 52). A part of the Argument of the fifth, the Sestiad containing this Epithalamion, runs thus :

She [Hero] sends for two betrothed lovers
And marries them, ...

.   .   .   .

She makes a feast, at which appears
The wild nymph Teras, that still bears
An ivory lute, tells ominous tales,
And sings at solemn festivals. (*Chapman*, ed. 1875, p. 81.)

91 6. *Tire.* Attire, dress.

91 9-12. *Love calls to arms*, etc. Cf. with these lines, which are very effective in their martial tread, Ben Jonson's refrain from the *Epithalamion* of *The Masque* of *Hymen* :

'Tis Cupid calls to arm
And this his last alarm.

91 13.   *Thy velvet hand.*   Cf. Lyly's "*Sleep with velvet hand,*" 21 3.
91 14.   *Day's outfacing face.*   Cf. note on 14 8.
91 23.   *Her balls of discord.*   Day is here likened to Eris with her apple of discord, which brought trouble among the gods ; as day by returning will bring separation to the lovers.

91 25–28.   *Day is abstracted here,* etc.   Day is here resolved into its essence, light or radiance, and here variously displayed in the three beautiful forms of Hero and the bridal pair, Alcmane and Mya.   Cf. Lodge's comparison of Rosalind's hair "to the clear in highest sphere," 30 1 ; and for the proper names see the Fifth Sestiad of *Hero and Leander* (ed. 1875, p. 82):

> Hero to shorten time with merriment
> For young Alcmane and bright Mya sent
> Two lovers that had long craved marriage rites
> At Hero's hands, etc.

91 28.   *Let Thetis thrice refine thee.*   The address is to Day, which is exhorted to be thrice refined by immersion in the sea before returning to shine upon the bride and bridegroom, Thetis the Nereïd being taken to represent the sea.

92.   *Munday and Chettle.*   For the former see 108, for the latter, 71.

92.   *Robin Hood's dirge.*   I read from Hazlitt's *Dodsley*, VIII, 249. Cf. *The Song of Robin Hood and his Huntsmen* in *Metropolis Coronata*, 1615, which Mr. Bullen considers sufficient to prove Munday's authorship of this poem. (*Lyrics from Elizabethan Romances,* p. xviii.)   The title of the play from which the song of the text is taken is an instance of the popular identification of real persons with fictitious characters. There were many plays of this class.

92 5.   *Primer.*   Book of devotion.
92 8.   *Flowers.*   Dissyllabic.   Cf. 21 13.

92.   *Three Men's Song.*   A song or catch for three voices.   The songs of this play were not originally printed in place.   I omit the stage directions as to repetition ; including, however, the line *Close with the tenor boy,* which, by reason of the rime, seems part of the poem.   Mr. Fleay absurdly doubts that this play is Dekker's, and refers its earliest performance to 1597.   (*Engl. Drama,* I, 125.)   I read from Pearson's *Dekker's Plays,* 1873.

92 5.   *Troll the bowl.*   Pass round, circulate.
92 7.   *Saint Hugh* was the patron saint of shoemakers.
92 13.   *King compass.*   Perhaps show the range or compass of your voice by singing out.

93. *Patient Grissell.* Chettle and Haughton collaborated with Dekker in this play. If any one doubts that these songs are Dekker's, let him compare them with the manner of Dekker's undoubted work on pp. 44–45.

93. *O Sweet Content.* Assuredly one of the most perfect and musical lyrics in the language. Note the effect produced by the various repetitions, and cf. in this respect the poems just cited above.

93 10. *Hey nonny nonny.* There are many instances of these meaningless refrains in the poetry of the day. In some cases, as in this, the poet appears to have reached the limit of coherent words and bursts into song of very joy. Cf. 52 4, 96 2, 123 6.

94. *A Passion,* etc. I read from Grosart's ed. of Essex, *Fuller Worthies' Miscellanies,* IV, 95. "This 'passion' is said to have been enclosed in a letter to the Queen from Ireland in 1599." (Hannah's *Courtly Poets,* p. 177.)

94 6. *Hips and haws.* The fruit of the wildrose and of the hawthorn.

94 7. *Still.* Ever. Cf. 14 9.

95. *As You Like It.* It would seem almost as if Shakespeare had deliberately set himself to outdo the beauty and spirit of the lyrics of Lodge's *Rosalind,* the original of the story of this play. See pp. 29–33 above.

95 10. *Live i' the sun.* Live out-of-doors, in freedom.

The omission of Jaques' parody of this song, which follows in the play, is no departure from the purpose of this book to print only whole poems.

95 5. *Thou art not seen.* I would commend a perusal of what the commentators have done to obscure the meaning of this phrase to any who would know to what depths the genus Shakespearian can descend. See Dr. Furness' Variorum ed. of *As You Like It,* p. 131.

95 7. *Holly.* An emblem of mirth. (Halliwell.)

96 14. *Waters warp.* "Either the change produced in them by the action of frost or the bending and ruffling of their surface caused by the wintry wind." (Wright.)

96. *It was a lover.* An early tune for this ditty is printed in Dr. Furness' Variorum ed. of this play, p. 262. See also Chappell, I, 114.

96 4. *Ring time* is Steevens' conjecture for *rang time,* a correction borne out by a MS. dated 1639, from which the music noted above was taken.

97. *John Donne.* "Educated at both universities and at Lincoln's Inn, a traveller, a man of pleasure, it has been thought a soldier, and probably for a time a member of the Roman Church; he seems, just

before reaching middle life, to have experienced some religious change, took orders, became a famous preacher, and [was] made Dean of St. Pauls." Such is Mr. Saintbury's summary. (*Elizabethan Literature*, p. 147.) Donne was held in the highest estimation among his contemporaries. Jonson's praise of him is well known, and excellent Izaac Walton loved the man and revered his memory. Drummond esteemed " Donne, among the Anacreontic lyrics [*i.e.*, lyrists], . . . second to none, and far from all second." (*Conversations with Ben Jonson*, Appendix, p. 50.) The best account of this remarkable man is to be found in Dr. Jessop's article in the *Dictionary of National Biography, s. v.* From it I quote the following : " He [Donne] seems to have had an extraordinary power of attracting others to himself ; there is a vein of peculiar tenderness which runs through the expressions in which his friends speak of him, as if he had exercised over their affection for him an unusual and indefinable witchery."

Donne's lyrics were in everybody's hands long before they were printed, and belong to the last decade of Elizabeth's reign. On this subject and on Donne's innovations of style see the *Introduction*, § 2. In the text I have followed Dr. Grosart, who prints mainly from the *Cosens MS.* In a few cases, however, all noted below, I have preferred other readings of the early editions.

The reader should observe that notwithstanding their extreme subtlety of thought in many places, the language of these poems of Donne is singularly clear and direct. Not only is his vocabulary, as a rule, free from the pedantry and the fantasticality of his age, but I shall venture to say that it would be difficult to find a meaningless inversion in his poetry.

97 2. *Mandrake root.* The root of a plant of the genus *mandragora*, which was popularly supposed to shriek on being pulled up. The resemblance of its forked structure to the human body is probably the ground of this superstition. (*Century Dictionary, s. v.*)

97 10. *Born strange sights to see.* In accord with the popular superstition, some are born with power to see things supernatural.

97 24. *And last till.* " And last so till " is the reading of the ed. of 1635.

98 3. *One other* I read on the same authority for *another* of the *Cosens MS.*

98 9. *Partial.* Trisyllabic, thus riming with *fall* and *all.* Cf. 102 23, 104 6, 116 29, and *Sh. Gram.*, § 479.

99 32. *To join them.* This is the reading of the *Steph. MS.* and the older edd., and seems altogether preferable to that of the ed. of 1669, *to*

join us, which Dr. Grosart defends. The antithesis lies in the contrast between *changing (i.e.,* exchanging) *hearts* and *joining them.*

99 7. *To use myself.* To practise or habituate myself. Cf. 98.

99 8. *By feignèd deaths to die.* The *Stephens MS.* reads: "Thus by feigned death to die."

99 13. *Fear not me.* Have no fears about me. Cf. 100 36.

100 21. *Come bad chance.* Subjunctive.

100 27. *Unkindly kind.* Cf. 14 8.

100 33. *Divining.* Foreboding. Cf. 119 16 and *forethink* in the verse below.

100 35. *Destiny may take thy part. I.e.,* Destiny may agree with thy foreboding.

100 8. *Make dreams truths. True* is the reading of the *Cosens MS.*

100 2. *Broke.* Broken. See *Sh. Gram.,* § 343.

101 19-20. *I must confess, etc.* Well may Mr. Saintsbury underscore these lines, containing as they do the finest compliment ever paid by lover to his beloved.

101. *The Message.* Note the freedom of the phrasing of this poem, which may be compared in this respect and in its perfect directness, with the Song above, p. 99.

101 8. *Still.* Forever.

102. *Upon Parting from his Mistress.* This poem, which is probably the most frequently quoted of Donne's, is often entitled *A Valediction forbidding Mourning.*

102 6. *Tear-floods . . . sigh-tempests.* Cf. 13 5, and see note there.

102 11. *Trepidation.* A motion which the Ptolemaic system of astronomy ascribes to the firmament to account for certain phenomena, really due to the motion of the axis of the earth. (*Cent. Dic.*) Cf. Milton, *P. L.* iii, 483. The singular is preferable to the plural of the *Stephens MS.*

102 14. *Sense.* Mere sensation.

102 15. *For that.* Because.

102 16. *Elemented it.* Composed it, were its elements.

103 23. *Expansion.* Donne generally makes two syllables of the termination *-ion,* riming with words like *one, alone, gone.* Cf. *partial* above, 98 9; 104 8, 125 1, 4, 126 13, 16; and Jonson's verse, 116 29.

103 25-36. *If they be two, etc.* It was the figure of these stanzas which inspired Dr. Johnson's well-known passage on "the metaphysical poets," a phrase which the Doctor borrowed from a hint of Dryden's. (*Discourse on the Original and Progress of Satire,* Cassell's *National Library,* No. 151, pp. 11-15.) "To the following comparison of a man

that travels and his wife that stays at home with a pair of compasses, it may be doubted whether absurdity or ingenuity has better claim." (*Lives of the English Poets*, *Cowley*, ed. Tauchnitz, p. 25.) This deliverance is worthy of a place beside the still more famous strictures on *Lycidas*. This figure of the compass is said to have been suggested by the "*impressa* of old John Heywood — Donne's maternal grandfather." There are several parallels of its use by Donne himself and by his contemporaries. See Donne's *Obsequies to the Lord Harrington's Brother* (Riverside ed., p. 127): —

> O soul! O circle, why so quickly be
> Thy ends, thy birth, and death closed up in thee?
> Since one foot of thy circle still was placed
> In heaven, the other might have securely paced
> In the most large extent through every path
> Which the whole world, or man, the abridgement, hath!

Also Jonson's *Epistle to Selden* (Riverside ed., p. 167), beginning: "You that have been Ever at home"; and Carew's *To Celia upon Love's Ubiquity*, ed. 1870, p. 159. I am indebted for these parallels to the Thesis of my late student, now my colleague, Dr. M. G. Brumbaugh, *A Study of the Poetry of John Donne*.

103 4. *Which*. Cf. 56 3.

104 14. *Love, if I love who loves not me*. The *Cosens MS.* reads *Love, till I lov'd her that lov'd me*.

104 18. *Purlieu*. Land added to the royal forest by unlawful encroachments; and hence here domain usurped, and not justly Love's.

104 20. *Ungod*. Cf. 64 4.

104 24. *Leave loving*. Cease to love. Cf. 17 29, 51 6.

104 26. *Which, since she loves before*, *i.e.*, already loves another, I am loath to have her love me, as in that case she would be false to her other love, and "falsehood is worse than hate."

104 1. *Whoever comes*. Cf. with this poem *The Relique*, in which the 'subtle wreath' is again alluded to in the words: —

> "A bracelet of bright hair about the bone."

We may agree with Mr. Saintsbury that the latter poem, "as a whole, is inferior to this."

104 6. *Unto heaven*. The *Cosens MS.* reads *Then to heaven*.

105 9. *The sinewy thread my brain lets fall*, *i.e.*, the spinal cord with its branching nerves.

105 20. *Others'*. *Other* is the reading of the *Cosens MS.*

105 23. *Bravery.* Defiance, or daring, in contrast with *humility* above.

105. *Henry Constable* was a Roman Catholic gentleman, who lived much in exile by reason of his religion. He was highly esteemed in his day, Bolton in his *Hypercritica* (ed. Haselwood, II, 250) observing that he "was a great master in the English tongue: nor had any gentleman of our nation, a more pure, quick, or higher delivery of conceit." I have preferred two little pastoral lyrics to Constable's sonnets, for which he appears to me to have been somewhat overrated. Both of these poems were first printed in *England's Helicon.*

105. *Damelus' Song.* This poem is set to music in Pilkington's *First Book of Songs and Airs,* 1605.

106 18. *In requite.* In requital.

106 4. *Wanton.* Sport, play.

106 5. *Herd.* Shepherd.

106. *Corydon's Supplication.* This poem does not seem to have been printed before its appearance in *England's Helicon.* For Breton, see above, p. 27.

106 1. *Silly.* Simple. Cf. 6 22.

107 5-6. *Power . . . hast got Upon.* Cf. *Anthony and Cleopatra,* i, 3, 23: "I have no power upon you"; we should say *over* you. See *Sh. Gram.,* § 191.

108. *Anthony Munday* was an actor, stationer's apprentice, "the Pope's scholar at the Seminary at Rome," a messenger to her Majesty's chamber about 1584-1592, city pageant maker, general writer and pamphleteer. That he was not without esteem among his contemporaries is shown by the fact that Meres alludes to him as "our best plotter" (*Palladis Tamia,* ed. Haselwood, p. 154), whilst Webbe (*A Discourse of English Poetry,* ed. Haselwood, p. 36) writes thus: "Anthony Munday, an earnest traveller in this art, and in whose name I have seen very excellent works, among which surely, the most exquisite vein of a witty, poetical head is showed in the sweet sobs of shepherds and nymphs: a work well worthy to be viewed and to be esteemed as very rare poetry." Mr. Bullen found great difficulty in believing Munday capable of anything so good as these two poems signed, "The Shepherd Tonie" and the *Dirge for Robin Hood,* above p. 92. But the discovery of an excellent song on the same redoubtable woodsman in an unquestioned Masque of Munday's has brought about a complete recantation. See the Introd. to *England's Helicon,* p. xvii, and *Lyrics from Elizabethan Romances,* p. xviii. There is an early copy of this poem in *Harl. MS.* 6910 (Bullen).

108 3. *More fine in trip.* Daintier in step.

108 13. *Curster than the bear by kind.* More shrewish or vixenish in disposition than the bear.

108 15. *Glib.* Smooth, slippery.

108. *Beauty sat bathing.* The fact that this poem also appears in Munday's translation, *Primaleon of Greece*, 1619, the poetry of which is not in the original, establishes the identity of Munday with "the Shepherd Tonie" of *England's Helicon.*

109. *Canzon.* For the form, canzon, consult *Introduction*, p. lviii. This poem is signed with Bolton's name in full. There are four other poems in *England's Helicon* signed "E. B.," doubtless by the same author. Bolton, who was a man of very great learning, is now chiefly remembered for his treatise, *Hypercritica, or a Rule of Judgment for writing or reading our Histories*, etc., about 1610, notable for its many acute comments on contemporary writers.

110. *A Palinode.* Not here a recantation or retraction as the term is usually employed, but a song which goes back or returns upon itself by means of a repetition of ideas. The first four lines set forth four successive comparisons which are gathered into application in the following three lines and clinched, so to speak, in the eighth line. The original themes are then again set forth with new variation, and again briefly applied in a concluding couplet. The second stanza works backward. Inverting the original order of the four themes it again rings successive variations upon them, this time in a larger scope, shows the relation of the themes to each other, and in the same number of lines and with similar stanzaic structure, concludes with the couplet of application. Cf. with this the 'sonnets' of Breton and Barley on pp. 66 and 82, and the notes thereon. See also Beaumont's poem beginning, "Like to the falling of a star," p. 170.

110 19. *Whenas.* When. Cf. 59 17.

111 24. *Vary.* Variegation, change or play of color. Cf. *Lear*, ii, 2, 85.

111 25. *Rathe.* Early. Cf. *Lycidas*, 142.

111 27-28. *So as.* Cf. 20 1-2 and see *Sh. Gram.*, § 275.

111. *John Dowland* was "a rare lutist," the height of whose contemporary reputation may be judged by Barnfield's sonnet on p. 87. Dowland was Bachelor of Music of both Universities and lutenist at one time to the King of Denmark. He resided much abroad. His earliest book appeared in 1597, his latest in 1612. The authorship of the words of Dowland's songs is, as in most of these cases, unknown.

111. *I saw my Lady weep.* Entitled *His Lady's Grief* in the reprint of the Percy Society, XIII, 69.

112. *Thomas Weelkes* was organist of Winchester College in 1600, and of Chichester Cathedral in 1608. His earliest collection appeared in 1597, his latest in 1608. Oliphant esteems him the best composer of his age. The verses of his books "are always bright, cheerful and arch." (Bullen.)

112. *Thou sent'st to me.* This poem was apparently first printed by Dr. Grosart in his ed. of Donne (II, 254) and by him ascribed to that poet. It cannot be his. These additional stanzas appear in that edition : —

> The heart I sent thee had no stain
> It was entire and sound ;
> But thou hast sent it back again
> Sick of a deadly wound.
>
> O, Heavens, how wouldst thou use a heart
> That should rebellious be,
> Since thou hast slain mine with a dart
> That so much honored thee.

Mr. Saintsbury calls these stanzas "a feeble amplification," and considers the earlier stanzas "less in the style of Donne than in that of Ben." (*Seventeenth Century Lyrics*, p. 305.)

112 1. *A heart was sound.* The *Oxford MS.* reads "a heart was crowned."

113. *Ben Jonson.* "Vigor of thought, purity of phrase, condensed and polished rhetoric, refined and appropriate eloquence, studious and serious felicity of expression, finished and fortunate elaboration of verse, might have been considered as qualities sufficient to secure a triumph for the poet in whose work all these excellent attributes are united and displayed ; and we cannot wonder that younger men who had come within the circle of his personal influence should have thought that the combination of them all must ensure to their possessor a place above all his possible compeers. But among the humblest and most devout of these prostrate enthusiasts was one who had but to lay an idle and reckless hand on the instrument which hardly would answer the touch of the master at all, and the very note of lyric poetry as it should be . . . responded on the instant to the instinctive intelligence of his touch. . . . As we turn from Wordsworth to Coleridge, as we turn from Byron to Shelley, so do we turn from Jonson to Herrick." (Swinburne, *A Study of Ben Jonson*, p. 97.) See *Introduction*, § 1.

113 4. *Division.* A rapid musical phrase generally sung on a single syllable and with one breath. Cf. *1 Hen. IV*, iii, 1, 211.

113 10. Notice the successful onomatopœia of this line.

113 10.   *To clear.*   To make bright, lighten.

114.   *His Supposed Mistress.*   The germ of this song can be traced to Martial's *Epigrams,* i, 58, quoted by Bell (*Songs of the Dramatists,* p. 113): —

> Qualem, Flacce, velim quaeris, nolimve puellam?
> Nolo nimis facilem, difficilem nimis.
> Illud, quod medium est, atque inter utrumque, probamus.
> Nec volo, quod cruciat; nec volo, quod satiat.   •

114 1.   *Discover.*   Make known, disclose.

114 9.   *Neither.*   Monosyllabic.   Cf. v. 20 below and see *Sh. Gram.,* § 466.

114 11–20.   Professor Winchester reminds me of the wonderful realization of the ideal of this stanza by Shakespeare in the "infinite variety" of his Cleopatra.

114 13.   *Froward.*   Perverse, willful.

114 14.   *Swowning.*   A form of *swooning.*

114 16.   *Purely jealous.*   Out and out jealous.   Because jealousy is an evidence of love, and would prove her constancy in moments of indifference.   See the verse below.

114 18–19.   *Then only constant,* etc.   That she should be constant only when I crave her is a virtue that should not save her, *i.e.,* keep her mine.   I would have her constant at all times, even when I am indifferent and do not demand her love.

114 19.   *Delicates.*   Charms, allurements.

115.   *Epode.*   This poem originally appeared in *Love's Martyr or Rosalin's Complaint. Allegorically shadowing the Truth of Love, in the constant Fate of the Phoenix and Turtle. A poem . . . now first translated out of the venerable Italian Torquato Caeliano by Robert Chester, . . . To these are added some new compositions of several modern writers, whose names are subscribed to their several Works; upon the first subject, viz.: The Phoenix and Turtle.*   Among these "best and chiefest of out modern writers," as they are elsewhere called, are Jonson, Marston, Chapman and Shakespeare.   This work has been reprinted among the *Publications of the New Shakspere Society,* Series VIII, No. 2.   The *Epode* was later included in *The Forest,* folio ed. of Jonson's works, 1616.

115 1.   *State.*   Status, equilibrium.

115 7.   *A guard . . . to watch and ward.*   Cf. a passage in Jonson's *Discoveries, Athenæum Press Series,* p. 13, and note p. 96, where a similar passage is referred to Plutarch, *Moralia (de Garrulitate).*

115 13.   *Affections.*   Feelings, emotions; Cf. v. 21 below, 207 25.

115 16. *Close, the close cause.* Cf. 14 ℵ. *Close cause,* secret cause. Cf. 126 22.

115 23. *Larum.* Alarm.

116 29. *Passions.* Trisyllabic. Cf. 98 9, 103 23 note, 101 ℵ.

116 41. *With whom, who rides. Whom* refers to *blind Desire* above, v. 37, here again personified, although treated as neuter in v. 39, *of whence 'tis born. Who* = whoever.

116 44. *Prove.* Experience.

116 45–49. *That is an essence . . . on lovers.* Mr. Swinburne extols this passage and vv. 55–65 below.

116 47. *A golden chain, etc.* Cf. Jonson's own later use of the same figure in *Hymenæi, a Masque,* 1606 (where a marginal note refers the thought to the *Iliad,* viii, 19) : —

> Such was the golden chain let down from Heaven;
> And not those links more even,
> Than these: so sweetly tempered, so combined
> By union, and refined.

116 52. *Different hearts.* Hearts opposed to love, or perhaps hearts opposed to each other.

117 63–65. *At suggestion of a steep desire . . . happiness.* Professor Kittredge suggests that *a steep desire* is here "a precipitous desire, a desire into which a man casts himself headlong"; and that *suggestion* be taken, as usually, *in malam partem,* and as equal to *temptation.* Hence : " Who, on the pinnacle of his joy, would cast himself headlong down to destruction for a desire that tempts him ? " Jonson's figure was evidently prompted by the temptation of the pinnacle of the temple.

117 69. *Luxury.* Lust.

117 73. *Sparrows' wings.* The sparrow being especially the bird of Venus, the goddess of sensual love.

117 87–90. *He that for love . . . he fears.* " Few of Jonson's many moral or gnomic passages are finer, says Mr. Swinburne." (*A Study,* etc., p. 102.)

118 101. *Feature.* The form of the whole body, shape. Cf. 81 169.

118 104. *How only she,* etc. How she bestows . . . her love on him alone.

118 113. *That knows the weight of guilt.* Cf. Seneca, *Hippolytus,* i, 162 f.: —

> Quid poena praesens, consciae mentis pavor;
> Animusque culpa plenus, et semet timens?
> Scelus aliqua tutum, nulla securum tulit.

11S. *A Book of Airs set forth to be sung to the lute, orpharion and bass viol, by Philip Rosseter.* The title further informs us that the work was printed " by the consent of Thomas Morley," who, after the expiration of the term of the patent granted to Tallis and Byrd, enjoyed a like monopoly of the publication of song-books. (Rimbault, pp. ix–xi.) For Rosseter, see below, p. 120 note.

118. *Thomas Campion* was educated at Cambridge and Grey's Inn, and published Latin Epigrams in 1594. His song-books were published between the years 1601 and 1617. In 1602 appeared his *Observations in the Art of English Poesy*, in which he attacked " the vulgar and inartificial custom of riming," and attempted to prove that English metrical composition was faulty in not following the classics. Campion was ably answered the next year by Daniel, who expressed his wonder that such an attack should proceed from one " whose commendable rimes, albeit now himself an enemy to rime, have given heretofore to the world the best notice of his worth." The evidence that Campion was not only the composer of the music, but the author of the words of the poems contained in his song-books, Mr. Bullen finds in Campion's address *To the Reader, Fourth Book of Airs:* " Some words are in these books which have been clothed in music by others, and I am content they then served their turn : *yet give me leave to make use of mine own."* In a similar address prefixed to the *Third Book of Airs:* "In these English airs I have chiefly aimed to *couple my words and notes lovingly together; which will be much for him to do that hath not power over both."* (Preface to *Lyrics from Elizabethan Song-Books*, p. xi.) For further information as to Campion, see Mr. Bullen's ed. of his *Works*, London, 1889.

11S. *In Imagine, etc.* I am indebted to Mr. Palgrave's *Golden Treasury of English Lyrics* for this apt title.

119 11. *As thou still black must be.* Since thou must ever remain black.

119 12. *Beams . . . turneth.* Cf. 25 37.

119 16. *Divineth.* Forebodes. Cf. 100 33.

119 20. *Proved.* Approved.

119. *When to her lute.* This poem also appeared in Davison's *Poetical Rhapsody*, in the next year. Cf. Herrick's imitation of this poem : *Upon Sappho sweetly playing and sweetly singing,* (ed. 1869, I, 151). Herrick may be suspected of having acquired not a little of his melody and simple sweetness from his fellow Hedonist, Campion.

119. *Thou art not fair.* Mr. Bullen informs us of two other versions of this poem. (Bullen's *Campion*, p. 15.) It has also been erroneously

assigned to Donne and to Sylvester. Dr. Grosart, who prints everything he can lay his hands on, includes it, of course, in his ed. of Donne
(II, 258).

120 5. *Soothe.* Flatter.

120 11. *A woman right.* A very woman. Cf. *M. N. D.* iii, 2, 302:
"I am a right maid for my cowardice."

120. *When thou must home.* "For strange richness of romantic
beauty," says Mr. Bullen, this "could hardly be matched outside of the
sonnets of Shakespeare." (*Lyrics from Elizabethan Song-Books*, p. xvi.)

120 4. *White Iope.* Cf. Propertius:—

> Sunt apud infernos tot millia formosarum;
> Pulchra sit, in superis, si licet. una locis.
> Vobiscum est Iope, vobiscum candida Tyro,
> Vobiscum Europe, nec proba Pasiphae, etc.

120. *Philip Rosseter* was Master of the Children of the Queen's
Revels, by patent dated Jan. 4, 1609-10, and, under that authority,
manager of the play-house in Whitefriars. Besides this work, Rosseter
published *Lessons for Consort: made by sundry excellent authors, etc.*
(Rimbault, *Bibliotheca Madrigaliana*, p. 17.)

120. *All is Vanity.* I assign this to Rosseter — at least as far as
the music is concerned — on the authority of the words of the table:
"Songs . . . made by Philip Rosseter." (Bullen's *Campion*, p. 25.)
Cf. also Rosseter's words in the dedication of this song-book, speaking
of Campion and his songs: "Yet hath it pleased him . . . to grant me
the impression of part of them: to which I have added an equal number
of mine own." (*Ibid.*, p. 3.)

121 11. *Vain opinion.* Mere repute founded on appearances.

121 12. *The world is but a play.* A very common sentiment of the
age, referable perhaps ultimately to Democrates: ὁ κόσμος σκηνή, ὁ βίος
πάραδος. Cf. also Petronius Arbiter (*Frag.* 10): *Quod fere totus mundus
excerceat histrionem.* Cf. *As You Like It*, ii, 7, 139; Chapman's *Bussy
D'Ambois*, i, 1; Jonson's *New Inn*, i, 1, and *Discoveries, Athenaeum
Press Series*, p. 36.

121. *Robert Jones* was a famous performer on the lute, and concerned, in conjunction with Philip Rosseter, in the management of the
theatre in Whitefriars. (Rimbault, as above, p. 18.) Jones, like Campion, may have been the author of the words of his songs.

122 13. *Hap.* Lot, fate.

122. *O mistress mine.* The music of this song is reprinted by Chappell (*Old English Popular Music*, I, 103) from Morley's *First Book of*

Consort Lessons, 1599. As this work contains only the music, it proves nothing as to the possible date of the words of the text.

122 11. *Sweet and twenty.* "That is, sweet kisses and twenty of them, twenty being used as a round number (cf. *Mer. Wives,* ii, 1, 203); or we may read with Theobald *sweet, and twenty,* making *sweet* a vocative. But to read *sweet-and-twenty* as a vocative with Boswell is certainly wrong." (*Clarendon Press Sh., Twelfth Night,* p. 109.) On the other hand Professor Winchester observes that "the Clarendon Press interpretation obscures the meaning of the next line, '*Youth's* a stuff will not endure.' Never is youth *sweeter* than at *twenty*: yet even then there are hints that it cannot long *endure.*" Notice that this poem is trochaic throughout, the interjections, *O,* of the first two lines being redundant.

122 2. *Cypress.* There is much ado among the commentators as to whether *cypress* means the customary branches strewn upon the grave, the wood of the coffin, or the crape material used for the shroud. The first seems the most probable interpretation, in support of which Mr. Aldis Wright refers to Drummond's *Sonnet* xx, *Twelfth Night,* as above, p. 119, and *Drummond* ed. 1856, p. 27 : —

> Of weeping myrrh the crown is which I crave
> With a sad cypress to adorn my grave.

122 7. *My part . . . share it.* "Though *death* is a *part* in which every one acts his *share,* yet of all these actors no one is so *true* as I." (Johnson.)

123. *Thomas Middleton,* a man of good birth and education, was sometime a student of Grey's Inn, a productive and highly successful playwright and writer of pageants, and, from 1620 to his death, chronologer of the city of London. Few of the lyrics of Middleton are altogether satisfactory; in all his work, like Massinger and some others, Middleton seems to inhabit that dangerous limbo that lies between the realms of the highest genius and the ordinary levels of a work-a-day world; making, it is true, an occasional flight into the former, but more usually contentedly trudging along the highways of the latter.

123 7. *Owe.* Own. Cf. 195 11.

123 10. *Wait.* Attend as cup-bearer.

123 11. *Phoebe here one night did lie.* Did Phoebe lie here one night.

124. *O Sorrow, Sorrow.* This dialogue form was very popular in the songs of the time. Cf. 162, 198, 199; and the following stanza from a recently discovered play of Heywood's (*The Captives or the Lost Recovered,* 1624, Bullen, *Old English Plays*): —

> O Charity, where art thou fled,
> And now how long hast thou been dead?
> O many, many, many hundred years.
> In village, borough, town or city
> Remains there yet no grace, no pity?
> Not in sighs, not in want, not in tears, etc.

The play from which the song of the text is taken was published in 1634, with the initials S[amuel] R[owley] on the title. A play called *The Spanish Fig*, which there is reason to believe (cf. Fleay, *The English Drama*, I, 128) was this play, was entered in the Stationers' Register in 1631 as Dekker's, and was, apparently, acted in 1602. The manner of this song seems to me peculiarly that of Dekker; note especially the short, end-stopped lines (see the *Hymn to Fortune*, p. 44), the brief questions and answers (*Sweet Content*, p. 93), and the repetition of verses 1, 15 and 16, with which compare "and bend and bend," 44 10; "O sweet, O sweet content," and "Work apace, apace," etc., 39 7-8.

124 4. *Furier face.* A face more like a fury. Mr. Bullen's emendation *fury's face* seems unnecessary.

124. *The Soul's Harmony.* This work is a series of 'divine sonnets,' in the Elizabethan sense of that term. Dr. Grosart prints — possibly on the authority of the original edition — as if he had a continuous poem before him. See his ed. of Breton, p. 5.

125 8. *But in her baby's clouts.* Only in her childish finery. Cf. 158 37.

125 14. *To thee.* For thee, or with a view to thee. See *Sh. Gram.*, § 186.

125. *Ode.* This poem has been assigned to Donne on early manuscript authority as well as on internal evidence. It was reprinted as an unpublished poem of his in *The Grove*, a collection of verse, 1721. Dr. Grosart does not appear to have been aware of the earlier and preferable version in the *Rhapsody*, which I have, of course, followed. (See Grosart's *Donne* II, 238.)

125. *Time and absence proves.* Cf. 25 37.

125 1. *Protestation.* Cf. 103 23 note.

125 9. *Affection ground.* Ground for affection. Some edd. read *affection's ground.*

126 19. *By absence.* Cf. with this last stanza, Carew's *To his Mistress Confined*, ed. 1824, p. 133:

> This eclipse
> Shall neither hinder eye nor lips;
> For we shall meet
> With our hearts, and kiss, and none shall see 't.

126 22. *Close.* Secret. Cf. 115 16.

126. *Joshua Sylvester's* contemporary reputation was sufficiently great to earn for him the epithet "the silver-tongued." This fame was based chiefly upon his translation of *Du Bartas His Divine Weeks and Days.* Drummond regarded Sylvester's translations as "excellent," but added, "he is not happy in his inventions : . . . his pains are much to be praised." (Appendix to *Jonson's Conversations, Sh. Soc. Pub.*, p. 51.) This sonnet is signed ' I. S.' in three of the four early editions of the *Rhapsody.*

127. *Madrigal.* Neither this nor the succeeding Madrigal have any signature affixed. Both appear in a section of the *Rhapsody* headed : *Divers Poems by Sundry Authors.*

127. *My love in her attire.* Well may Mr. Saintsbury exclaim : " This could not easily be bettered ! " Mr. Bullen refers us for a parallel to the following verses of Clément Marot, which I take the liberty of quoting from him :

DE MADAME YSABEAU DE NAVARRE.

Qui cuyderoit desguiser Ysabeau
D'un simple habit, ce seroit grand' simplesse ;
Car au visage a ne sçay quoi de beau,
Qui faict juger tousjours qu'elle est princesse :
Soit en habit de chambriere ou maistresse,
Soit en drap d'or entier ou decouppé,
Soit son gent corps de toile enveloppé,
Tousjours sera sa beauté maintenue ;
Mais il me semble (ou je suis bien trompé)
Qu'elle seroit plus belle toute nue.

Mr. J. M. Thomson, quoted by Mr. Bullen, refers us still further to Aristænetus, *Epist.* i, and Plato's *Charmides*, 154 D). (Bullen's ed. *Poetical Rhapsody*, II, 196.)

127 2. *Feater.* Neater, nicer. Cf. 76 27.

127 7. *Sith.* Since. Cf. 63 13, 179 11.

127. *An Epitaph.* Salathiel Pavy acted in *Cynthia's Revels* and in the *Poetaster*, 1600 and 1601 ; he probably died in the latter year. (Gifford.) Mr. Swinburne justly remarks on this epitaph : " For sweetness and simplicity, it has few if any equals among his lyrical attempts." (*A Study of Ben Jonson,* p. 97.)

128 11. *Filled zodiacs.* Full years.

128 17. *So, by error to his fate . . . consented.* Cf. Martial, lib. x, epig. 53 :

Ille ego sum Scorpus, clamosi gloria Circi,
Plausus, Roma, tui, deliciaeque breves;
Invida quem Lachesis raptum trieteride nona,
Dum numerat palmas, credidit esse senem.

"Jonson must have read *inscia* for *invida*, if he did not intentionally depart from his original." (Cunningham.) This is but one of innumerable instances of Jonson's ability "to convert the substance or riches of another poet to his own use," to quote Jonson's own words. (*Discoveries, Athenæum Press Series,* p. 77.)

128. *How should I.* The traditional music of this song is printed by Dr. Furness in his Variorum ed. of *Hamlet,* I, 330. Cf. the song attributed to Raleigh, p. 3 of this volume.

128 3. *Cockle hat.* Hat decorated with cockles or scallop-shells, which were worn by pilgrims as the badge of their vocation. Cf. 129 1.

128 4. *Shoon.* Shoes. An archaic form in Shakespeare's day.

129 10. *Larded.* Garnished, set out.

129. "*Sir Walter Raleigh,*" says Naunton (*Fragmenta Regalia,* ed. Arber, p. 47) "was one, that, it seems, Fortune had picked out of purpose, of whom to make an example, or to use as her tennis-ball, thereby to show what she could do; for she tossed him up of nothing, and to and fro to greatness, and from thence down to little more than to that wherein she found him, a bare gentleman." See on this ever fascinating and typical character Charles Kingsley's suggestive essay, *Sir Walter Raleigh.*

129 1. *Give me my scallop-shell.* This poem is one of some halfdozen to which attaches the legend that it was "made by Sir Walter the night before he was beheaded." More reasonable is the explanation of Canon Hannah, who dates the poem "during Raleigh's interval of suspense in 1603," when the fallen courtier was smarting under the injustice and brutality of the King's Attorney, Sir Edward Coke, just after the iniquitous trial for high treason. Canon Hannah adds: "The grotesque imagery which disturbs its solemn aspirations may remind us of the more galling of the annoyances from which he knew that death [alone] would set him free." (See especially verses 35-42, and Hannah's ed. of *Raleigh,* pp. 221 and xiv.) It would be difficult to find a poem more truly representative of the age of Elizabeth, with its poetical fervor, its beauty and vividness of expression, its juggling with words, and its daring mixture of things celestial with things mundane.

129 1. *Scallop-shell.* Cf. 128 4.

129 3. *Scrip.* The pilgrim's pouch or traveling bag.

129 9. *Palmer.* A pilgrim who had returned from the Holy Land, had fulfilled his vow, and brought a palm branch to be deposited on the altar of the parish church. (*Cent. Dic.*)

129 16. *Milken hill.* Perhaps hill of plenty, running with milk and honey. Cf. wooden, woolen, and the older English ashen treen, etc.

129 17. *A-dry.* Cf. 26 9. We still say athirst.

129 22. *Fresh.* Freshly.

130 25. *Suckets.* Sweetmeats, delicacies of any kind.

130 42. *Angels.* The familiar Elizabethan pun on the popular name for the angel-noble, a coin first struck by Edward IV, and varying in value from 6*s.* 8*d.* sterling to 10*s.* Cf. 189 32.

131 58. The lines :

> Of death and judgment, heaven and hell
> Who oft does think must needs die well,

usually appended to this poem, are undoubtedly the trite comment of some moralist copyist.

132. *Thomas Bateson,* "practitioner in the art of music," was organist at Chester and Dublin, and the author of two books of madrigals. (Oliphant, p. 212.)

132. *Song of the May.* Cf. Herrick's beautiful elaboration of this familiar theme in *Corinna's Maying.* The popular custom of May-day can hardly be better described than in the words of the redoubtable Puritan, Philip Stubbes in his *Anatomy of Abuses,* 1595, p. 109: "Against May-day, every parish, town, or village assemble themselves, both men, women, and children, and, either all together or dividing themselves into companies, they go to the woods and groves, some to the hills and mountains, . . . where they spend all the night in pleasant pastimes; and in the morning they return, bringing with them birch boughs and branches of trees to deck their assemblies withal. But their chiefest jewel they bring from thence is the may-pole, which they bring home with great veneration, as thus, etc. . . . And thus equipped, it was reared with handkerchiefs and flags streaming on the top, etc. . . . And thus they fall to banquetting and feasting, to leaping and dancing about it as the heathen people did at the dedication of their idols."

132 1. *Springs . . . makes.* Cf. 25 37, 65 36.

133. *Take, O take.* Fletcher in his *Bloody Brother,* v, 2, quotes these verses, adding the following stanza of his own :

> Hide, O hide those hills of snow,
> Which thy frozen bosom bears,
> On whose tops the pinks that grow
> Are of those that April wears!

But first set my poor heart free
Bound in icy chains by thee.

Mr. Swinburne is very indignant and abusive of the "earless owners of
fingers" who have thought these lines by any possibility Shakespeare's.
(*A Study of Sh.*, p. 205.)

133. *To Celia.* The leading thoughts of this familiar song have
been traced to scattered passages in the love letters of Philostratus the
Sophist. Gifford quotes the passages in question. (See his ed. of
Jonson, VIII, 268.)

134. *Tobias Hume*, a musician and soldier, spent much of his life in
the services of Sweden. He entered the Charter-house as a poor brother
in 1629 and lived on to 1645. Rimbault (*Bibliotheca Madr.*, pp. 21 and
25) accredits him with another book besides this. Some particulars of
his later life will be found in *Notes and Queries*, Ser. II, VII, 369.

134 1. *Fain would I change.* With pardonable enthusiasm Mr. Bullen
remarks on this exquisite song : "I have found no lines of more faultless beauty, of happier cadence or sweeter simplicity, no lines that more
justly deserve to be treasured in the memory while memory lasts." Mr.
Palgrave has included this poem in the new ed., 1892, of his *Golden
Treasury of English Lyrics* under the title *Omnia vincit.* I have preferred Mr. Bullen's title.

134 4. *That that.* The thing which.

134 18. *I know thee what thou art.* Abbott explains this idiom,
which Shakespeare uses frequently, by regarding *thee* as the object and
"the dependent clause a mere explanation of the object." *Sh. Gram.*,
§ 414.

135. *Thomas Heywood* was by far the most voluminous of the
dramatists of his age, and belonged to the class that wrote for bread
and dealt with Henslowe. Besides his dramas, Heywood wrote many
pageants and considerable prose of the pamphlet class. The loss of
his *Lives of All the Poets*, if indeed it was ever published, is much to be
deplored. Charles Lamb, in delight at Heywood's exquisite sense of
pathos and delicate insight into the human heart, dubbed him "a prose
Shakespeare." But even Heywood is not all prose, as this musical song
is sufficient to attest. This poem was also printed in the author's
Dialogues and Dramas, 1637.

135 16. *Stare.* Starling.

136 1-2. *On whose eyelids sit*, etc. Cf. Spenser, *Faery Queen*, ii, 3,
25 : "Upon her eyelids many graces sat . . . working belgards and
amorous retrate." Cf. also Ford and Dekker's *The Sun's Darling*,
iii, 2. I am indebted for these parallels to Professor Kittredge.

136. *Michael Drayton* was probably of Cambridge, as his earlier inti-
mates were Lodge and Daniel. I quote Meres' contemporary estimate
of his personal character : " As Aulus Persius Flaccus is reported
among all writers to be of an honest life and upright conversation, so
Michael Drayton (*quem toties honoris et amoris causa nomino*) among
scholars, soldiers, poets, and all sorts of people, is held for a man of
virtuous disposition, honest conversation, and well governed carriage,
which is almost miraculous among good wits in these declining and
corrupt times, when there is nothing but roguery in villanous man,
when cheating and craftiness is counted the cleanest wit and soundest
wisdom." (*Palladis Tamia*, 1598.) Drummond remarked that : " Drayton seemeth rather to have loved his Muse than his Mistress; by, I
know not what artificial similes, this sheweth well his mind but not the
passion." (Appendix, *Jonson's Conversations*, p. 50.)

136 11. *I hold it vile that vulgar wit affords.* *I.e.*, What vulgar wit
affords I hold vile.

136. *Fair stood the wind.* This poem must be distinguished from
the author's epic entitled *The Battle of Agincourt*, a far less valuable
work. The title, *To my friends*, etc., is Drayton's own. I have preferred the earliest version of this best of English martial lyrics ; its
very rudeness makes it more soldierly. Drayton afterwards filed it as
was his wont, and somewhat spoiled it in the polishing. Of this poem
Lowell writes : " It runs, it leaps, clashing its verses like swords upon
bucklers, and moves the pulse to a charge." (*Spenser, Prose Works of
Lowell*, ed. 1894, IV, 280.)

136 2. *Advance.* Hoist, raise.

137 5. *But put unto the main.* Ed. 1619: " But putting to the main."

137 14. *With those oppose his way.* Note the omission of the relative.
The later ed. reads : " With those that stopped his way."

137 15. *Whereas the gen'ral.* " Where the French gen'ral lay."
Later ed.

137 17. *Which* refers to the French general. Cf. 56 3.

137 18. *As Henry to deride.* As = as if. Cf. v. 92 below. The later
version reads : " King Henry to deride."

137 21. *Which.* The mandate that Henry send his ransom. *Neglects*,
disregards.

137 28. *Amazed.* Confused with fear. Cf. 66 15.

137 34. *Rest.* Resolution. Cf. *Mer. of Venice*, ii, 2, 110 : " I have
set up my *rest* to run away," *i.e.*, I have made up my mind, resolved.

138 37. *I will.* Notice the proper use of will here to denote deter-
mination.

138 41. *Poyters.* I retain the old spelling of this word, as it denotes the contemporary English pronunciation.

138 50. *Vaward.* Vanguard.

138 52. *Henchmen.* Here simply followers.

138 64. *Trumpet to trumpet spake.* Cf. with this passage especially *The Charge of the Light Brigade.* Closer metrically is Longfellow's *Skeleton in Armor.*

138 68. *Unto the forces.* Ed. 1619: "To our hid forces."

139 71. *Archery.* Bowmen. ●

139 73. *Spanish yew.* The favorite wood in the manufacture of bows.

139 76. *Piercing the wether.* Probably to be construed with *serpents,* and meaning that the arrows stung as suddenly and fatally as a snake strikes a wether.

139 82. *Bilbows.* Swords; so called from the Spanish town Bilboa, where excellent cutlery was made.

139 88. *These were men.* Ed. 1619: "Our men were."

139 92. *As.* As if. Cf. v. 18 above.

139 93. *Who* = And he; the later version reads *and.*

140 103. *That yet a maiden knight.* Ed. 1619: "Though but a maiden knight," thus avoiding the repetition of the word *yet* in the next verse.

140 108. *Still.* Ever.

140 111. *Right doughtily.* Cf. 65 22, 37.

140. *Cherry Ripe.* I read with Mr. Bullen's ed. of *Campion.* This poem was subsequently published in Robert Jones' *Ultimum Vale,* 1608, and in Campion's own *Fourth Book of Airs,* 1617. Cf. with this Herrick's poem of the same title. (Hazlitt's *Herrick,* I, 17.) 'Cherry Ripe' was a popular street cry of the age. Cf. Jonson's *The New Cry:*

> Ere cherries ripe and strawberries be gone,
> Unto the cries of London he'll add one;
> Ripe statesmen, ripe: they grow in every street;
> At six and twenty, ripe.

141. *John Daniel,* apparently the brother of Samuel Daniel, the poet. Little is known of John beyond the fact that he was later one of the court musicians of Charles I and the publisher of his brother's works in 1623. (Rimbault, *Musa Madr.,* p. 24.)

141 3. *Notes.* Records.

142 15. *Repose me.* "Many verbs, which are now used intransitively, were used by Shakespeare reflexively." *Sh. Gram.,* § 296.

142. *Death be not proud.* "The tenth sonnet of Donne, beginning 'Death,'" writes Wordsworth to Dyce (*Prose Works*, ed. 1876, III, 332), "is so eminently characteristic of his manner, and at the same time so weighty in thought, and original in the expression, that I entreat you to insert it." Mr. T. Hall Caine considers this "the weightiest, most forceful and full-thoughted of all the many English sonnets written on the subject." (*Sonnets of Three Centuries*, p. 276.)

142 8. *Rest of their bones, and souls' delivery.* These words are in apposition with *thee* in the verse above.

142 12. *Swell'st thou.* *I.e.*, with pride.

143. *Fair Maid of the Exchange.* "The vexatious but indispensable Mr. Fleay," as some one has recently called him, assigns this play variously to Lewis Machin and Jervais Markham. (*The Engl. Drama*, II, 219 and 329.) The play is certainly not Heywood's.

143 6. *Sing . . .* (that) *she may not lower.* Note the omission of the conjunction.

143 14. *Strain.* Cf. a similar use of *shrill*, 135 13.

143 23. *Still.* Perhaps here with something of its modern sense, *even yet.* Cf. 14 9.

143 25.–32. This poem is much bettered by the omission of this last stanza. The Elizabethans, like some of the poets of other times, did not always know when to stop.

144. *Thomas Ford* was a musician in the suite of Prince Henry, and later in the court of Charles. He died in 1648. (Oliphant.) Rimbault mentions only this one work of Ford's.

144. *Love's Steadfastness.* The poem appears with this title in *The Golden Garland of Princely Delights*, 1620. Ford's music is given by Chappell, *Old English Popular Music*, p. 129.

144 1. *Ye.* Cf. 71 2.

144 10. *Compare.* Comparison. Cf. 49 2.

145. *John Webster* was born free of the Merchant Tailors' Company, and was probably a cloth-worker as well as a playwright. We know next to nothing of his life except the fact that he labored for Henslowe in company with Dekker, Heywood, Middleton and others.

145 1. *Call for the robin-redbreast*, etc. "I never saw anything like this funeral dirge," says Charles Lamb, "except the ditty which reminds Ferdinand of his drowned father in the *Tempest*. As that is of the water, watery; so this is of the earth, earthy. Both have that intenseness of feeling, which seems to resolve itself into the element which it contemplates." (*Specimens of English Dramatic Poets*, ed. 1835, I, 251.)

145 3. *And with leaves . . . do cover.* Cf. Shakespeare's use of the same popular superstition, *Cymbeline*, iv, 2, 225.

145 2. *Pink eyne.* Small eyes: "Some haue myghty yies and some be pynkyied. *Quidam pregrandibus sunt luminibus, quidam peti.*" Horman's *Vulgaria*, 1519, fo. 30, vᵒ. (Hudson.)

145 3. *Vats.* The folio reads *fats.* I modernize for the sake of intelligibility.

146 9. *Finèd.* Refined.

146 12. *Dainty tied.* Daintily tied. Adjective for adverb. Cf. *Sh. Gram.*, § 1. Cf. 154 15.

147 1. *Hark, hark, the lark.* Cf. *Sh.'s Son.*, xxix, 84 12.

147 4. *Chaliced.* Cup-shaped.

147. *Dirge.* This song is assigned to two singers in the play, Guiderius and Arviragus, sons of Cymbeline, disguised under the names of Polydore and Cadwal. The first stanza is sung by Guiderius, the second by Arviragus, the last two in alternate lines, beginning with Guiderius, save for the last two verses of each stanza, which are sung together.

147 14. *Thunder-stone.* A common word for thunder-bolt. (Hudson.)

147 15. *Censure rash.* Hasty, adverse judgment; *adverse* being here implied in the context, and not resident in the meaning of *censure.*

147 18. *Consign to thee.* "Seal the same contract with thee, *i.e.*, add their names to thine upon the register of death." (Steevens.)

148 19. *Exorciser.* "Sh. always uses this word to signify one that raises spirits, not one that lays them." (Mason.)

148. *The Maid's Tragedy.* Mr. Fleay assigns this play to 1612, Mr. G. C. Macaulay to 1609. (*Francis Beaumont, a Critical Study*, p. 195.)

148 7. *Lie lightly, gentle earth.* Cf. the familiar phrase of Latin monuments: *Sit tibi terra levis*, and Martial, *Epigrams*, v, 34 : —

> Nec illi,
> Terra, gravis fueris : non fuit illa tibi.

See also Jonson's *Epig.* xxii, *On my first daughter*, which Mr. Fleay assigns to the year 1593 : —

> This grave partakes the fleshly birth,
> Which cover lightly, gentle earth.

Still another parallel in a *Sonnet on the Death of Beaumont*, was pointed out by Dyce, in the *Introductory Essay* to his ed. of Beaumont and Fletcher, I, 28.

148. *All in Naught.* Oliphant considers this poem a translation from the Italian, but gives no reference. (*Musa Madr.*, p. 187.) In form the poem is really a quatorzain, although divided into two stanzas of equal length, showing the influence of that popular form in length and metre, although not preserving its other features. This poem is notable in another respect, from the fact that, although an undoubted lyric, only the concluding couplet of each stanza rimes. In this respect it may be compared with Jonson's *Æglamour's Lament*, p. 194.

149. *Thomas Ravenscroft* was the editor of three works entitled respectively *Pammelia*, *Deuteromelia*, and *Melismata*, published between 1609 and 1611. These collections differ materially from those of the writers of Madrigals in including catches, rounds, canons. *A Brief Discourse*, 1614, includes verses on "five usual recreations: hunting, hawking, dauncing, drinking, enamouring." See Oliphant, *Mus. Madr.*, p. 256, and Linton, *Rare Poems*, p. 260. Oliphant, *ib.*, p. 232, denies that Ravenscroft was concerned in *Deuteromelia* or *Pammelia*. The music of this song is given by Chappell, as above, p. 77.

150 7. *Bullyboy.* A jolly fellow; cf. *M. N. D.*, iii, 1, 8: "What sayst thou, *bully* Bottom?"

150 6. *Noises.* Disturbances making for notoriety.

151. *Simplex Munditiis.* Cf. with this poem Herrick's *A sweet disorder in the dress* (*Selections from Herrick*, 1882, p. 24), and the anonymous *My love in her attire doth show her wit*, p. 127 of this volume. This song is modelled on some Latin verses of Jean Bonnefons: "Semper munditias, semper, Basilissa, decores," etc., which form part of his work entitled *Pancharis*. Gifford has also pointed out an imitation of this poem as late as Flecknoe, which he quotes, ed. Jonson, III, 348.

151 1. *Still to be neat.* Always to be finical, over-careful in dress.

151 10. *Taketh me.* Captivates me.

151. *The Muses' Garden*, etc. This song-book is apparently now hopelessly lost. In 1812 Beloe printed six songs from it — all that now remain — in his *Anecdotes of Literature and Scarce Books*, 1807-12, VI, 162-69. These Mr. Bullen has included in his volume, *More Lyrics from Elizabethan Song-Books*.

151 7. *Toy.* Trifle. Cf. 4 36.

151 11. *Self-proof.* Proof of your own, experience. Cf. Shakespeare, *Rich. II*, ii, 3, 80: "Self-born arms," arms sprung from amongst us, civil-war.

152 17-18. *Love's martyr*, etc. Professor Kittredge suggests: Taking *confessor* "not in the sense of shrift-father but in the sense of one who makes public confession of his faith in a religion (Edward the Confessor

and the like)," the passage may be paraphrased: "Those who profess and suffer for Love (*Love's Martyrs*) often at the last confess to their being, as it were, devotees of Care."

152 7–9. *How many walls.* Cf. 17 3.

152 14. *Charàcters.* The accent, as usual, on the penultimate. Cf. 177 5.

153. *Beaumont and Fletcher.* I pefer the old-fashioned designation, wherever possible. If we are to accept Mr. G. C. Macaulay's reasonable theory, this play is largely the work of Beaumont, and was written about 1610. (*Francis Beaumont*, p. 50.)

153 2. *Whiles.* Genitive of *while*, during the time when. Cf. *Sh. Gram.*, § 137.

153 12. *Enow.* Enough. Both forms were common. So decisive a wrench of accent as we seem to have here is very unusual in such smooth versifiers as both Beaumont and Fletcher.

153. *Tethys' Festival.* This Masque was celebrated at Whitehall, June 5, 1610, on the occasion of the creation of Henry, Prince of Wales; Inigo Jones, the famous architect, was Daniel's coadjutor. (*Daniel's Works*, ed. Grosart, III, 304 *sqq.*) The title is Mr. Bullen's.

154 15. *Sudden.* Suddenly. Cf. 146 12.

154 18. *Length it.* Lengthen it. Cf. 58 10.

154. *A Sea Dirge.* Cf. Charles Lamb's note on this poem and Webster's *Dirge*, p. 145 above.

155 5. *After summer merrily*, *i.e.*, in pursuit of summer like the swallow. (Dyce.)

155 2. *Against the sun.* Opposite to the sun. Cf. the same expression, 161 4.

155 4. *Won.* Dwell.

155 6. *Walls of clay.* A common building material of the day for humbler houses. See Harrison's *A Description of England*, Camelot Series, pp. 114–115.

155. *Love's Immortality.* Oliphant has a note on this madrigal in which he quotes these lines, by way of parallel, from the *Diana* of Montemayor, "thus rendered by Sir Philip Sidney":—

> On sandy bank of late
> I saw this woman sit;
> Where, 'sooner die than change my state.'
> She with her finger writ.

Oliphant continues: "the point, however, is not concluded as in Byrd's version." (*Musa Madr.*, p. 37.)

155. *The Forest.* These two songs are numbered i and vii of this collection of Jonson's.

156. *That women,* etc. This song was written for the Countess of Pembroke in penance for maintaining her Lord's opinion against hers. (Drummond, *Conversations,* as above, p. 25.) Mr. Fleay puts the date of its composition as early as 1605. (*The English Drama,* I, 321.) "Beaumont," says Mr. Swinburne, "must have taken as a model of his lighter lyric style the bright and ringing verses on the proposition 'that women are but men's shadows.'" (*A Study,* as above, p. 103.) Professor Kittredge calls my attention to the following striking parallel from an *Eclogue* of Bernardino Baldi (1553–1617) entitled *I Metitori* (vv. 122–125): —

> Fatta appunto la donna è come l'ombra
> De' nostri corpi, che seguita, mai
> Arrivar non si lascia; ed a colui,
> Che s'invola da lei sempr' è a le spalle.

156 2. *The screech-owl and the whistler shrill.* Cf. *The Faery Queen,* ii, 12, 36 : —

> Fatal birds about them flockèd were
> .   .   .   .   .   .
> The ill-faced owl, death's dreadful messenger.
> .   .   .   .   .   .
> The whistler shrill, that whoso heares doth dy.

157 6. *Competent.* Sufficient, enough for one, even of your rank, in the grave.

157. *Phillada flouts me.* "The air [*Phillada flouts me*] is referred to as 'a new tune' in *The Crown Garland of Roses,* 1612." (Linton, *Rare Poems,* p. 261.) I take my text from the reprint of *Wits Treasury,* ed. 1658, *Musarum Deliciae,* Hotten, London, 1817.

157 11. *Alack.* Cf. 44 2. *Well a day* = alas; an altered form of *well a way.*

158 19. *To the wine.* "Up to the time at which the wine was served and the women left the table," Linton explains. Perhaps the meaning is no more than "Will got her to accept his treat of wine" though she would not dine with me.

158 28. *Entertain me.* Consider me, receive me [as thy lover].

158 34. *A bag full of shreds.* Possibly bits of ribband or cloth, preserved for patchwork or for weaving.

158 35. *Goods.* Linton emends "guedes" for the rime's sake.

158 37. *Clout.* Kerchief. Cf. 125 8, where, however, the term is used of like trifles generally.

158 38. *Blue Coventry.* The *Century Dictionary* defines this, "a blue thread of a superior dye, used for embroidery." This would apply very well here, but scarcely to Drayton's shepherd's 'breech of Cointree blue." (*Ballad of Dowsabel.*) It is probable that the term applies rather to the color than the material. "Coventry blue stuffs were as famous as Lincoln green," comments Mr. Bullen.

159 47. *Death strikes me with his dart!* Cf. the second stanza of Lyly's *Vulcan's Song*, p. 22, which well expresses the plight of Phillada's lover.

159 53. *Whigge.* A sort of sour buttermilk or acidulated whey. *Whilst thou burst.* Until, up to the time when. Not an uncommon idiom. Cf. *Twelfth Night*, iv, 3, 28: "He shall conceal it *whiles* (till) you are willing it shall come to note." *Sh. Gram.*, § 137.

159 54. *Ramble-berry.* More usually bramble-berry.

159 58. *Weaver's skin.* Surely quite as good as Mr. Linton's emendation, *weevil's skin.* It is possible that *wether's skin* of Ritson is nearer the true reading.

160. *John Fletcher* was the son of Dr. Richard Fletcher, afterwards Bishop of London. He was probably educated at Cambridge, and led to authorship by his younger associate, Beaumont, and through the encouragement of Jonson and Chapman. Fletcher collaborated with several other playwrights besides Beaumont. The plays attributed to their joint authorship succeeded to the supreme popularity which Shakespeare had long enjoyed, and held the stage until Restoration times, and after.

160. *A Bridal Song.* The weight of authority is against the Shakespearian authorship of this beautiful song. It is certainly much in Shakespeare's manner; but there are other cases in which Fletcher has caught at least the outward style of his great master. Mr. Bullen indicates the general feeling of doubt in giving the song "tentatively to Fletcher," as he puts it ; adding, "but I have a strong suspicion that it is by Shakespeare." (*Lyrics from Elizabethan Dramatists*, p. 40.) Cf. with this song the song from *Valentinian*, *Now the lusty spring is seen*, p. 172.

160 4. *Maiden pinks.* Fresh pinks.

160 9. *With her bells dim.* Mr. W. J. Linton unnecessarily emends "with harebells slim."

160 12. *Larks'-heels.* The nasturtium; also explained as the larkspur.

160 15. *Their sense.* Sense is here plural. Cf. ll 3.

161 20. *Chough hoar.* This is the reading of Seward; the old edd. read *clough hee* or *clough he.*

161. *Orlando Gibbons* was "batchelor of music and organist to his Majesty's honorable Chapel in ordinary."

161 6. *Hour.* Dissyllabic. Cf. 21 13, 43 10.

161. *Francis Beaumont.* The particulars of the life of Beaumont are, like those of so many of his contemporaries, quite beyond our reach. We know that he had all the advantages of gentle nurture, an excellent education, a small competence, and the devoted — at times almost deferential — friendship of his most celebrated seniors in literature. See an excellent monograph on Beaumont by Mr. G. C. Macaulay, London, 1883.

161. *Song for a Dance.* This is Mr. Bullen's title; the poem is entitled *First Song* in the Masque.

162. *Praise of Ceres.* Mr. Fleay places the performance of this play in 1595. The evidence is doubtful, although everything points to a date earlier than 1613. I curtail the unnecessary repetition of the last word of the first and third lines of each stanza, printed, doubtless for the sake of the accompanying tune, thus :

> Sing their harvest home, home, home.

162 8. *Champians.* Champaign, open country.

162. *What is Love.* This song with certain variations is found in *The Knight of the Burning Pestle.* Mr. G. C. Macaulay considers that Beaumont had a share in *The Captain.*

162 7. *Prove.* Try it, test it.

163. *Melancholy.* It has long since been remarked that this poem suggested Milton's *Il Penseroso.* There is a reply to Fletcher's verses by Dr. William Strode, published in *Wit Restored,* 1658 (Reprint, 1817, p. 184), a piece of small merit, but it is hardly probable that this had any effect in suggesting Milton's companion piece, *L'Allegro.*

164. *King Henry VIII.* I accept the orthodox date of Dyce, Collier and Delius on this much mooted question. Mr. Fleay assigns Shakespeare's version of the play to 1609 and the rewritten drama by Fletcher and Massinger to 1617. (See his *Life of Sh.,* pp. 68-69.) Notice the freedom of the phrasing of this poem, especially the first stanza.

164 5. *As.* As if.

164 9. *Lay by.* Ceased, rested.

164. *Two Books of Airs.* Mr. Bullen assigns this book to the year 1613 on the internal evidence of an allusion to the death of Prince Henry. (*Lyrics from Elizabethan Song-Books,* p. xv.)

164. *Awake, awake.* "Henry Vaughan is the one English poet

whose devotional fervor found the highest lyrical expression; and Campion's impassioned poem 'Awake, awake,' . . . is not unworthy the great Silurist ": thus writes Mr. Bullen in the same place.

165 9. *Yields but the model of a span.* Cf. 206 1-2.

165. *Sic Transit.* I take the title for this poem from Mr. Palgrave, who has included it in his *Golden Treasury*, ed. 1892.

165 11. *Part of my life.* *I.e.*, Night is a part of life, because, although spent in sleep which is *feigned death* and the negation of activity (*in that you life deny*), its purpose is *life sweetly to renew.*

165. *Hymen's Triumph, a Pastoral Tragi-Comedy,* was performed at Somerset House at the marriage of Lord Roxburgh to Mistress Jane Drummond; "'solemn and dull' writes Mr. Chamberlain." (Fleay.)

166. *Sir Henry Wotton* was a man of excellent birth and education who left England for a time in consequence of the fall of his patron, the Earl of Essex. His service in disclosing to James, while he was yet in Scotland, a plot against that monarch's life, procured him royal favor, and he was afterwards employed on many diplomatic missions. Wotton was highly esteemed in his day as a statesman, a writer, and an amiable and honorable man. (Condensed from Nicolas' Introduction to *The Poetical Rhapsody*, p. cxviii.)

166. *Overbury's Wife and Characters,* 1614. This was the fourth edition.

166. *The Character of a Happy Life.* I take my text of this exceedingly popular poem from *Reliquiæ Wottonianæ*, 1672, the third ed., with certain changes, the sources of which are noted below. The poem exists in many versions, MS. and printed, for an account of which see Hannah's *Poems of Wotton, Raleigh and Others*, 1845, pp. 28-31. Cf. with this poem in general tone that of Essex, p. 94. In *Notes and Queries* (Series I, IX, 420) a question is raised as to whether these lines are the translation of a similar German poem, the work of George Rudolf Weckherlin, whose *Oden und Gesänge* appeared in 1618 and 1619, his *Gaistliche und weltliche Gedichte*, in 1641 and 1648, and who died in 1653, in London. The poem in question, entitled *Kennzaichen eines glückseeligen Lebens*, appears in Müller's *Bibliothek deutscher Dichter des siebzehnten Jahrhunderts*, ed. Leipzig, 1823, and also in *Georg Rudolf Weckherlin's Gedichte herausgegeben von Hermann Fischer*, I, 148. The volume last mentioned contains also a translation of Daniel's *Ulysses and the Siren;* elsewhere Weckherlin has translated Raleigh's *Lie* literally, though prosaically, and without reference to its English original. It is not probable that the borrowing was Wotton's. The personal acquaintance of the two writers is established by a long complimentary poem of Weckherlin's *An Herrn Heinrich Wotton, Engelländischen Rittern* (ed. Fischer, I, 231).

166 6. *Still prepared.* Ever ready.

166 8. *Of princes' grace or vulgar breath.* This is the reading of a copy in the handwriting of Jonson, which was found by Collier at Dulwich College. (See his *Memoirs of Alleyn*, p. 53.) Drummond tells us of Jonson : "Sir Edward [*i.e.*, Henry] Wotton's verses of a happy life he hath by heart." (*Conversations*, p. 8.)

166 9. In this verse I read with the same, as well as other MSS., *envieth* for 'envies,' and *whom* for 'that.'

166 10. In this verse I follow again the Jonson MS.; the text of *Rel. Wotton.* is hopelessly corrupt.

166 13. *Rumors.* The reading of the Jonson MS., and other authorities. Collier's faulty copy reads *humors*, which G. F. Warner corrects. *Catalogue of the Manuscripts and Muniments of Alleyn's College of God's Gift at Dulwich*, 1881, pp. 59–60.

166 15. *State.* Estate, position in life.

167 20. *Well-chosen.* The reading of all versions save that of *Rel. Wotton.*, which has *religious.*

167. *William Browne* of Tavistock was educated at Oxford and the Inner Temple, and was, in his youth, intimate with Jonson, Selden and Drayton ; but little is known of his life. In literature, he is the chief of that group of writers which has been dubbed 'the School of Spenser,' although the influence of the Drayton of the *Polyolbion* and *The Muses Elizium*, seems to me scarcely less an element in Browne's pastorals. I take my text of Browne from *The Poems of William Browne of Tavistock*, edited by Gordon Goodwin, 1894.

167. *The Inner Temple Masque* was first published by Thomas Davies in his ed. of Browne, 1772. (Goodwin, I, xi, f.)

167. *Song of the Siren.* Lowell tells us that these beautiful verses were suggested by the sirens' song to Sir Guyon in the *Faery Queene.*

> 'O thou fair son of gentle Faëry,
> That art in mighty arms most magnified
> Above all knights that ever battle tried,
> O turn thy rudder hitherward awhile,
> Here may thy storm-beat vessel safely ride ;
> This is the port of rest from troublous toil,
> The world's sweet inn from pain and wearisome turmoil.'

> With that the rolling sea, resounding swift
> In his big bass, them fitly answerèd.

(See Lowell's *Prose Works,* the Essay on Spenser, IV, 349; and *Faery Queene,* ii, 12, 32; cf. also Daniel's well-known *Ulysses and the Siren,* ed. Grosart, I, 270, and *Odyssey,* xii, 180 *seq.*

167 4. *Passengers.* Here is the older sense of a wayfarer or traveler.

167 5. *Perfumes . . . which make the Phoenix' urn and nest.* The aromatic herbs with which the Phoenix built its nest on preparing to die in the flames; hence appropriately an urn as well as nest. Cf. Lactantius, *Elegia de Phoenice* and Herrick, *A Nuptial Song on Sir Clipseby Crew* (*Hesperides,* ed. 1869, I, 119):

> The phoenix nest,
> Built up of odors, burneth in her breast.
> Who therein would not consume
> His soul to ash-heaps in that rich perfume?
> Bestroking Fate the while
> He burns in embers on the pile.

167 8. *Oppose.* A play on the two meanings of the word, to set or place opposite and to resist.

167 15. *The compass Love shall . . . sing.* An evident play upon the two meanings of the word *compass. Sing compass* would then mean : (1) tell the points of the compass, the nautical instrument, cf. v. 18 below; and (2) show the range of your voice in singing; cf. *ring compass,* 93 13 above.

167 16. *As he, i.e.,* Love, *goes about the ring.* Love, moving from Siren to Siren, is likened to the needle of the compass moving from point to point.

168. *The Charm.* This poem was quoted with appreciation by Warton in his *History of English Poetry* (ed. Hazlitt, III, 321), first published in 1777–81 ; Warton was also the first to suggest Milton's relation and debt to Browne.

168 6. *Mandragoras.* Cf. mandrake, 97 2.

168 7. *Simples.* Medicinal herbs so named as forming a single or simple ingredient in a compound.

168 9. *Coil.* Tumult, disturbance. Cf. 196 22.

168 15. *Moly.* Cf. *Odyssey,* x, 305.

168 17. *Jaspis.* Jasper, supposed by the ancients to have the virtue of breaking a spell or charm.

168 18. *Sagest Greek. . . . .* The song is broken off by the continuance of the action of the Masque.

168. *George Wither,* the early friend and companion of Browne, is one of the poets whom the untimely death of Prince Henry hurried into

song. His best work is contained in *Fidelia, The Mistress of Phil'arete*,
and *The Shepherd's Hunting;* in later years he degenerated into a
mere pamphleteer of unexampled "moral garrulity and tedious length."
Wither was praised by Charles Lamb for his heptasyllabic trochaics,
and contrasted, in his poetry and character, with Robert Burns. (*On
the Poetical Works of George Wither, Works of Lamb*, II, 405.)

168. *Shall I wasting.* "I have transcribed this song *verbatim et
literatim* (for it is too precious not to be given exactly as it first saw
the light)," says Mr. W. T. Arnold, "from the original edition of
Fidelia in which it first appeared. Mr. W. C. Hazlitt in his *Handbook
to Early English Literature* assumes the existence of an edition in
1617, before the well-known second edition in the latter part of the
same year; but adds : — 'This first edition is supposed to have been
privately printed. No copy is at present known.' There is, however,
a copy of this treasure in the Bodleian Library. As I write, the title
page of it is before me: — *Fidelia, London*, Printed by *Nicholas Oakes*,
1615." (Ward's *English Poets*, II, 96.) I need scarcely add that I
have followed this version. This poem was extremely popular and
led to many imitations and parodies; the most famous of these were
Jonson's, and the one attributed to Raleigh (printed in Hannah's ed. of
that poet, p. 82; and see Arber, *Engl. Garner*, IV, 577).

169 9. *Seely.* Simple, innocent. Cf. 6 22.

169 14. *Pelican.* In allusion to the popular fable that the pelican
feeds and revives its young with its own blood.

170. *Poems.* The chronology of the poems ascribed to Beaumont
— those not in the plays — is unascertainable; as, with the exception
of *Salmacis and Hermaphroditus*, which is doubtless not his, none of
his non-dramatic works were published until 1640. Indeed the evidence
as to all of these poems is more or less apocryphal, as the publisher
certainly included many things not possibly Beaumont's.

170 15. *For me.* As far as I am concerned, or perhaps the very
common (Lat. abl. of price): exchange me for him. Cf. 'I would not
change for thine,' 133 ℵ.

170 18. *Their* referring to *he or she*, a common modern colloquialism.

170. *On the Life of Man.* On this poem Hazlitt enthusiastically exclaims : "'The silver foam which the wind severs from the parted
wave' is not more light or sparkling than this : the dove's downy
pinion is not smoother and softer than the verse . . . the poetry of
that day . . . often wore a sylph-like form with Attic vest, with faëry
feet, and the butterfly's gaudy wing. The bees were said to have come,
and built their hive in the mouth of Plato when a child ; and the fable

might be transferred to the sweeter accents of Beaumont and Fletcher."
(*On the Age of Elizabeth,* ed. Bohn, p. 173.)   Cf. this poem with those of
similar structure on pp. 66 and 109 above.   It has been attributed to
Bishop King, and weakly imitated by Simon Wastell in his *Microbiblion,*
1629.   (See Ellis, *Specimens of the Early English Poets,* II, 319.)

171.   *On the Tombs, etc.*   This is regarded as probably Beaumont's
by Mr. Macaulay.   (*Francis Beaumont,* as above, p. 199.)

171 5.   *Lie, had realms.*   Note the omission of the relative.

172.   *The Bloody Brother ; Valentinian.*   I again follow Mr. Fleay
as to the probable date of the performance of these two plays.

172 12.   *Fall with the leaves still in October.*   This familiar simile,
which I trust has long survived any fidelity to the actual habits of the
American college youth, was early imitated by John Hilton, *Ayres or
Fa-las for Three Voices,* 1627 : —

> If any so wise is
> That sack he despises,
> Let him drink his small beer and be sober ;
> Whilst we drink sack and sing
> As if it were spring,
> He shall droop like the trees in October.

173 15.   *Cherries kissing as they grow.*   Cf. Campion's poem, *Cherry
Ripe,* 140 above.

173 17.   *Even ripe below.*   Evenly ripe, or perhaps ripe even below,
i.e., on the side furthest from the sun.

173.   *Care-Charming Sleep.*   Fletcher has certainly succeeded in ringing a new melody out of this old and popular theme in these tender and
delicate lines.   Cf. 50, note.

173 5.   *Light.*   The folios read *sweet.*

173 7.   *Sing his pain.*   Assuage his pain by singing.   (Mason.)

173 3.   *Lusty grapes.*   Browne uses the same adjective. 177 21.

173 5.   *Mazer.*   A beaker, or bowl.

174.   *What Wight he Loved.*   Cf. with this poem, Crashaw's, *Wishes
to his Supposed Mistress, Works, Library of Old Authors,* p. 133.   This
poem is much in the manner of Wither : a characteristic explainable by
Wither's intimacy with Browne, *The Shepherd's Pipe* being the joint
production of the two poets.

174 3.   *Move.*   Here = exist.

174 8.   *As.*   That.

175.   *Lansdowne MS.* 777 bears date 1650.   These poems were
first printed in 1815 by Sir S. Egerton Brydges at his Lee Priory Press.

I have placed them thus early as unquestionably most of Browne's poetry was written in his youth.

175 5–7. *Love, that to the voice,* etc. Love, that is near to the voice which breaks from your ivory pale, need not fear, etc.

175 13. *Still.* Cf. 14 9; and below, vv. 19, 20. 177 17.

176 32. *Brief.* Abstract.

176. *A Round.* "Catch Round or Roundelay, and Canon in unison, are, in music, nearly the same thing. In all the harmony is to be sung by several persons; and is so contrived, that, though each sings precisely the same notes as his fellows, yet, by beginning at stated periods of time from each other, there results a harmony of as many parts as there are singers." (Chappell, *Early English Popular Music,* I, 66, note.)

176 7. *Then here's,* etc. The numerals denote the singers, as the word *all* denotes the chorus. Cf. Dekker's *Three Men's Song,* 92, above. This song was apparently very popular, as in *Poor Robin's Almanac,* 1699, it is alluded to as well known : "Now [June] is the time when farmers shear their sheep . . . and yet for all this, the old song is in force still and ever will be:
        Shear sheep that have 'em cry we still."
                        (Bullen in *Browne,* ed. Goodwin, I, xxxiii.)

176 12. *Not I.* The MS. reads *nor* I.

176 14. *No hogs are in my ground.* A proverb.

177. *Cælia* is the title of the second section of the *Lansdowne MS.* It consists of fourteen sonnets, all in the Shakespearian form.

177 3. *Wight.* Mortal, being. Cf. 23 4.

177 5. *Characters.* Cf. 152 14.

177 7. *Ta'en.* Taken ; a familiar Middle English contraction.

177 10. *As.* As if. Cf. 164 4.

177 13. *Fair.* Fair one. Cf. Daniel's use of this adjective as a noun in the same sense as here, 51 15.

177. *Visions.* The seven poems constituting this, the fifth section of the MS. are "closely imitated from Spenser's *Visions of the World's Vanity* and his translations of the *Visions of Bellay.*" (Goodwin.)

178 12. *Their proper use.* Their own special or peculiar use.

178 14. *So.* Such.

178. *For her gait.* This little song was first printed with two sonnets from the same MS., by Mr. Goodwin in his ed. of Browne, I, 226.

178 3. *State's sake.* State = dignity of bearing or carriage. Cf. Sidney's use of the same word, 11 5 above.

179. *William Drummond, Poems.* The text of the later edd. of Drummond is probably more hopelessly and carelessly inaccurate than

that of any other early English poet approaching his rank ; this is especially true of Cunningham's ed. of 1833 and Turnbull's in the *Library of Old Authors.* I have collated each of the poems contained in this collection with the first folio of the poet's collected works "published at Edinburgh in 1711 under the superintendence of Bishop Sage and Thomas Ruddiman." (Masson, *Drummond of Hawthornden,* Preface, p. vii.) I have also had access, through the kindness of Marshall C. Lefferts, Esq., of New York, to his copy of *The Most Elegant and Elaborate Poems of that great Court-wit Mr. William Drummond etc.,* 1659, the readings of which agree closely with the folio just mentioned. By these means several readings have been restored in even these few poems. Each is noted below. I have not been able to see any of the earlier separate edd. of Drummond.

179 7. *Impórtune.* Accent on the penult. *Who like case pretends.* Who offers or presents a similar condition.

179 10. *Thou . . . complains.* Cf. 84 5 and the note thereon.

179 11. *Sith.* Drummond generally employs this form for *since* (sithence), which had come to be the prevailing form in the England — if not the Scotland — of his day. Cf. 63 13, 127 7, 180 2, 11, 181 5.

179 14. *Sighed.* Later edd. read *sobbed.*

179 4. *Gracing grace.* Cf. note on 14 8.

179 5. *In fair Paestana's,* etc. Later edd., *In flowery Paestum's field perhaps you grew.* Notice Drummond's admirable use of melodious proper names in this madrigal. Paestum, a town in Lucania, was celebrated for its beautiful roses, Mount Hybla in Sicily, for its honey ; the plains surrounding Enna, also in Sicily, were of remarkable fertility and on them was situate a temple to Ceres. Lastly, Mount Tmolus, Asia Minor, was famed for its wine, saffron, and precious minerals.

180 11. *Blissed.* Cf. *Ballad of Dowsabel* (*Drayton's Select Poems,* ed. Bullen, p. 5): " There's never shepherd boy that ever was so *blissed,*" and 37 28 above.

180 8. *Fatal lot.* Death.

180 1. *Thy head with flames.* I have inverted the first and second lines of this sonnet to preserve the arrangement of rimes.

180 1. *Thy mantle.* Main finds a parallel to this in Spenser's *Son.,* lxx.

180 2. *Turn'st.* Return'st. Notice the play upon this and the more usual modern meaning of the word in v. 8.

180 8. *Sweets in sours.* *In* = into.

180 13. *Neglected virtue.* *Virtue neglected* would be the more usual modern order of the case absolute.

180 14. *Thine. I.e.,* thy virtues.

181. *Life a Bubble.* The concluding lines of this madrigal have often been printed:

> For even when most admired, it in a thought,
> As swelled from nothing, doth dissolve in naught.

181. *To his lute.* The general idea of this sonnet may have been suggested by Sidney, *Arcadia:* Grosart's *Sidney,* III, 8:

> My lute within thyself thy tunes enclose,
> Thy mistress' song is now a sorrow's cry. (Main.)

181 1. *Thou did grow.* Cf. 84 5, 132 1, 179 10.

181 3. *Immelodious winds.* Perhaps winds not having melody in themselves. "I cannot but think," says Hazlitt, after quoting several of the sonnets of Drummond, "that his sonnets come as near as almost any others to the perfection of this kind of writing, which should embody a sentiment and every shade of a sentiment, as it varies with time and place and humor, with the extravagance or lightness of a momentary impression, and should, when lengthened out into a series, form a history of the wayward moods of the poet's mind, the turns of his fate; and imprint the smile or frown of his mistress in indelible characters on the scattered leaves." (*On the Age of Elizabeth,* ed. Bohn, p. 181.) Those interested in the facts which underlie the subjective expression of poets, will find the story of Drummond's love and loss in Professor Masson's excellent, if somewhat voluble, *Drummond of Hawthornden,* pp. 43–53.

181 4. *Ramage.* A wood-song. (Nares' *Glossary,* s. v.)

182 6. *Grim grinning king.* Cf. Milton, *P. L.* ii. 846: "Death grinn'd horrible a grisly smile."

182. *Phyllis.* I am not certain that this little trifle may not have appeared in print in its author's life-time. Professor Kittredge calls my attention to the fact that it is taken from Marino, *Madrigal* xxxi.

182 2. Drummond uses this verse elsewhere, *Poems,* Part I, *Madrigal* xl:

> Like the Idalian queen,
> Her hair about her een.

After a reasonable eulogy of Drummond's prose, the preface to the ed. 1656 continues: "Neither is he less happy in his verse than prose : for here are all those graces met together that conduce anything towards the making up of a complete and perfect poet, a decent and becoming majesty, a brave and admirable height, and a wit so flowing that Jove himself never drank nectar that sparkled with a more

spritely lustre." This preface is signed E[dward P[hillips], Milton's
nephew, the author of the *Theatrum Poetarum*. (*Drummond of
Hawthornden*, p. 472.)

182. *Wouldst thou hear.* "The name of the lady upon whom this
most exquisite epitaph was written is unknown. Jonson wished it
concealed, and the secret seems to have been carefully kept until the
means of tracing it were lost." (Gifford's *Jonson*, VIII, 233.) Mr.
Fleay assigns the writing of this epitaph to *c.* 1602. (*The Engl. Drama*,
I, 320.) Cf. an epitaph of Browne's on Mrs. El. Y. (ed. Goodwin,
II, 343):

> Underneath this stone there lies
> More of beauty than are eyes
> Or to read that she is gone,
> Or alive to gaze upon.
>
> She in so much fairness clad,
> To each grace a virtue had;
> All her goodness cannot be
> Cut in marble. Memory
> Would be useless, ere we tell
> In a stone her worth. Farewell.

183. *The Triumph of Charis.* Mr. Fleay holds that nine of the ten
lyrics entitled *Charis* are referable to a Masque at Court in 1608.
(*The Engl. Drama*, I, 324.) The first stanza of this song was omitted
in the version of *The Devil is an Ass.* This poem has been variously
estimated: it certainly is very unequal. Hazlitt, in his *Lectures on the
Age of Elizabeth* (ed. Bohn, p. 207), dissects the last five verses, and
finds in them illustrations alike of "imagination," which "consists in
enriching one idea by another, which has the same feeling or set of
associations belonging to it in a higher degree," and "the quaint and
scholastic style," which "consists in comparing one thing to another by
the mere process of abstraction." Mr. Swinburne, too, indulges in
some eloquent and violent strictures upon Jonson's metre, declaring:
"His anapæsts are actually worse than Shelley's: which hope would
fain have assumed and charity would fain have believed to be impossible." (*A Study, etc.*, p. 104.)

183 10. *Through.* •Perhaps this word should be pronounced *thorough*
both times for the metre. Cf. *M. N. D.*, ii, 1, 3: "Thorough bush,
thorough brier."

183 15. *Forehead smoother.* An earlier and preferable reading to *forehead's smoother.*

184 19. *As.* That. *Alone there.* We should say 'there alone' or 'only.' *Triumphs.* The pronunciation of this word exhibits a divided usage in the age of Elizabeth. Cf. *Rich. III*, iii, 4, 91, and *Julius Caesar*, i, 1, 56.

184 19-20. *As alone there triumphs,* etc. Professor Kittredge sends the following explanation of these two verses: "In her face is present, in triumphant beauty, the supreme result (*all the good, all the gain*) of that balance of the warring elements which makes up human life and indeed the universe itself. The four elements are in themselves inconsistent and at war (as in chaos). The universe exists as a cosmos by virtue of a balancing of them. Every human body is, similarly, the resultant of the discordant elements ('Does not our life consist of the four elements?' says Sir Toby, *Twelfth Night*, ii, 3, 9). In my lady's face, then, the supreme result of the balance of those substances that make up the universe manifests itself in triumphant beauty."

184 21-34. Cf. Suckling's imitation of this stanza, entitled *A Song to a Lute* (*Poems of Suckling*, American ed., 1876, p. 7):

> Hast thou seen the down i' th' air,
>   When wanton blasts have tossed it ;
>   Or the ship on the sea,
>   When ruder waves have crossed it ?
> Hast thou marked the crocodile's weeping,
>   Or the fox's sleeping ?
> Or hast thou viewed the peacock in his pride,
>   Or the dove by his bride,
>   When he courts for his lechery?
> O so fickle, O so vain, O so false, so false is she !

184 28. *Nard.* More commonly spikenard. See Hazlitt's criticism of this figure. (As above, p. 208.)

184. *The Vision of Delight.* This Masque was presented at Court, Christmas of this year, the Queen taking a part. It is probably the Masque at which Pocahontas was present. See Captain John Smith's abstract of his petition to Queen Anne concerning Pocahontas. (*Works of Smith*, ed. Arber, p. 534.)

184 1. *Fant'sy.* The intermediate form between *phantasy* and *fancy*.

184 3. *Figures.* Images, forms of fancy.

184 6. *Fleam.* Phlegm, one of the four humors of which the human body was thought to be composed.

185. *Thrice toss,* etc. This fine sonnet is attributed to Thomas Campion in the Harleian MS., 6910, fol. 150, and was published by him in his *Third Book of Airs*, about 1617, in a version, which, omitting the

tenth and twelfth lines, converts the remaining into a succession of couplets. On the other hand, it is included amongst "Remains never till now imprinted," in the *Works of Joshua Sylvester*, ed. 1633. Dr. Grosart, the editor of Sylvester, feels very certain that the sonnet belongs to his author. (*Works of Sylvester, Chertsey Worthies*, II, 325, and I, xxvii f.); whilst Mr. Bullen, the editor of Campion, is none the less sure that "Sylvester has not a shadow of claim to it." (*Lyrics from Elizabethan Song Books*, Revised ed., p. 220.) See, however, Main's *Treasury*, p. 276, on the subject. As to the charms here recited, cf. Virgil, *Ecloga* viii, *Pharmaceutria.*

185. *Now winter nights.* Mr. Bullen records this as his favorite poem of the collection, *Lyrics from Elizabethan Song Books*, xvi.

185 4. *Airy.* Open to the air, breezy.

185 7. *Amaze.* Bewilder, daze. Cf. 66 15.

186 10. *Wait on.* Attend.

186 23. *Toys.* Trifles. Cf. 4 36.

186. *Silly boy.* Notice Campion's perfect mastery over the long trochaic line and the effect of the choice of metre. I have given 1617 as the date of the *Third*, as well as the *Fourth*, of Campion's *Books of Airs* on the authority of Mr. Bullen's ed.; in some of his earlier editings he assigned them to 1613.

186 1. *Silly.* Here probably *seely*, innocent.

186 3. *Are bereaved.* Destroyed, cut off. Rarely thus used.

186 6. *Artless.* Without guile. All is guileless that you now say.

187 10. And thy lively pleasant cheer, dejected (*i.e.,* changed to dejection), shall read grief on earth.

187 16. *Envying.* This is the usual Elizabethan accent of the verb. Cf. *Taming of the Shrew*, ii, 1, 18.

188 17. *That will still be free.* *I.e.,* true love will ever be free.

188. *Even Such is Time.* These verses also appear in *Reliquiæ Wottonianæ*, the only poem of the several therein ascribed to Raleigh which is undoubtedly his. "That his faith," says Oldys, "was no less steadfast in the hopes of a resurrection, we are convincingly assured by those verses, which, this last night of his life, he probably wrote also here, in the gatehouse, — they being found there in his Bible." This story is more probable of this poem than of any of the other poems to which it has been applied.

188. *Farewell, ye gilded follies.* This poem has been variously assigned to Donne and others. Cf. *The Complete Angler*, ed. 1653, p. 243, and *MS. Ashm.* 38, in which latter it is called "Doctor Donns valediction to the worlde." Later edd. of the *Angler* suggest: "Some

say written by Dr. Donne, *and some say, written by Sir Harry Wotton.*"
Raleigh and Sir Kenelm Digby have been likewise suggested. The
" bold and insolent vein " is not unlike Sir Walter, but there is no real
authority for ascribing the poem to him. Cf. with the general tenor of
this poem the *Passion of my Lord of Essex*, p. 94 above and also verses
to *Master Hugh Holland*, published in Dowland's *Second Book of Song
and Airs*, 1600 (*Lyr. Eliz. Song Books*, p. 31), beginning :

> From Fame's desire, from Love's delight retired,
> In these sad groves an hermit's life I lead,
> And those false pleasures, which I once admired,
> With sad remembrance of my fall I dread, etc.

188 3. *Pure clay.* Mere clay.
188 8. *Merely but* = but. *Veins.* Dispositions.
189 9. *Alone.* In modern English *only, no more than.*
189 17. *Unkind.* Unnatural, with probably a play upon the more
unusual meaning of the word.
189 18. *Mind.* A by-form of *mine.*
189 31. *Minion.* Darling.
189 31. *Vie angels with India.* Vie, here a technical term from the
game of gleek or primero, signifying to wager on a hand of cards.
Hence here to wager angel-nobles to an amount such as India, with all
her wealth, would not be able to equal or 'cover.' Cf. note on 130 42.
190 52. *Affect.* Strive after, 'cultivate.'
190 4. *Retire.* Withdraw or draw out.
191 3-4. *Ever ruing*, etc. Ever pitying those poor hearts, which are
still *pursuing their loves, i.e.,* wooing and as yet without requital.
192. *A Nymph's Passion.* Mr. Swinburne remarks that this poem
" is not only pretty and ingenious, but in the structure of its peculiar
stanza may remind a modern reader of some among the many metrical
experiments or inventions of . . . Miss Christina Rossetti." The structure of this stanza of Jonson really exhibits the influence of Donne.
Cf. his *Witchcraft by a Picture* (Riverside ed., p. 292) and his *Confined
Love (ibid.,* 283), in both of which the arrangement of rimes is identical
with this poem.
192 7. *A narrow joy is but our own.* Note the omission of the
relative.
192 10. *Jealous mad.* Mad with jealousy.
192 20. *I doubt he is not known.* I fear, suspect his real excellence
is not known, and, on the other hand, fear much more, etc. For this
use of the word *doubt* cf. *Mer. Wives*, i, 4, 42.

193. *The Hour-glass.* This song was written for Drummond at his
request and sent to him in Scotland. (See *Conversations*, as above,
p. 38.) Whalley refers the suggestion of the subject to a Latin epigram
by the Italian poet, Jerome Amaltheus, beginning :

Perspicuo in vitro pulvis qui dividit horas,
Dum vagus angustum saepe recurrit iter.
Olim erat Alcippus, etc.

Herrick, in a poem of the same title (*Hesperides, Library of Old Authors*,
I, 44), has applied this conceit to "lovers' tears," which

In life-time shed
Do restless run when they are dead.

193. *The Dream* Mr. Swinburne considers "one of Jonson's most
happily inspired and most happily expressed fancies"; not losing even
here, however, that tone of eccentric patronage which pervades so
much of this rhapsodic and ecstatic criticism, he concludes : "the close
of it is for once not less than charming." (*A Study*, as above, p. 105.)

193 6. *Attempt awake.* The folio reads *attempt t' awake.* The
emendation is Gifford's.

194 13. *Sleep['s].* The folios and subsequent editions read *sleep so
guilty.*

194 14. *As.* That.

194. *The Sad Shepherd.* The date of the composition of *The Sad
Shepherd* is beyond definite settlement. But many have doubted that
the play was really written towards the close of Jonson's career. Mr.
Fleay identifies it with *The May Lord* mentioned to Drummond in
1619, and assigns it to 1615. Goffe, who died in 1627, imitated *The
Sad Shepherd* in his *Careless Shepherd*, performed in 1629. I do not
feel sufficiently certain of Mr. Fleay's identification to accept his date ;
but include this selection in my period without hesitation. (See Fleay,
Chron. Biog. Hist. I, 379 f.)

194. *Æglamour's Lament.* These verses have all the 'notes' of the
lyric except rime. It would be hard to draw a line which should ex-
clude them. I am indebted to the suggestion of Professor Winchester
that they, as well as several other selections, were not omitted. Another example of the unrimed lyric will be found in the song, *All in
Naught*, p. 148 above. It may be worthy of note that in both of these
cases there is a return to rime in the concluding couplets.

194 6. *Blow-ball.* The downy head of the dandelion.

194 9. *As she had sowed them*, etc. Cf. 12 13.

194. *Since there's no help.* This famous sonnet appeared first in the
collected folio of Drayton's Works, 1619, p. 273, and is numbered 61 of
the sonnets, *Idea.* "From Anacreon to Moore, I know of no lines on
the old subject of lovers' quarrels, distinguished for equal tenderness
of sentiment. . . . Especially may be observed the exquisite graceful-
ness in the transition from the familiar tone in the first part of the
sonnet to the deeper feeling and the higher strain of the imagination at
the close." (Henry Reed, *British Poets,* I, 241.) It is interesting to
know that this was a favorite sonnet with Rossetti. In a letter to Mr.
T. Hall-Caine he writes:—"As for Drayton, his one incomparable
sonnet is the *Love Parting.* That is almost the best in the language, if
not quite." (*Recollections of D. G. Rossetti,* quoted by Mr. Bullen in his
Selections from the Poems of Michael Drayton, p. 195.) Cf. the subject
of this sonnet with the *Canzonet* below; the two poems must have been
written about the same time; possibly upon the same occurrence. It
appears that under the pseudonym of his 'fair Idea, soul-shrin'd Saint'
Drayton concealed the identity of his mistress, Anne Goodeere, the
daughter of his patron, Sir Henry Goodeere, of Powlesworth Abbey.
The lovers were eventually separated, and Drayton never married.

195. *The Crier* and the *Canzonet* following appear for the first time
in the fol. of 1619. The implication of Mr. Bullen that they are to be
found in the undated ed. of 1605 must be a mistake, as I do not find
them in that edition, in the edition of 1606, nor in the reprints of these
editions by the Spenser Society. (See Bullen's *Selections from the
Poems of Drayton,* p. 8.)

195 5. *O yes, O yes, O yes.* Hear! hear! the introductory words of
a proclamation, here that of the crier, to secure silence.

195 9. *Pain.* Pains.

195 11. *Owe.* Own. Cf. 123 7, 15.

195 16. *It was a tame heart* (hart) *and a dear* (deer). Cf. 78 67,
85 14, 130 42, 180 2, 5, 8 for like instances of puns.

195 18. *Haunt.* Custom, habit. Cf. Chaucer, *Canterbury Tales,
Prologue,* 447.

195 19. *Hardly.* With difficulty. Cf. 90 5.

196 8. *Stervèd.* Killed with want or privation ; partaking here more
of the modern signification of the Old English verb, *steorfan,* to die.

196 10. *Azure riverets branchèd.* Drayton uses the same phrase in
The Baron's War, cvi, 56, 2 : "Whose violet veins in branchèd riverets
flow."

196 14. *Prevented.* Anticipated.

196 17. *Clip.* Embrace.

196 22. *Coil.* Disturbance. Cf. 168 9.

196 23. *Nice.* Here with considerable tinge of the old meaning, foolish, trifling.

197. *Thomas Vautor.* Of Vautor we know no more than that he was Bachelor of Music and author of this book of songs.

197. *Sweet Suffolk Owl.* Cf. Shakespeare's well known song, p. 43 above and Tennyson's imitation of it : " When cats run home and light is come."

197. *Martin Peerson* was Bachelor of Music and author of a second book of songs entitled *Mottects or Grave Chamber Musique,* etc., 1630. This last contains a *Mourning Song of six parts for the Death of the late Right Honorable Sir Fulke Greville . . . Lord Brooke,* etc., and a dedication to the same nobleman. The work must have been in contemplation at the time of the assassination of Greville, two years earlier ; and discloses him, a patron and lover of art to the very close of his life.

197. *Lullaby.* This poem, as Professor Kittredge puts it, is "the ultimate expression of a mother's worship of her baby, her gratitude that it is hers, and her wish that she may be a perfect mother."

198 19–22. *Yet as I am,* etc. " Yet such as I am and so far as my powers extend, I must and will be thine, though it is true that all I am and can be is too little (too small a gift) in return for the gift that thou hast vouchsafed to make to me — namely, thyself. *Vouchsafe* carries out the spirit of the first stanza (' my sov'reign,' etc.)."

198 11. *Seld-seen.* Seldom seen.

199. *A woman will have her will.* Cf. the quest of the condemned knight in *The Wife of Bath's Tale.*

199 11. *Toys.* Trifles. Cf. 4 36, 151 7, 186 23.

199. *A Dialogue.* This poem and the last selection of this volume were first printed by Mr. Bullen in his *More Lyrics from Elizabethan Song Books,* 1888, from a MS., I, 5, 49, in the Library of Christ Church College, Oxford. Mr. Bullen gives no dates nor further particulars ; but by inference the *MS.* belongs to the early seventeenth century and probably falls within the period covered by this book. Cf. note on the poem, *guests,* 207, below.

200. *On his Mistress, Elizabeth.* This was the eldest daughter of James, "who, in the Low Countries and some parts of Germany," writes Howell (*Familiar Letters,* ed. Jacobs, p. 112), "is called the Queen of Boheme, and for her winning princely comportment the Queen of Hearts." She took great interest in the court entertainments of her father's reign, appearing in Daniel's masque, *Tethys' Festival.* To the festivities of her marriage with the Elector Palatine, Frederick V, in

1613, many poets of the day contributed: Chapman, Beaumont, Campion, Heywood, Donne and Wither. Her later life was one of much trial and vicissitude, through which she appears to have preserved the amiability and something of the levity of the Stuarts. This poem was printed "in a vacant page, before the other songs" of Este's collection. (Rimbault, as above, p. 48.)

    200 l. *You meaner beauties of the night.* Cf. Carew's lines *To his mistress confined,* (ed. 1824, p. 133):

        O think not   .   .   . .

        .   .   .   .

        My wandering eye

        Can stoop to common beauties of the sky.

The date of the writing of this poem was assigned by Freeman (*Kentish Poets,* I, 215).

    201. *Underneath this sable hearse.* This famous epitaph is found in *Lansdowne MS.* 777, with other epitaphs of Browne's; it also appears "in a middle seventeenth century MS. in Trinity College, Dublin," there subscribed, 'William Browne.' In Aubrey's *Memoirs of Natural Remarks on Wilts* (ed. Britton, 1847 p. 90), this epigram is said to have been "made by Mr. William Browne, who wrote the Pastorals," (*Notes and Queries,* Ser. I, III, 262); and Mr. Goodwin has lately found a passage, in which Browne himself apparently alludes to his authorship of this very epitaph. It is in his *Elegy on Charles, Lord Herbert,* a grandson of the Countess, and runs:

        And since my weak and saddest verse

        Was worthy thought to grace thy grandam's hearse,

        Accept of this.

Returning to the epitaph, it was first published in Osburne's *Traditional Memoirs of the Reign of King James,* 1658, p. 78, and also included in the *Poems* of the Countess' son, William, Earl of Pembroke and Sir Benjamin Rudyerd in 1660, p. 66; but "in neither volume is there any indication of authorship." Ben Jonson's claim to it, although the epitaph must be acknowledged to be much in his manner, rests solely upon Whalley's allegation of tradition, and on the fact that it has usually been included amongst Jonson's works by his editors: first by Whalley. (See his ed. of Jonson.) In both the MSS. above mentioned the second stanza follows. It is so inferior that Mr. W. C. Hazlitt believes it not to be Browne's, but the Earl of Pembroke's. (See Hazlitt's ed. of Browne, II, 373.) But as Mr. Goodwin has put it, "it must be remembered that Browne has occasionally marred his work by not knowing when to stay his hand." (Goodwin's Browne, II, 257.) The concluding conceit is by no means foreign to Browne's mode of thought. See especially his Epitaph *On one drowned in the snow*, Hazlitt's Browne, II, 339. I have therefore given both stanzas of the epigram in the text.

201 1. *Hearse.* The canopy of open work or trellis set over the tomb, and used to support candles at times of ceremony. Here = *tomb.*

201. *Hence away, you Sirens.* I take my text from the Spenser Society's Reprint of *The Mistress of Phil'arete, Poems of George Wither*, p. 814. There is a second, decidedly weaker version of this facile poem. Wither was often troubled with pangs of conscience for the levity of his earlier Muse; it may have been in one of these moments that he reduced his Sirens to one, and somewhat prudishly covered their antique nakedness.

201 4. *Prove.* Test, make trial of.

202 16. *Ray.* Radiance, light.

203 42. *Mates with him.* Enjoys like privileges, is his equal.

203 44. *There's noble hills.* A noun in the plural was often used as the logical subject of *is*. Cf. *Hen. V*, iv, 6, 32: "There is salmons in both."

203 52. *Greatest-fairest.* Wither had not lost the great Elizabethan daring in the formation of compounds. Cf. *never-touchèd thorn*, v. 34 above; and see 13 5, note.

204 73. *That coy one in the winning.* That one who is coy while winning or, as we say, while being won. This phrase almost amounts to a compound.

204 85–90. *Few attempt to gain favor with her.* And if a lover should be so bold as to woo (*complain*), she is not to be gained at a word.

204 96. *You labor–may.* You will find it a great labor.

205. *Flowers of Sion.* The text is here, as above, from the first folio collected edition, 1711.

205 1. *Brandons.* Torches. The fol. and the earlier collected ed. of 1656 read *tapers. Brandons* is apparently the earlier reading. See Main, *English Sonnets*, p. 432 f.

205 4. *Out-weep.* Cf. 13 5, note.

205 5–8. These locks, the gilt (*i.e.*, the golden and guilty) attire of blushing deeds; waves (of hair and of the sea) curling to shadow deep (conceal in their depths) wrackful shelves (ship-wrecking reefs); rings (ringlets of hair), which wed souls, etc., do now aspire to touch thy sacred feet.

205. *The Book of the World.* Main quotes besides a parallel in Daniel's *Defence of Rime*, the following lines from *Wither's Motto*, 1621 (as above, p. 325) : —

> For many books I care not ; and my store
> Might now suffice me, though I had no more
> ·Than God's two Testaments, and therewithall
> That mighty volume which we world do call.

205 9–12. Main likewise refers the reader for a parallel to these lines to *Astrophel and Stella*, xi : —

> For like a child that some fair book doth find,
> With gilded leaves and colored vellum plays,
> Or at the most on some fine picture stays,
> But never heeds the fruit of writer's mind, etc.

206. *The world's a bubble.* In the first ed. this poem was signed 'Ignoto.' It was first ascribed to Bacon in Farnaby's *Florilegium*, 1629, p. 10 ; elsewhere it has been variously ascribed to Raleigh, Donne, and to Henry Harrington. Although it compares rather favorably with Bacon's translations of the Psalms, in view of the fact that it is little more than a translation, and peculiarly in accord with the passionless worldliness that marks the character of the Lord Chancellor, I see no reason to doubt his authorship of it. The whole poem is a paraphrase of a Greek epigram attributed to Poseidippus, by others to Plato, the comic poet, or to Crates the Cynic, beginning :

> Ποίην τις βιότοιο τάμοι τρίβον; εἰν ἀγορῇ μὲν
> Νείκεα καὶ χαλεπαὶ πρήξιες · etc.

See *Anthol. Graeca*, IX, 359. I am indebted for this parallel to my friend and colleague, Professor Lamberton.

206 1. *The world's a bubble.* Cf. Drummond's Madrigal, *Life, a Bubble*, p. 181, above.

206 2. *Less than a span.* Cf. 165 8–9.

206 8. *Limns.* Paints.

207 25. *Affections.* Emotions, feelings. Cf. 115 13, 21.

207 29. *Noise.* Tumult, disturbance. Cf. 150 6.

207. *Guests.* "This magnificent descant," as Mr. Saintsbury calls it, was discovered by Mr. Bullen, and first printed in his *More Lyrics from Elizabethan Song Books* from the MS. K. 3. 43. 5 in the library of Christ Church College, Oxford. Well may Mr. Bullen declare that "verse so stately, so simple, so flawless, is not easily forgotten." Both Mr. Bullen and Mr. Saintsbury have surmised that Henry Vaughan is the

author. But as Thomas Ford, who set these words to music, was a musician in the suite of Prince Henry in 1607, and on the accession of Charles was appointed one of the king's musicians, dying, evidently a very old man, in 1648; and as Vaughan's earliest published work is dated 1650, I think that we may safely place this poem within our period. Mr. Bullen suggests that these verses may have once formed part of a longer poem. I have printed them for the first time in the stanzas which their structure demands.

208 7-18. "Few could have dealt with common household objects — tables and chairs and candles and the rest — in so dignified a spirit," comments Mr. Bullen.

208 10. *Order taken.* Arrangements made.

208 14. *Dazie.* A canopy of state. Mr. Bullen reads *dais.*

208 30. *Still lodge.* Ever lodge.

INDEX OF FIRST LINES.

This Index contains, besides the poems of the text, those which, belonging to this period, are quoted entire in the Introduction and Notes. Such poems are indicated by an asterisk.

INDEX OF AUTHORS AND EDITORS.

Names printed in Roman letters denote authors; those in italics, editors; the dates following are those of birth, earliest authorship and death. When the editor is unknown, MS. or other source is given. Original titles are printed in Roman; those assigned by others than the author, in italics; first lines are put in quotation marks.

INDEX OF INTRODUCTION AND NOTES.

ADVERTISEMENTS

ATHENÆUM PRESS SERIES.

ISSUED UNDER THE GENERAL EDITORSHIP OF

PROFESSOR GEORGE LYMAN KITTREDGE, *of Harvard University,*

AND

PROFESSOR C. T. WINCHESTER, *of Wesleyan University.*

IT is proposed to issue a series of carefully edited works in English Literature, under the above title. This series is intended primarily for use in colleges and higher schools; but it will furnish also to the general reader a library of the best things in English letters in editions at once popular and scholarly. The works selected will represent, with some degree of completeness, the course of English Literature from Chaucer to our own times.

The volumes will be moderate in price, yet attractive in appearance, and as nearly as possible uniform in size and style. Each volume will contain, in addition to an unabridged and critically accurate text, an Introduction and a body of Notes. The amount and nature of the annotation will, of course, vary with the age and character of the work edited. The notes will be full enough to explain every difficulty of language, allusion, or interpretation Full glossaries will be furnished when necessary.

The introductions are meant to be a distinctive feature of the series. Each introduction will give a brief biographical sketch of the author edited, and a somewhat extended study of his genius, his relation to his age, and his position in English literary history. The introductory matter will usually include a bibliography of the author or the work in hand, as well as a select list of critical and biographical books and articles. *See also Announcements.*

Sidney's Defense of Poesy.

Edited with an Introduction and Notes by ALBERT S. COOK, Professor of English in Yale University. 12mo. Cloth. xlv + 103 pages. By mail, 90 cents; for introduction, 80 cents.

William Minto, *Late Prof. of Literature, University of Aberdeen:* It seems to me to be a very thorough and instructive piece of work. The interests of the student are consulted in every sentence of the Introduction and Notes, and the paper of questions is admirable as a guide to the thorough study of the substance of the essay.

Ben Jonson's Timber: or Discoveries

Made upon Men and Matter, as they have Flowed out of his Daily Readings, or had their Reflux to his Peculiar Notions of the Times.

Edited, with Introduction and Notes, by FELIX E. SCHELLING, Professor in the University of Pennsylvania. 12mo. Cloth. xxxviii + 166 pages. Mailing price, 90 cents; for introduction, 80 cents.

THIS is the first attempt to edit a long-neglected English classic, which needs only to be better known to take its place among the best examples of the height of Elizabethan prose. The introduction and a copious body of notes have been framed with a view to the intelligent understanding of an author whose wide learning and wealth of allusion make him the fittest exponent of the scholarship as well as the literary style and feeling of his age.

Edward Dowden, *Prof. of English, Trinity College, Dublin, Ireland:* It is a matter for rejoicing that so valuable and interesting a piece of liter- atu.. as this prose work of Jonson should be made easily accessible, and should have all the advantages of scholarly editing.

Selections from the Essays of Francis Jeffrey.

Edited, with Introduction and Notes, by LEWIS E. GATES, Instructor in English in Harvard University. 12mo. Cloth. xlv + 213 pages. By mail, $1.00; for introduction, 90 cents.

THE selections are chosen to illustrate the qualities of Jeffrey's style and his range and methods as a literary critic. The introduction gives a brief sketch of the history of Reviews in England down to 1802 and suggests some of the more important changes in critical methods and in the relations between critic and public which were brought about by the establishment of the *Edinburgh Review.* This volume is especially valuable for classes that are beginning the independent study of literary topics and methods of criticism.

Charton Collins, *London, Author of "Bolingbroke and Voltaire," "Jonathan Swift," etc.:* The intro- duction gives succinctly and clearly all the facts which enable students to understand Jeffrey's character- istics as a man, his relative position to his contemporaries, his excellence, his deficiencies and his limitations. . . . I have no hesitation in saying that the book supplies a real want, and supplies it excellently.

Old English Ballads.

Selected and edited, with Notes and Introduction, by Professor F. B. GUMMERE of Haverford College. 12mo. Cloth. xcviii + 380 pages. By mail, $1.35; for introduction, $1.25.

THE aim has been to present the best of the traditional English and Scottish ballads and also to make the collection representative. The texts are printed with no "improvements" whatsoever, and but few changes in arrangement. The *Gest* of Robin Hood is given entire, not only for its intrinsic merits, but to assist in the study of epic development. The pieces have been arranged by subject, but not divided into groups or classes. The glossary will be found full, but simple. Philological details have been given only when the explanation of the passage rendered them necessary. The notes have been prepared according to the same principle, — the elucidation of the text and the thought. The introduction presents a detailed study of popular poetry and the views of its chief critics, with notes on metre, style, etc.

Selections from the Poetry and Prose of Thomas

Gray.

Edited, with Introduction and Notes, by WM. LYON PHELPS, Instructor in English Literature at Yale College. 12mo. Cloth. xi + 179 pages. By mail, $1.00; for introduction, 90 cents.

THIS volume contains all of the poems of Gray that are of any real interest and value, and the prose selections include the *Journal in the Lakes* entire, and extracts from his Letters of autobiographical and literary interest. The Introduction, besides containing a Life of Gray, a Bibliography, etc., gives a summary of his historical significance, with a critical review of his work. A special feature will be an article on *Gray's Knowledge of Norse*, by Professor Kittredge of Harvard. The text is taken directly from the original editions, and is printed entire with scrupulous accuracy. The Notes on the Poems explain every doubtful or obscure passage, all allusions to historical or literary matters, and give the most important parallel passages with exact references. The Notes on the Prose are very brief, and simply explanatory. This volume of Gray, besides being adapted for the general reader, will be especially useful in schools and colleges.

HIGHER ENGLISH.

[*See also Classics for Children, pages 2 to 5.*]

Lessons in English.

Adapted to the study of American Classics. A text-book for High Schools and Academies. By SARA E. H. LOCKWOOD, formerly teacher of English in the High School, New Haven, Conn. 12mo. Cloth. xix + 403 pages. Mailing price, $1.25; for introduction, $1.12.

Thanatopsis and Other Favorite Poems of Bryant.

Prepared especially to accompany Lockwood's Lessons in English. 12mo. Paper. 61 pages. Mailing price, 12 cents; for introd., 10 cents.

THIS is, in a word, a practical High School text-book of English, embracing language, composition, rhetoric, and literature. It presents in simple and attractive style, the essentials of good English ; and, at the same time, develops a critical literary taste, through the study of American Classics.

The plan provides for a course in English extending over the pupil's first year and a half in the High School, the work being preparatory to the study of English Literature as usually pursued in schools of this grade. These "Lessons" include the most important facts concerning the History and Elements of the Language, Common Errors in the Use of English, the Study of Words, Rules for the Construction of Sentences, Figures of Speech, Punctuation, Letter-Writing, Composition, and Biographical Sketches of the seven authors particularly studied, — Irving, Bryant, Longfellow, Whittier, Hawthorne, Holmes, and Lowell.

Katharine Lee Bates, *Professor of English, Wellesley College, Mass.:* While the treatment of the various subjects included is thorough, sound and clear, the art of the teacher is most happily displayed throughout. English study guided by this volume can hardly fail to be at once profitable and delightful.

F. A. Hill, *Prin. English High School, Cambridge, Mass.:* The book opens to me like a very sensible, practical and attractive book; and I may say that the author has hit the nail pretty squarely on the head.

James Winne, *Prin. High School, Poughkeepsie, N. Y.:* The more I examine it and other books, the more I like it. As yet I have found no text that I like so well as Lockwood's.

C. G. Dunlap, *Prof. of English, Kas. State University:* I know of no text-book on elementary English so satisfactory to me as this. Any student who masters it is soundly prepared in elementary English.

R. E. Blackwell, *Prof. of English, Randolph-Macon College, Virginia:* I was so pleased with the book that I put it into my preparatory class. It has stirred more interest in the study of English than any book I have ever used in that class.

The Practical Elements of Rhetoric.

By JOHN F. GENUNG, Ph.D., Professor of Rhetoric in Amherst College. 12mo. Cloth. xiv + 483 pages. Mailing price, $1.40; for introd., $1.25.

THE treatment is characterized by good sense, simplicity, originality, availability, completeness and ample illustration.

It is throughout constructive and the student is regarded at every step as endeavoring to make literature. All of the literary forms have been given something of the fulness hitherto accorded only to argument and oratory. No important principle has been presented without illustrations drawn from the usage of the best authorities.

Genung's Rhetoric, though a work on a trite subject, has aroused general enthusiasm by its freshness and practical worth. Among the many leading institutions that have introduced it are Wellesley, Smith, Vassar Colleges; Cornell, Johns Hopkins, Vanderbilt, Northwestern Universities; and the Universities of Virginia, North Carolina, Illinois, Minnesota, Kansas, Michigan.

C. F. Richardson, *Prof. of English, Literature, Dartmouth College, and author of a History of American Literature:* I find it excellent both in plan and execution.

Miss M. A. Jordan, *Prof. of Rhetoric, Smith College, Northampton, Mass.:* The critic is conscious of a feeling of surprise as he misses the orthodox dulness. The analysis of topics is clear, the illustrations are pertinent and of value in themselves, the rules are concise and portable.

T. W. Hunt, *Prof. of Eng. Literature, Princeton College, Princeton, N. J.:* It impresses me as a philosophic and useful manual. I like especially its literary spirit.

W. H. Magruder, *Prof. of English, Agricultural and Mechanical College of Mississippi:* For clearness of thought, lucidity of expression, aptness of illustration,—in short, for real teaching power,—I have never seen this work equalled.

A Handbook of Rhetorical Analysis.

Studies in Style and Invention, designed to accompany the author's *Practical Elements of Rhetoric.* By JOHN F. GENUNG, Ph.D., Professor of Rhetoric in Amherst College. 12mo. Cloth. xii + 306 pages. Mailing Price, $1.25; Introduction and Teachers' Price, $1.12.

THIS handbook follows the general plan of the larger text-book, being designed to alternate with that from time to time, as different stages of the subject are reached.

J. H. Gilmore, *Prof. of Rhetoric, University of Rochester, N. Y.:* This strikes me as a very significant attempt to open a road that college students especially need to travel.

C. L. Ehrenfeld, *Prof. English, Wittenberg College, Springfield, Ohio:* Its actual use in class work has confirmed my former favorable judgment of it.

Selections in English Prose from Elizabeth to
Victoria. 1580-1880.

By JAMES M. GARNETT, Professor of the English Language and Literature in the University of Virginia. 12mo. Cloth. ix + 701 pages. By mail, $1.65: for introduction, $1.50.

THE selections are accompanied by such explanatory notes as have been deemed necessary, and will average some twenty pages each. The object is to provide students with the texts themselves of the most prominent writers of English prose for the past three hundred years, in selections of sufficient length to be characteristic of the author, and, when possible, they are complete works or sections of works.

H. N. Ogden, *West Virginia University:* The book fulfills my expectations in every respect, and will become an indispensable help in the work of our senior English class.

F. B. Gummere, *Prof. of English, Haverford College:* I like the plan, the selections, and the making of the book.

Macaulay's Essay on Milton.

Edited, with Introduction and Notes, by HERBERT A. SMITH, Instructor in English in Yale University. 12mo. Paper.   pages. Mailing price,   cents; for introduction,   cents.

A CONVENIENT and well-edited edition of Macaulay's masterly essay on Milton. The introduction and notes are especially valuable to students.

DeFoe's History of the Plague in London.
Journal of the Plague Year.

Edited by BYRON S. HURLBUT, Instructor in English in Harvard University. 12mo. Cloth.   pages. Mailing price,   cents; for introduction,   cents.

THE book is intended to meet the requirements of students preparing to take the college entrance examinations, and to supply a convenient edition for general use.

Biography.   Phillips Exeter Lectures.

By Rev. PHILLIPS BROOKS, D.D. 12mo. Paper. 30 pages. Mailing price, 12 cents; for introduction, 10 cents.

Minto's Manual of English Prose Literature.

Designed mainly to show characteristics of style. By WILLIAM MINTO,
M.A., Professor of Logic and English Literature in the University of
Aberdeen, Scotland. 12mo. Cloth. 566 pages. Mailing price, $1.65;
for introduction, $1.50.

THE main design is to assist in directing students in English
composition to the merits and defects of the principal writers
of prose, enabling them, in some degree at least, to acquire the one
and avoid the other. The Introduction analyzes style: elements
of style, qualities of style, kinds of composition. Part First gives
exhaustive analyses of De Quincey, Macaulay, and Carlyle. These
serve as a key to all the other authors treated. Part Second takes
up the prose authors in historical order, from the fourteenth century up to the early part of the nineteenth.

Hiram Corson, *Prof. English Literature, Cornell University :* Without going outside of this book, an earnest student could get a knowledge
of English prose styles, based on the
soundest principles of criticism, such
as he could not get in any twenty
volumes which I know of.

Katherine Lee Bates, *Prof. of
English, Wellesley College:* It is of
sterling value.

John M. Ellis, *Prof. of English
Literature, Oberlin College:* I am
using it for reference with great interest. The criticisms and comments
on authors are admirable — the best,
on the whole, that I have met with
in any text-book.

J. Scott Clark, *Prof. of Rhetoric,
Syracuse University:* We have now
given Minto's English Prose a good
trial, and I am so much pleased that
I want some more of the same.

A. W. Long, *Wofford College, Spar-
tanburg, S.C.:* I have used Minto's
English Poets and English Prose the
past year, and am greatly pleased
with the results.

Minto's Characteristics of the English Poets,

from Chaucer to Shirley.

By WILLIAM MINTO, M.A., Professor of Logic and English Literature
in the University of Aberdeen, Scotland. 12mo. Cloth. xi + 382 pages.
Mailing price, $1.65; for introduction, $1.50.

College Requirements in English.

Entrance Examinations.

By Rev. ARTHUR WENTWORTH EATON, B.A., Instructor in English in
the Cutler School, New York. 12mo. Cloth. 74 pages. Mailing
price, 90 cents; to teachers, 80 cents.

The Art of Poetry:

The Poetical Treatises of Horace, Vida, and Boileau, with the translations by Howes, Pitt, and Soame.

Edited by ALBERT S. COOK, Professor of the English Language and Literature in Yale University. 12mo. Cloth. lviii + 303 pages. Mailing price, $1.25; for introduction, $1.12.

Bliss Perry, *Prof. of English, Princeton College:* The fullness and accuracy of the references in the notes is a testimony to his patience as well as his scholarship. . . . I wish to express my admiration of such faithful and competent editing.

Shelley's Defense of Poetry.

Edited, with Introduction and Notes, by ALBERT S. COOK, Professor of English in Yale University. 12mo. Cloth. xxvi + 86 pages. Price by mail, 60 cents; for introduction, 50 cents.

John F. Genung, *Prof. of Rhetoric, Amherst College:* By his excellent editions of these three works, Professor Cook is doing invaluable service for the study of poetry. The works themselves, written by men who were masters alike of poetry and prose, are standard as literature; and in the introduction and notes, which evince in every part the thorough and sympathetic scholar, as also in the beautiful form given to the books by the printer and binder, the student has all the help to the reading of them that he can desire.

Cardinal Newman's Essay on Poetry.

With reference to Aristotle's Poetics. Edited, with Introduction and Notes, by ALBERT S. COOK, Professor of English in Yale University. 8vo. Limp cloth. x + 36 pages. Mailing price, 35 cents; for introduction, 30 cents.

Addison's Criticisms on Paradise Lost.

Edited by ALBERT S. COOK, Professor of the English Language and Literature in Yale University. 12mo. Cloth. xxvi + 200 pages. Mailing price, $1.10; for introduction, $1.00.

V. D. Scudder, *Instructor in English Literature, Wellesley College:* It seems to me admirably edited and to be welcome as an addition to our store of text-books.

"What is Poetry?" Leigh Hunt's Answer to

the Question, including Remarks on Versification.

Edited by ALBERT S. COOK, Professor of the English Language and Literature in Yale University. 12mo. Cloth. 104 pages. Mailing price, 60 cents; for introduction, 50 cents.

Bliss Perry, *College of New Jersey, Princeton, N.J.:* Professor Cook's beautiful little book will prove to the teacher one of the most useful volumes in the series it represents.

The Beginnings of the English Romantic Movement.

A Study in Eighteenth Century Literature. By WILLIAM LYON PHELPS, Ph.D., Instructor in English Literature, Yale University. 12mo. Cloth. viii + 192 pages. Mailing price, $1.10; for introduction, $1.00.

THIS book is a study of the germs of English Romanticism between 1725 and 1765. No other work in this field has ever been published, hence the results given here are all the fruit of first-hand investigation. The book discusses, with abundant references and illustrations, the various causes that brought about the transition of taste from Classicism to Romanticism — such as the Spenserian revival, the influence of Milton's minor poetry, the love of mediæval life, the revival of ballad literature, the study of Northern mythology, etc. It is believed that this book is a contribution to our knowledge of English literary history ; and it will be especially valuable to advanced classes of students who are interested in the development of literature.

Archibald MacMechan, *Professor of English, Dalhousie College, Halifax, N.S.:* It is a valuable contribution to the history of English literature in the eighteenth century.

Barrett Wendell, *Professor of English, Harvard University:* All along I have thought it among the most scholarly and suggestive books of literary history. . . . It is certainly based on an amount of original study by no means usual.

Studies in the Evolution of English Criticism.

By LAURA JOHNSON WYLIE, Graduate Student of English in Yale University. 12mo. Cloth. viii + 212 pages. Mailing price, $1.10 ; for introduction, $1.00.

THE critical principles of Dryden and Coleridge, and the conditions on which the evolution of their opposite theories depended, are the subjects chiefly discussed in this book. The classical spirit is first traced from its beginnings in the sixteenth century to its adequate expression by Dryden ; the preparation for a more philosophic criticism is then sought in the widening sympathy and knowledge of the eighteenth century ; and, finally, Coleridge's criticism is considered as representing the reaction against the philosophy of the preceding school.

A Primer of English Verse.

By HIRAM CORSON, Professor of English Literature in Cornell University. 12mo. Cloth. iv + 232 pages. By mail, $1.10; for introduction, $1.00.

THE leading purpose of this volume is to introduce the student to the æsthetic and organic character of English Verse — to cultivate his susceptibility to verse as an inseparable part of poetic expression. To this end, the various effects provided for by the poet, either consciously or unconsciously on his part, are given for the student to practice upon, until those effects come out distinctly to his feelings.

J. H. Gilmore, *Prof. of English, University of Rochester:* It gives a thoroughly adequate discussion of the principal forms of English verse.

The University Magazine, *New York:* Professor Corson has given us a most interesting and thorough treatise on the characteristics and uses of English metres. He discusses the force and effects of various metres, giving examples of usage from various poets. The book will be of great use to both the critical student and to those who recognize that poetry, like music, is constructed on scientific and precise principles.

Analytics of Literature.

A Manual for the Objective Study of English Prose and Poetry. By L. A. SHERMAN, Professor of English Literature in the University of Nebraska. 12mo. Cloth. xx + 468 pages. Mailing price, $1.40; for introduction, $1.25.

THIS book was written to embody a new system of teaching literature that has been tried with great success. The chief features of the system are the *recognition of elements*, and *insuring an experience of each*, on the part of the learner, according to the laboratory plan. The principal stages in the evolution of form in literature are made especial subjects of study.

Edwin M. Hopkins, *Instructor of English, University of Kansas:* I am delighted with the fruitful and suggestive way in which he has treated the subject.

Bliss Perry, *College of New Jersey, Princeton, N.J.:* I have found it an extremely suggestive book. . . It has a great deal of originality and earnestness.

Daniel J. Dorchester, Jr., *Prof. of Rhetoric and English Literature, Boston University:* It is a very useful book. I shall recommend it.